Also by Annie Liontas

Let Me Explain You

sex with a brain injury

ON CONCUSSION AND RECOVERY

annie liontas

SCRIBNER

NEW YORK   LONDON   TORONTO   SYDNEY   NEW DELHI

Scribner

An Imprint of Simon & Schuster, LLC

1230 Avenue of the Americas

New York, NY 10020

First Scribner hardcover edition January 2024

SCRIBNER and design are registered trademarks of The Gale Group, Inc., used under license by Simon & Schuster, LLC, the publisher of this work.

Simon & Schuster: Celebrating 100 Years of Publishing in 2024

For information about special discounts for bulk purchases, please contact Simon & Schuster Special Sales at 1-866-506-1949 or business@simonandschuster.com.

The Simon & Schuster Speakers Bureau can bring authors to your live event. For more information or to book an event, contact the Simon & Schuster Speakers Bureau at 1-866-248-3049 or visit our website at www.simonspeakers.com.

Interior design by Kathryn A. Kenney-Peterson

Manufactured in the United States of America

10 9 8 7 6 5 4 3 2 1

Library of Congress Cataloging-in-Publication Data has been applied for.

ISBN 978-1-6680-1554-4
ISBN 978-1-6680-1555-1 (ebook)

for the walking wounded
who keep on
& for Sara

She was not well, but she had been sicker before. A crisis had passed. And something wrong had been set right. But there was something else, something monstrous in that rightness. And that was what she wanted to remember.

—Joy Williams, *The Changeling*

No head injury is too severe to despair of, nor too trivial to ignore.

—Hippocrates, c. 400 BCE

contents

sex
with a
brain
injury

the life cycle of a concussion

It starts with a big bang. It comes from the sky: a meteor, a falling object, a box. It comes out of nowhere, a car, a baseball, an opponent's fist, a partner's fist, an officer's baton, a player's helmet, the banned *Kanibasami* throw during the girls' judo tournament, a skateboard crash, a roller coaster, the blast of an IED, a low-sitting shelf, a low-hanging branch, a rogue wave, a 2x4. Or you fall off your bike on a quiet road.

You do not pass out. You aren't likely to, less than 10 percent of concussions result in loss of consciousness (this happens only if the rotational forces at the junction of the midbrain and thalamus result in a disruption of the system that regulates your sleep-waking—that is, you get hit at just the right spot). Later, you will wish you *had* passed out for just a minute or two, as proof to you and everybody else that something happened. You will secretly wish that there was blood, not too much blood, not like a whole brain bleed. Just, like, a touch of Halloween-style makeup.

Your brain, which is the texture of butter, ricochets around in its own liquids. It slams against the wall of the skull. The axons that connect the white matter of the brain—each a tiny filament less than 1/100th of a human hair in diameter—fray and tear. The headaches, the dizziness, these will come soon enough. Right now, you are freaked because something is up with your eyes. You were told by the cartoons that you'd see stars, but actually the world is retreating, as if the air is taffy being pulled and stretched, the world in present tense and you several seconds behind.

Your friend answers the phone call you don't remember making, scrapes you off the pavement, stealing glances at you in the passenger seat because he's nervous you'll fall asleep, or worse. You try to be the same person you were before you fell off your bike, crack a joke about how hard your head must be, only you're not sure if you actually spoke out loud or if you said the joke twice or if your friend was actually the one who made the joke. This is called, you are told, confusion. At the hospital, if you're lucky, you're put through a CT scan. The CT scan does not show a thing, because technology cannot yet detect the microscopic axonal injury of concussion. The scans come back normal. The formal diagnosis is "traumatically induced transient disturbance of brain function," but the people who treat you now and in the coming months interchangeably use the words "concussion," "mild head trauma," and "traumatic brain injury" so that when you leave with the paper that says what you have and what you should do—which you cannot read, why can't you read? You were in the Acorn group in second grade, which means you have been praised for your reading abilities since age seven and are pretty sure you've only gotten better since then—you are lost. You realize you have no idea what a concussion is, really.

Your knowledge about TBI—traumatic brain injury—comes from the movies or the news. The one about the skiing accident, the horrific car pileup, the boxer's career-ending match, the brilliant lawyer-doctor-professor-soldier-architect who can no longer feed himself and must learn how to walk again with the help of the doting wife. To you, "traumatic" suggests debilitating disability. The images scrolling through your mind are categorized as "severe TBI," an injury that ranks 3 to 8 on the Glasgow Coma Scale (GCS) and likely results in amnesia, slurred speech paralysis, or days of unconsciousness. Think of Tracy Morgan, comatose for two weeks after a speeding Walmart truck crushed his limousine, followed by five months in a wheelchair. Conversely, if you had a moderate TBI, you would have likely passed out for twenty minutes to six hours, and upon waking might face permanent cognitive limitation or emotional lability—9 to 13 on the Glasgow Coma Scale. Think of Roseanne Barr, who talks about how her family took in Holocaust refugees; how, after she was hit by a car at age sixteen and impaled by a hood ornament, she was never the same. "It's still you," Barr says, "but it's an artificial intelligence you."

You are not Tracy Morgan or Roseanne Barr. Apparently, what you have is far less tragic, is in fact minor, which is why they put a little "m" in front of it and call it "mild TBI." Tiny baby teeny-weeny mTBI, a.k.a. concussion, a.k.a. not something that the Glasgow Coma Scale is very much help with since it only evaluates loss of consciousness. You think of these three categories of brain injury as three separate boxes—*severe, moderate, mild*—when in reality they are more like steps down to the same dark, haunted basement.

The doctor who treats you likens what you've got to "a bad hangover," prescribes Tylenol.

You return to work, because the pamphlet says you should be good in two or three days. Here come the headaches, the sensation that your head is full of gauze, distortions in your periphery. You catch the start of people's sentences, but by the time they get to the question you're supposed to answer, or the thing you're supposed to remember the next time you see your colleague or boss, you forget what's been said. You still can't read—the words on the page refuse each other like oil and water. So you fake it. When you do finally get reading back, you can't recall what the paragraph is about when you get to the bottom. You can't draw a clock. The numbers get all bunched up, 7 to 12 are crammed together like the condiments on a fridge shelf—and that is definitely not where 6 goes. Even your little nephew knows the 6. You walk outside on your lunch break, and the sun brings new hurt. The whooshing cars, screaming birds, the trash truck, snippets of chatter, lawnmower—it's all a grind in your head. You have to cross the street because the guy in front of you is wearing a neon-patterned shirt. Your mother calls, you can't listen to her for two minutes before nausea sets in.

You always thought migraines were an exaggeration, maybe even a romantic notion, and now you know that you were simply stupid and condescending in your illusion of your perfect, contiguous health. You give your supervisor a letter from your doctor indicating that the fluorescent bulbs are an impediment to doing your job; she looks at you askance. If you were a Black woman, that supervisor's look would be outright suspicious, and maybe you couldn't even get the doctor to give you a note. You don't know how to tell your bosses that scrolling causes glitches in your brain, that the overhead lights make you wilt, that a gif brings on a wave of motion sickness. You are tempted to tell the leadership about the woman with migraines from Vineland, New Jersey, who is suing the Cumberland County Board of Social Services for not moving her desk to a window and for then firing her when she couldn't work. But you can't afford to lose this paycheck. So you take secret breaks in the supply closet, lying on the floor with damp office-kitchen paper towels draped over your eyes, then go home and wrap a blue scarf around your head. The tinnitus is always there in the background, a remix of buzz saw and elevator music. You're sure this noise in your head is what is responsible for the invention of the car alarm, the fire alarm, the alarm clock. You've never had triggers before, but these will stick with you: light, noise, movement, plus new vulnerabilities that evolve.

Maybe you are one of the lucky ones, met with unconditional love and people who continue to come around (even if they think you're exaggerating a little bit, which you let slide because you also think they're exaggerating when they call out sick). Or maybe you understand Virginia Woolf, who, writing from her own sickbed, tells you friends change during illness, "some putting on a strange beauty, others deformed to the squatness of toads." You miss all the jokes, all the fun, and suddenly you realize that your friends have moved on, made new friends who can go out at night or sit in the sun and drink tequila. The last time you went to the beach, the sun made swallowing a problem, and you had to play it down in front of others, even as you were panicking and thinking to yourself, Lord please don't let me die choking on a ham sandwich like Mama Cass. You are as guilty as your friends: you don't want to be around you, either. Case in point, the last six months you've had "Mambo Number Five" stuck in your head for days at a time. You have the constant feeling of needing to go away—to be gone.

By now, you realize the pamphlet left out that a concussion means mood swings, disequilibrium, disorientation, disinhibition, distance between you and others, vacant staring. No brain is the same, thus no brain injury is the same. You will understand that a TBI, even a tiny baby mild one, a concussion, is true to its Latin derivation and "shakes violently." Your dreams are full of blood. Sometimes you wake up in the middle of the night, not remembering your name. You sit up, heart pounding, sheets smelling of rotting apples, and wonder who this person is in your place.

The concussion might have started off as particles finer than human hair, but now it is a giant donut-shaped disk of gas and dust. When gravity and other forces cause material within to collide, it becomes a full planet. You are your own planet, and that concussed person over there is their own planet, and that one over there is their own planet.

You are all part of the same ever-expanding universe, yet you are always apart.

ooooo

Improbably, you get hurt again. You are in a store, in the infant section. A car seat falls off a high shelf and because your back is turned, you don't see it coming. Splayed on the tile floor, you ask the blinding track lights, How stupid can I be? Two teeny-tiny-baby mild traumatic brain injuries in one year? More improbably—might we say *incredibly*—just a few months after the second injury, you get a third mTBI: a heavy potted plant falls off its shelf. Are shelves the problem here? No, the trouble with head injuries and potato chips: the odds aren't great that you'll stop at just one. The pamphlet failed to warn you, and you do not know to explain to others, about this new vulnerability, how after one concussion you are one-to-two times more likely to get a second one, how after a second concussion, you are two-to-four times more likely to have a third, and how if you've had a third . . . well, just don't.

The first accident, people can understand. The second injury within a year, you all called bad luck. The third, though, seems so impossible as to be a lie. You could say, I wasn't in my right mind. You could say, I am slower at cause and effect now. You could say, I was looking right at the heavy object on the shelf but at the same time I couldn't see it. Instead, you say nothing.

Most people doubt anything is wrong with you, including the doctors. Maybe they have never heard of Mary's Room, the thought experiment wherein Mary lives in a black-and-white room, knows everything there is to know about color and can offer thorough scientific explanations about it, though she has never seen color herself. One day, by error, Mary sees a red apple. This is the first time she has ever seen red with her own eyes. Does Mary learn something new about color, having now experienced it? (Does reading about sex and never having it mean you know all there is to know about sex?) Is seeing red merely an extension of knowing about red, or are there, according to educator Eleanor Nelson at TED-Ed, "non-physical properties and knowledge which can only arise from conscious experience"? And if science can't explain what knowledge explosion is happening in Mary when she bites into this red, red apple, then maybe the doctors—even the neurologists—have no idea what is going on with your brain. Maybe they have no idea what it's like to be you.

What it's like to be you: every single object above eye-level is now a meteor, and you are the dinosaur in its path.

For the first eleven months, you are a mess. The next six months, a different kind of mess. Your polyvagal nerve is all wiry. You recall a line from *Jurassic Park* ("The point is, you are alive when they start to eat you"). Sometimes you faint or nearly faint, usually you cry—you used to feel superior to people who cried in public—but mostly your response is *fight*. At the grocery store, in traffic, at a parent-teacher conference, at a barbeque, at brunch. You never understood angry people, but now you are one of them. If you are Henry VIII, your head injuries kick off years of intense rage and murder; in 2021, Yale scientists posit that following jousting accidents the king suffered from the same condition as some NFL players, and that his infamous bloodthirst might in part be explained by injury. You go home and ask your family if they're afraid of you, and sometimes the answer is yes. You take off your wife's head again and again.

A meme tells you: A disco ball is hundreds of pieces of broken glass put together to make a magical sphere of light. You aren't broken. You are a disco ball.

In a year, maybe, you'll get better. In two years, maybe it'll be even better. In three years, surely, things will be back to normal. But by years four, five, you know better than to plan for normal. You are terrified to hit your head—even a small bump. You begin to collect stories of people who've had ten, twelve teeny-tiny-teeny-weeny mild traumatic brain injuries, urban legends that are all too true. Years in, you can no longer do crowds, spice, alcohol, concerts, intense exercise, hunger, temperature regulation, movie screens, maps, math, recipes, anything which requires holding on to two things in your mind at once. You screw up an important meeting with your editor even though it was the focus of a fifty-minute therapy session the night before—and, surprise, you are now an introvert (that one, you don't mind so much). You will likely carry your new limitations into your twilight years, cognitive abilities declining at a faster rate than others your age, but maybe that also means you will eat better, try yoga, pick up Sudoku or a foreign language, look quietly and intensely at the color of a single flower petal that you once would have walked right over. You might have an ongoing aversion to Ping-Pong, luggage carousels, the roller coasters you used to love, traffic at night, snow, but that's okay, the world is full of amazing stuff. Come for the shock, stay for the awe.

When something good happens, even if it's small, you treat it like a feast. When a global pandemic sweeps through, you're extra cautious, but you are not undone by the isolation. You are no longer afraid to be alone. It is not that you have been brought closer to death, but how raw we must be to live at all. How strange that the thing that nearly broke you creates within you a new place for the light to go.

ооооо

Maybe you are UFC Joe Rogan, Super Bowl MVP Mark Rypien, Lady Gaga, Angelina Jolie, Jackie Chan, Brene Brown, George Clooney, Justin Bieber, Pope Benedict XVI, pro-surfer Shawn Dollar, or Ben

Driebergen, winner of the thirty-fifth season of *Survivor*. Maybe you are among the 10 percent of the 3.8 million athletes or motorists concussed each year. Maybe you are one of 415,000 wounded vets—maybe a woman in combat, recovering in silence. A person who is incarcerated and therefore seven times more likely to get a head injury than those who retain their freedom. A college kid after a night of drinking. Maybe you are one out of every two people experiencing houselessness who also has a brain injury, likely injured before you lost your home. Maybe you jumped out of a plane for your twenty-first birthday, and it was the wind that concussed you. Maybe you are a transgender youth attacked at school. Maybe you are still recovering from COVID-19, and your doctor told you that, though you never hit your head, you're exhibiting clinical and neurochemical signs synchronous with mild brain injury. You are probably not Abraham Lincoln or Harriet Tubman, but now you know a shadow of their suffering after concussion. And, maybe, when you envisioned your life and all the things you'd ever do, you couldn't imagine the will that you would have to summon just to get through a day.

Your injury, you would give it back, of course you would. But now you understand something others don't: something about life, how it requires, in Woolf's words, a language that is "more primitive, more sensual, more obscene." (*Brutal*, she wrote in an earlier draft instead of *primitive*, and sometimes, you think, yes, brutal.) You will marvel at all that you still do not know, and all that you do not know you do not know, but you will also see beauty you too often ignored. You will cry, but also you will laugh harder, so hard it hurts your ribs. You have fallen through a trapdoor you never suspected existed—a special door not seen by the untrained eye—and what it shows you is what only the angels can envy—how people suffer, how they go on despite it. This will feel, some days, like the most precious gift.

Whoever you are—you know.

sex with a brain injury

The best way to picture it is this: that's my wife on our bed, and there's a tree stump on top of her. The funny thing is she is really into the tree stump, even though the stump can't do too much, except maybe crush her with its weight.

I am trying to figure out how to move. I am above my wife, and I am stuck. I don't know how to get myself out of this position, which looks similar to a dog when it's raising its leg to take a piss. The problem is my brain has stopped telling me what to do. My wife touches my arm, What do you need?

ooooo

The only times I've moved through holy water are on the page, on the dance floor, on the ice, and when I'm with my wife.

I used to be good at sex. This is not something people like me are supposed to say, and it's a secret I've held close, one I'll only tell you now because that sense of freedom has been taken from me.

It started in seventh grade when I was sitting atop the doghouse and Sean C kissed me and asked, Where did you learn that, do you watch dad movies? At some point I understood that I had a hidden intelligence, and it had to do with attunement. From then on, I decided I was only going to share it with people I liked. That's how I caught my wife—sex and poetry, and the promise of more sex through poetry.

Is it really that different now? a friend asks. Listen, do you know what happens to me if I shake the orange juice too hard? Do you know what happens if I drink coffee? When chicken is fried anywhere in the apartment building, the smell overpowers me for days. Fried chicken and legs in the air, fried chicken and her exposed throat. It wakes me at two a.m. It rubs itself on our bedsheets. Some nights, my mind cannot tell her skin from the chicken's.

How do I put this? Orgasms make my head explode.

∞∞∞∞

For as long as I have known lust, it is as if a boar is barreling through my body, hot breath, tusks raised. What is in me will not be quieted. D'Angelo on the speaker, streetlights glowing aluminum through the gauzy curtains. One nice kiss, and then it cannot be called kissing, this is gulping, searching out something far below, no coming up for air. My body over hers, thighs straddling hers, heat between us causing a melting—except that I am solid as a boulder. I smell the dirt on us. I use my fingers, my nose, my lips, whatever she permits. She wriggles away, twists back. We will get to oblivion but first we will sweat.

Only now, sometimes, we have to stop as soon as we get going. My wife gets out of bed naked to grab an icepack for the back of my head.

Arousal migraines: the occurrence of migraines in circumstances which activate, arouse, annoy, and jangle. In these moments, Oliver Sacks tells us, "we may recognize the following: light, noise, smells, inclement climate, exercise, excitement, violent emotion, somatic pain"—fucking, clawing, grabbing, needing, sucking, moaning, mounting, demanding, exploding.

Over time, I become afraid of my head. I become the dormant volcano the tiny people fear, so that I am both seething earth and the people's constant terror of the next invisible tremor.

∞∞∞∞

I had many early sexual fantasies in which I was a lumberjack coming home to a beautiful woman and a woodstove. When S and I began to have sex, the reality wasn't as far from the fantasy as you might think.

My wife's hair. How it tickles my face and chest. The light fuzz on her navel, the skin that is soft as limestone in spots and a lovely rough in others. The moodiness of her eyes. How she attracts the darkness of the room to them, binds me to it.

Sex on an average day was about dropping into your own skin while sinking into your lover's. Sex gave me the type of confidence I usually admired in an actor who walks breezily out onto the stage. But after the injury, out of the bend of my mind, a new animal self emerges, cannot tell time, sees only shadow and light, touch as refraction.

Sometimes it's the anxiety—the ankle bracelet of any brain injury—that makes all contact out of the question. How many people are afraid of sex? That it will hurt, even as we ache for it?

∞∞∞∞

I miss fucking. I miss throwing my wife on the bed, against the headboard, which for us is usually just a wall because we have never actually owned a headboard. I miss the strap-on, which fits me like a body part from a past life, or a future one. She in the streets, they in the sheets. But now I barely recognize myself.

Fucking is collision, derailing, two speeding objects encountering one another in unknown territory. Fucking is rubber on blacktop. Fucking means getting hit in the head sometimes. It happens. It happens to you, too, you get hit in the head all the time, you just never notice. I hope when you reel back from the explosion of lights and ecstatic throbbing, it's not out of pain.

She says it will be like that for us again. Soon.

ooooo

A head injury will take a lot from you. Loud music, perfume, storms, sprinting, pride, but what it takes from your partner is unbearable. The gruesome statistic somebody shares, as if they've been listening to accidents on a police scanner, or a news report on *Morning Edition*: you know 48 to 78 percent of marriages fall apart after brain injury, don't you?

Weeks pass. We both stop asking for it. It's the migraines, it's the tinnitus, it's the nausea, it's the receding self and a disturbed sense of object permanence. It feels too much like going to your favorite restaurant and choking on each bite.

During this time, I hide a lot from my wife, much of my pain.

Now, when she comes in for a kiss, there are two of her. She's a beautiful blur.

Am I a blur? Are we a blur, to her?

At a work gathering, I slip. I call my wife my sister, and somebody I barely know sneers. I hate him for it, hate myself, actually. All my "queer fears" splattering in my face like grease off a spitting pan—and we are still so, so young.

It is winter. We are on a getaway to Rehoboth Beach, Delaware. We buy Milano cookies, wine for her. The whole point of the trip is high-quality shrimp cocktail, then sex. We are a few minutes in, foreplay, kissing, I hit second base, the bra I like because it forms tiny fists of lace. We start to forget our grievances, the agonies of the last few years. Then she accidentally elbows me in the head, as easy as knocking a glass off a table. She starts to cry. Her hands cover the bottom half of her face. I'm fighting to console her through the fog that turns my tongue into a thick plunger. The swelling instrument that is my brain. I can't believe how weak I am, my whole skull a soft spot like a baby's. I want to leave Rehoboth and find a cave and cause an avalanche. Instead, I hold her through the humiliation, anger.

Sex is leaving and its opposite.

ooooo

"Queerness does not have to be healthy to be human," Melissa Febos writes in *Body Work*. "We do not have to earn our humanity by being any kind of perfect . . . Every sex scene that we write has the potential to expand a reader's entire conception of goodness."

ooooo

Some people with brain injuries have no trouble fucking. Others, even after mild head trauma, cannot become aroused at all. Some get aroused all the time, without wanting to. At a meeting for people like me, I bring up sex, and those around me nod, as if we all lost the same close friend.

These days, I think about football players—any of the 300,000 who this year alone will get concussed. What it must be like to be the wife, or the mistress, or the undisclosed lover lying beside them, listening to them breathe.

ooooo

I know why my friends think sex should be the same. It's because I look the same. People like me, you usually can't tell us apart from people like you. In some ways, we would rather you didn't. But if you slam into us with your car doors or your bodies, we might not be able to get up right away.

We bring up the Rehoboth incident to the couples' counselor. She looks at us like we're freaks, or like she's trying to sort out why our foreplay includes my wife clubbing me with a dildo. She artificially softens her voice to mask her fear of lesbian sex, how it makes her confused and squeamish. What we bring into the room—lust, implicit fragility—is beyond her imagination.

We fire the couples' counselor.

I inhabit the trap my body has become because there is nowhere else to go, just as someone who is lonely believes they can fall in love again.

ooooo

Is it crazy to say that I hear the sparkly purple dildo call to me from across the store, like a sword or a wand, whispering that it belongs to me/I belong to it? I buy it, even though it's the last one on the shelf and strangers' hands have been all over it. The shop owner cleans it with something that might be cornstarch, and I carry it home in a dusted white baggie.

In the bedroom, alone, I strap on the sparkly purple dildo. My whole body turns sparkly purple. This is not my first strap-on, nor the biggest—there is nothing salaciously new here—yet I fill with the effervescence of a teenager. I smile so big I have to clap my hands over my mouth. Is this what they mean by hope?

ooooo

I am on all fours, once again. Trying to figure out how to move. Okay, not a tree stump. A cardboard box crushed at one corner; so sodden that it can't support its own weight. This time, we crack up. We have been here before; we've been here for years. My wife guides me onto my back. She does something nice with her tongue. Heavy smell of snow at the window, glint of silverware or firelight. This secret room has been here all this time, how have I only just discovered it. My hand gliding down her back, is it possible I could get used to this view?

There is a different rhythm to what my wife and I do, lake water on a shore. This is a new kind of patience my wife is teaching me.

But still I carry it in me, the desperation of a colt.

One night, I climb on top of her. I do not know where this urge comes from, I am not ready when it arrives. I become deaf to fears about being careful. My heart is hammering and might kill me. My eyes are hot. The noise in my throat so violent, I'll be hoarse later. I do not stop. I ram through flashing alarms to get to her. I am claimed by a force so much greater than me that it totals my coursing blood. There is her surprise, and something else, too—her blind need, as taut as my own, pulled to the surface and no longer able to hide. No oxygen, no caution, only clutching one another through the perilous seconds.

When I break through, it is for no less than this: I will have my life.

doubt, my love

Don't turn away. Keep looking at the bandaged place.
That's where the light enters you.

—Rumi

My wife and I gazed at each other across the tree and tinsel, and we said, This is our last Christmas together, isn't it? Back then, I must have been especially hard to come home to. Most days she would walk through the door and I'd be in bed, the blue scarf wrapped around my head to keep out the light. No TV, no drinks at a bar, no strolls through the city holding hands. I was too weak for any of that. It was years like this, me in sickness, her in doubt. I remember a fight over a tea bag. I remember days being jealous of the sick cat. After a decade and a half, we had never really had the opportunity to truly disappoint one another. Now my head injuries had turned us into strangers, me wondering who had roamed into the house, she thinking the house empty until she turned on the lights. It baffled her, why I was not getting better. There was nothing I could say that would erase that look on her face. We had become suspect to one another, opposites of who we were when we fell in love, my strength turned to weakness, her kindness receding into quiet. No wonder they make you put it in the vows. Not "till death do us part"—the "in sickness and in health." The warning is right there on the label.

Like most people, I didn't read the warnings.

ooooo

Doubt, like a river, has two banks: that which separates cannot easily be crossed.

ooooo

Thomas, in front of the other apostles, said *I don't believe you.* Jesus walked right up to him, pointed to the juicy place where the spear had entered, and replied, Go ahead, stick your hand in there. Stop doubting, believe. This was the only thing that convinced Thomas that his friend Jesus was what he said he was: this proof of blood. Touching it with his fingers, seeing red, laying hands on the warm, wet rib.

ooooo

Each year, three million people are admitted to the emergency room for brain injuries. Most of those do not show up on a CT scan or MRI. There is no bandage, no blood, no cast. The wound is invisible. Poor judgment, memory loss, emotional volatility, ringing in the ears—laid out like this, of course, these seem less like signs of brain trauma, more like hysteria.

ooooo

My wife loves anything with a beating heart. Once, walking through Newark to work, we had a tiff because she "didn't like walking by the chicken factory when they were delivering the chickens." When we play the game of Who Would You Have Been in a Past Lifetime, some people with egos—ahem, me—say "emperor." S says "Happy turtle in a little pond." When we play the game of Who Would You Have Been in 1600s

America, I say "Fire Tender," S says "The lesbian who lives at the top of the hill and ends up burned at the stake for a witch." She is unaware of her power over others, but you can hear the awe in the voices of friends and colleagues when they talk about her. S, an architect, takes me on tours of her construction sites in Philly, showing me the bright new playgrounds with the spraygrounds, pointing out the spinning thing the kids are crazy for, and I understand how lucky we all are to know her.

We met in college. Dancing was what got S to notice me back then—me in black pleather pants, her in a black pleather skirt. Sometimes, when we aren't sure what to say to one another, we let the rhythm take over. Our bodies loosening, *oh yeah, I remember you*. We've moved twelve times in nineteen years, helped each other through graduate degrees, slept in a single hospital bed when we both got food poisoning, scraped together to buy a house of our own. Our friends call us soul mates and roll their eyes about it. Sometimes I run into S on the street without expecting to, for a split second don't recognize her, think: "She's hot." I look at her face and see changing weather patterns, storm clouds, sun breaking through. I watch her hang back at parties until there is a predictable silence, and then she throws a zinger that people reference months later. The last time we played Bananagrams, she let me go for twenty minutes piecing together my three-syllable words before announcing she'd won: every one of her words invented, hysterectomy spelled as "hiztorktmee." S teaches me to take myself less seriously. She, the funniest person in the room, laughs at my jokes. This is how we stay in love.

S insists that she will go before me—and I'll be left here alone, boring myself to death. If we are to make it, it will be through laughter, which for us can be as potent as sex.

But I don't know if we are going to make it.

———

My third year into recovery, I take a free yoga class open only to people with head injuries. The teachers help us work through dizziness, balance. The lights stay dim. We do a lot on our backs. We wear sunglasses and lean on walls. One man, a fireman, is on leave, the butt of his department's jokes. One is a college kid who, half weeping, thanks his buddy Sam for coming with him today. One is a woman who has been fired from the job she loved, having used up her sick time. Her mother joins her for every class, an older woman from the Caribbean who on the first day tried out some stretches, pushing her body into unfamiliar shapes. Every day after, the mother sits in a metal folding chair and watches. She speaks blessings over us: How they suffer God, give them their peace.

I am stunned by this woman's act of love, so whole. This generosity from a complete stranger, with tears in her eyes, who sees not only her daughter's pain, but the pain of strangers.

∞∞∞

In her groundbreaking work *The Body in Pain*, Elaine Scarry writes, "For the person in pain, so incontestably and unnegotiably present is it that 'having pain' may come to be thought of as the most vibrant example of what it is to 'have certainty,' while for the other person it is so elusive that 'hearing about pain' may exist as the primary model of what it is 'to have doubt.' Thus pain comes unsharably into our midst as at once that which cannot be denied and that which cannot be confirmed." Pain, language—the things that make us most human are too often what alienate us, keep us apart.

∞∞∞

Have you heard this one? asks Dr. Ann Marie McLaughlin. A professor is lecturing a group of neurology students on brain injury. Stopping at slide one, she says, Patient A shows signs of anxiety and depression.

Slide two, Patient B, complains of chronic migraine. At the third slide, the professor notes, This one has trouble concentrating, headaches, and fatigue. The professor asks, What do they all have in common?

A student at the front tentatively raises his hand. He answers: They're all making it up.

ooooo

In 1916, 1918, 1919, 1922, 1923, and 1925, Virginia Woolf was confined to her bed with influenza. Afterward, she was in such pain that only extreme intervention—tooth extraction—brought relief. Dr. Fergusson, her practitioner, worried about her nervous system and her heart. Woolf often expressed emotional tumult as physical symptom: "Such 'sensations' spread over my spine & head . . . the horror—physically like a painful wave about the heart." Do we dare doubt her?

ooooo

Five: the magic number in head injury, which doctors often refuse to speak aloud. Most people will recover from a head injury in a few weeks or months, but for many others, it can take five years or far, far longer until you're wholly or even partly back in the world. Part of the sentence is not knowing how long the sentence is. In the meantime, there are pharmaceuticals, ice, boiled ginger, frankincense, quiet rooms, body work, acupuncture. There are the fits of anxiety and anger, the irrational fear of bed bugs, the constant vigilance—paranoia—that the next head injury is just around the corner. There is having to explain the failures of your body to those closest to you over and over again, even when you know they won't understand.

I ask S to join me at the yoga class, to prove that I, too, have someone at home who would sit for an hour on a metal chair, or join in the poses like the friend Sam. But I must not ask her in the right way—never quite express what it would mean to have her in that room with me, the leap of faith she would take simply by skipping out on work and crossing the threshold of the South Philly studio—and she never comes. Instead we go to an appointment that is supposed to save us but is nearly the end of us. There are throw pillows, dimmed lights, a couch that feels as if it has no bones in it, an unlit candle that smells of spoiling fruit, and yet all I feel is the hardness of the room. I look from my wife to the couples' therapist, back to my wife. They doubt me, every word. Their eyes as unblinking and fixed as the rule of law. When I speak, they look right past me to the blank wall, as if what I'm sharing is shadow puppetry.

ooooo

Disability, whatever our gross assumptions and beliefs about it, carries legitimacy, whereas chronic illness, especially when it cannot be seen, raises flags. My condition is unbelievable until I put on sunglasses indoors; then people clock me—even if they don't want to. I trade symptoms with others like me—Do you ever get the feeling that an airbag went off in your head? Do you feel like your brain is a block of melting ice?—each of us desperate for reconciliation. Even then, I feel us eyeing each other, working out what is real, what is fiction.

In *Notes from Sick Rooms*, Virginia Woolf's mother Julia Stephen, a nurse, takes the "stance of radical unknowingness" and tells us that illness and injury should have "the leveling power of death." She notes that "the smell of the snuffed candle, the too-hot towel after the bath, the too salty beef tea, the under-filled water cushion, the absence of 'gentle hush' in the sick room are examples of the physical torments that cause the patient to suffer." When she talks about "invalid's fancies"—those absurd, sometimes raving complaints about physical discomfort—she urges us not to dismiss them, for we cannot say for sure what the unwell are dealing with. Language, a simulacrum, fails us in sickness, as it fails us in nearly all things.

Even so, when I can read again, I go to books, because that is where I have always gone. The medical texts say, Have we told you the one about the guy with the iron pole in his head? What an injury! Then I go to the survival stories, but the survivors say, Have we told you how they said we'd never walk again? Look at us now, racing across mountains and rivers to win bronze medals! But where is everybody else, the ones who aren't outliers, the people like me who, even before all this, couldn't much hack a lazy river? Where are the drunk college kids who made a bad decision on a balcony and the mediocre drivers who got rear-ended and the construction worker thinking about his sandwich who accidentally got brained, and what type of person gets hit by a potted plant, anyway, and where is Lady Gaga? Where is George Clooney in all of this? If every one of us wrote our own book, maybe then they'd finally believe us.

Somebody in my family says, "Jeez, you act like such an old person now."

ooooo

One windy day, two years into recovery, a bit of bark flies off a tree and hits me in the head. It sends me to bed for hours. My wife picks it up off the counter, examines it. This? she asks. Are you sure it was this? Truthfully, I am as confounded as she is. It weighs nothing. Surely, it is nothing.

Dr. M, my general practitioner, is as tidy as a dinner napkin and wears a look of genuine concern anytime I enter the exam room. We text often. Dr. M is one of the good ones. Yet even Dr. M cannot bring himself to agree with me about my pain. On our call after the bit of bark, he says, Are you sure this isn't just anxiety?

Doubt hangs perpetually in the space between belief and disbelief. It is usually employed anagogically—we doubt God most of all, even as we feel the ache of our own private god-shaped hole, a knowing sensed mostly through absence. In premodern Western theology, doubt emerges as "the voice of an uncertain conscience." Doubt, in the Age of Enlightenment, is the tool of the evolving mind. There can be no new knowledge without the space that doubt—sometimes cruelly—excavates.

Descartes, in his *Meditations*, shows us that doubt can be unsettling, corrosive, even annihilating, yet it is the only path to truth. No peace without contrition, no contrition without examination, no examination without doubt. To illustrate his point, he gives an example of a basket full of apples. If we suspect some are rotten, don't we have to dump the whole basket? Inspect every apple for brown spots? Make sure the disease doesn't reach the whole bushel? We have no choice, Descartes tells us, but "to demolish everything completely and start again right from the foundations," for a single falsehood "threatens to spread falsehood." When I return to Descartes, I cannot help but remember that doubt binds us to one another. To doubt is to hesitate, to hesitate is to think, to think is to reason, to reason is to bring ourselves in communion with the uncertainties of others, and what could be more human?

When Dr. M announces he's moving out of the country, I give him a signed copy of my first book. He is jubilant. Oh, you're a real writer, he says. I didn't realize!

When things between us are at their worst, my wife says, Are you sure this isn't in your head?

Even the word "doubt," with its impossible "u" and silent "b," makes us balk.

If there is a heaven—if it opens itself to us—it must be the place where we are as undeniable as the smell of bread.

ooooo

On display at the Museum of Fine Arts in Boston: Handsome Hyacinth, dying because of a game gone wrong, a wild windy day. Apollo, bent over him, mourning his lover. But this was no accident, it is the west wind god, also in love with Hyacinth, who killed him. Zephyros used the wind to strike Hyacinth, perhaps because his words failed him, he did not know how to say, Come to me, be with me.

My love, I do not want your pale sorry. I want to be understood.

ooooo

"Somatization disorder" is defined as a form of mental illness that manifests in the body, often as pain. Somatoform disorders, depending on who is doing the defining, include hypochondriasis, conversion disorder, pain disorder, Lyme disease. The classification has been used by insurance companies in court cases, specifically in regard to TBI, to suggest that the plaintiff is not actually experiencing what she is experiencing. The injury is not the problem. Rather, catastrophizing presents as greater vulnerability to pain. What the plaintiff is complaining about, the lawyer says, is actually anxiety, or depression, or stress—obviously preexisting—projected into physical symptoms. This is overestimation, overblown imagination, expectation as etiology. Somatization disorder, a synonym for what was once called hysteria, is psychogenetic: it's all in your head.

I do not know what somatization is—have to look it up—when it is used on me.

ooooo

But how can we blame our loved ones when they have been made to doubt?

The systemic codification of doubt started long ago, before average households had electrical light or indoor plumbing, years before the car was invented, before the world wars, in the time that people still dreamed of flight and the best we could achieve was a glider pulled by a horse on a beach. It was the advent of the train in the 1800s—that icon of modernity that might in fact be the first real modern clock, "compressing travel length and distance," to obliterate any definition of time known to the mind and body—that birthed the very concept of trauma. Then, for the next two hundred years, we fell all over ourselves denying trauma even exists.

It will be of little surprise when I tell you that American insurance companies, those insidious enterprises that made their money insuring slave ships and their captains, are most responsible for our skepticism of other people's pain. The railway insurance companies and their stakeholders are the ones, according to trauma researcher Roger Luckhurst, who convinced us that hurt people are not actually hurt, that we honest taxpayers are being duped by fakers and rogues trying to scam the system. Insurance companies taught us to be suspicious of people who are in pain.

Even after clocks were standardized to railway timetables, traveling by train was dangerous and chaotic. During westward expansion, as Robert C. Reed explains in *Train Wrecks*, the federal government encouraged flimsy, cheap railroad construction through the land grant policy, giving rail companies property and funding so long as the lines were complete. There were no standard gauges, which meant that trains sometimes ran on tracks anywhere from four to six feet wide, and often in both directions on single rails. In 1875, 1,201 train accidents were reported. In 1880, just five years later, that number increased to 8,216, a jump of 584 percent. Many people died, but also, for the first time in history, hundreds were walking away from horrific accidents without a scratch only to later contend with "disordered memory . . . melancholia . . . the sudden loss of business sense." We were suddenly grappling with the collective experience of trauma, defined by Luckhurst as the confrontation between the general public and industrialization.

Widespread trauma had been experienced by nineteenth-century factory workers, much of it kept from the public, but never on this scale, nor had it impacted so many people across classes and industries. A theory arose that "traveling at speed might have concussive effect on the nervous system, whilst the violent jarring of the body in an accident might induce permanent but invisible damage." They named the condition "railway spine"—what Charles Dickens suffered in 1865 after a bridge derailment, when all train cars but his own fell into a ravine. (Dickens: "I am not quite right within, but believe it to be an effect of the railway shaking.")

Railroad tycoons began to lose "millions [of dollars] in law cases where they suspected juries were already biased to favor individual victims over large railroad corporations in an era of anti-trust agitation." Groups like the National Association of Railway Surgeons, funded by the railways and insurance outfits, arose to contest the claims of victims. They equated the condition with hysteria ("a form of disease imitation . . . neuromimesis, or malingering") and accused victims of faking it for payouts. They did not call it somatization then, but "factitious PTSD."

From this point, it was easy for the medical industry to dismiss the work of trauma researchers such as Hermann Oppenheim who, in 1886, delivered a lecture entitled "The meaning of fright for the diseases of the nervous system." Following World War I, traumatic neurosis— experienced in staggering numbers by soldiers coming home with "shell shock," the combat version of railway spine—were largely excluded from medico-legal assessments. Conversely, in 1961, "accident neurosis" became defined as a syndrome that was largely "motivated by hopes of financial and other rewards, and which shows considerable improvement following the settlement of compensation." While "post-trauma concussion state" was coined in 1939, and "post-concussion syndrome" was in use by 1941, with PTSD entering into official diagnosis in 1980—no universally accepted definition of post-concussive disorder exists.

Many people—and courts—still think it is made up.

ooooo

I have doubts, too. I don't think our marriage is going to survive. One day—my birthday—I start crying, the croissant going to pieces in my hands. I think it's just mine, this secret of our undoing. But such knowledge, even unspoken, invades any relationship. S feels the growing distance between us—and looks away.

Every night, I pack a bag, and every morning I unpack it. The leaving happens over and over again, but only in my mind, because I do not have the resolve or physical endurance for self-preservation. *If you had checked into a hotel, if you had gone to your sister's. How easy it would be to save yourself, if only you were up for it.* The leaving is a form of the conditional to which I return—*if, if, if*—even—especially—once I start to get better.

It's not just my marriage—I begin to question all my connections, as one does in periods of isolation. I doubt the point of my work, my place in the world—how necessary it is—my own resilience. There are good days and bad days, and maybe that is the problem: the good ones erase credibility, the doubt spreads. I am enveloped in such a great fog. I go to a brain trauma support meeting and, because of the looks I get, the horror stories I hear, start edging toward the door. I'm not really hurt, not like these people, I think. I should not be asking about free yoga. The guest speaker—a woman injured so severely on a bike ride that doctors didn't think she'd walk again, and who announces herself as Executor of the Mind Your Brain Foundation—turns to me, says, We're all on the same ship.

You have to understand, a friend admits to me over the phone—I've heard all about your brain injury, and I still have no idea what a brain injury is. Even if I get my own brain injury, I'll still have no clue.

My friend adds, Only the doctors refuse to admit they don't know.

Kevin Pearce, former snowboarder, agrees: "A brain injury is to doctors like the ocean floor is to oceanographers. The mysteries of both, they remain so vast and so unknown."

ooooo

Haven't we learned yet? The blank space is never empty. There are a million conversations taking place in the silence, naked to the eye.

Between any two neurons, there exists a tiny, tiny gap. This is called a synapse, and it is where the talking happens. This might be best imagined as two asterisks separated by white space. See * *.

In the brain, a single neuron can have thousands of these gaps into which it constantly sends messages. One type of neuron, the Purkinje cell, deep in the cerebellum, has 100,000 synapses. What is there to say? This is pain, this is touch, this is movement, this is what we have learned, this is where we are going, look up, this is where I am * * where are you. A neuron sends out its signal in an act of chemical synapse, initiating an electrical response, exciting or inhibiting the other neuron.

My * throws out a flare to your *, hoping for a response.

The injured self, wanting to be heard, emerges in all kinds of ways. Sometimes temper tantrum, sometimes dirge, sometimes raw memoir, noise from a window, lyricism. We write the whole body, the symptom, claustrophobia. The injured self is the integrated self, and will not be confined.

In a single human being, there are more than 125 trillion synapses in the cerebral cortex alone, about the number of stars in fifteen hundred Milky Way galaxies. What this means is that we are not just lying in wait for others, but that in our very selves, we live most often in the in-between.

**
**
**

It is okay to be between. Where else is there to go?

ooooo

Twelve-year-old Araminta Ross, called "Minty" but perhaps best known to us as Harriet Tubman, is sent to the dry goods store on errands. Another enslaved person is discovered to have left the property without permission, and the overseer demands young Harriet help restrain him. She refuses. The overseer throws an object, missing the man, hitting her—a two-pound lead scale counterweight to the head. It is a vicious blow. The brain injury changes everything.

No medicine, no time for rest. Forced back to work, hauling muskrat traps shoeless through frozen swamps, Harriet Tubman is overcome by seizures, headaches—even migraines, a diagnosis not yet named in the 1800s though the symptoms appear as far back as some 3,000 BCE Mesopotamian poems. The untreated head trauma yields periods of cataplexy, hypersomnia, possibly even narcolepsy. The slave master is brutal, and while many layers of clothes can absorb the brunt of his violence, there is nothing to protect from further blows to the head. Biographer Sarah Hopkins Bradford notes, "The day's work must be accomplished, whether the head was racked with pain, and the frame was consumed by fever, or not; but the day came at length when poor Harriet could work no more." Harriet Tubman flees north at twenty-seven, walking the ninety miles to freedom and Philadelphia on foot.

Harriet Tubman begins to see visions. She will be out one minute—not even realizing she had fallen asleep—and the next, she is listening to God. She has vivid dreams of flying over water that seem to be missives from her Maker. The visions tell her how to keep her and others safe, especially when she begins her nightly rounds on the Underground Railroad. Thirteen trips, seventy enslaved men and women and children. Do these people believe she is communing with God? They believe in her—in the pistol she packs, the paregoric she administers to babies to keep them quiet, and when she knocks out her own infected tooth when it risks a mission. They believe she is a man when she dresses up as one, that she is a free, middle-class woman when she dons a silk dress. She sets out to free her countrymen on Saturdays ("Wanted" posters aren't printed until Monday, and this gives her a head start), sends out her signal—* *. They respond * *—and in a single night, Harriet Tubman has converted another doubter.

Frederick Douglass, in one of his letters to Harriet Tubman, writes: "I have wrought in the day—you in the night . . . The midnight sky and the silent stars have been the witnesses of your devotion to freedom." In 1859, in an early act of the Civil War, she sparks an armed revolt of enslaved people, helping abolitionist John Brown plan the raid on Harpers Ferry (though the night it happens, she is home ill). In 1863, General Tubman leads three hundred black soldiers in the Combahee River Raid, the first woman-led armed expedition of the war, liberating more than seven hundred of her people in South Carolina.

Yet the nightly devotions come at great sacrifice: thirteen years after the injury, writes biographer Sarah Hopkins Bradford, Harriet Tubman is still in agony. In the 1890s, at Massachusetts General Hospital, she undergoes brain surgery for migraines, but the pain never stops. Neither does she. Tubman opens a restaurant-laundry, runs businesses out of her own home, trains entrepreneuring black women. She works alongside Susan B. Anthony for women's suffrage, largely uncredited. She opens a nursing home on her own property in Auburn, New York, taking care of others until it is her time to go. There is no room for doubt, only action.

It is the very condition of Harriet Tubman's vulnerabilities—her enslavement, her injuries, her blackness in America, her fragile humanity—which make her brave, and which ultimately call her to reach out to those weaker, less protected than she. It is those perceived weaknesses, not their denial, that make her superhuman. Doubt need not be annihilation, Harriet Tubman teaches us. All we have to do is turn it into belief.

ooooo

When we think of Thomas the Apostle, we think of someone miraculously cured of doubt. Jesus, by showing himself to his friend, grants him undeniable proof. Belief is the opposite of faith, unmade without doubt. Still, I wonder if it's so simple for the man we now deem a saint. I wonder if, even in that moment of divine illumination, a darker shadow overcame him. If in touching the very wounds of the Son of God, Thomas was overwhelmed by a new, cataclysmic doubt to overcome—within himself.

The single gift of these voices in your head—doctor, family, wife— all saying the same thing, is that a little light goes on. You've never trusted yourself before, but now, stranded in the interstitial, you're the one you listen to.

ooooo

I used to say my wife was a saint. I don't say that anymore. No one should have to live with that hanging over them.

Some years into recovery, I have a bad weekend. Lightning strikes in the same spot in my head, over and over. My trigeminal nerve acting up. My wife says, I've never seen you in pain like this. I think, that's because I didn't let you, you didn't want to, we sat on our opposite riverbanks and stared at each other across the tide that kept rising. And then I really start looking at us and realize: my doubt in S far predates her. I've told myself I could be married so long as I still depended mostly on myself. I've spent most of my adult years with S, am deeply devoted to her, and had no idea that the reason so much of that was possible was because of how much I've held back. It begins to dawn on me, the lack of faith implicit in such an arrangement.

Most marriages exist not between doubt and belief but in certain denial—in mutual, even convenient disbelief. That is, until reality comes crashing in. Too often, we mistake stasis for stability when, really, it is in risk where we truly learn to know one another. We are the distance between **.

It is not only me who stays. She does, too, going through her own madness, trying to make sense of us in this gibberish. The supreme act is not the falling in love, it is checking for it day after day, like a letter in the mail or a sign from above. Without meaning to, we find each other's rawest vulnerabilities: after being together for over a decade, our relationship finally begins. Years pass, we learn that somehow you can emerge from devastation and estrangement far less willing to contort yourself into a false shape, even for love, which after all is love.

Four years into recovery, I land an interview for a position with healthcare, in a city that is hours away. I turn to my wife, blurt out, I really need this job. She puts down her book, looks at me, and says, I will always take care of you.

ooooo

"When you are in doubt," Carl Jung writes, "you have the greatest opportunity to unite the dark and light sides of life." He contends, "Doubt is creative if it is answered by deeds."

On a particularly bad night, standing up to brush my teeth is too much. My wife holds me up on the toilet, her fingers interlaced around my head so I don't pass out and hit it on the porcelain. She and my best friend wheel me into the living room in the office chair because I can't make it the fifteen feet. After my friend leaves, I realize I have to pee. It's my wife's idea, this act of empathic imagination: she holds the orange pot under me, the one we use to cook spaghetti. When I'm done, she cleans it.

We lie in bed together, blue scarf on my head, her leg curled around me, waiting it out.

ooooo

On our last day at the yoga class, our teacher tells us she has had twelve concussions. Twelve! I think in disbelief—what can twelve possibly feel like? The teacher says, *My twelve might not feel as bad as your three*—and this is the first incredible act of faith I witness that day. The second happens when the woman on the metal folding chair stands up. She clears her throat, looks at her daughter with such tenderness, and says, Before I came here and listened to all of you, I thought she was faking it. For over a year, this loving mother, who has shown up to our class week after week, did not believe in her daughter's pain. What has brought her here is not proof, but devotion.

And then, moments later, the third revelation, clear as the word of God: I understand my wife's doubt does not belong only to her, but to everybody—my family, my doctor, my country—to me, too. Because who is to say I would have believed her, believed any of you, before all this.

So go ahead, doubt, my love.

ooooo

Kierkegaard says for one to truly love God, one must doubt God. But Kierkegaard also tells us that there is not enough evidence in the world to convince us that God, or even love, is real. "Faith involves making the commitment anyway," he says. To doubt means to earn our belief when it finally arrives. To leap is to have the courage to doubt.

duplicity

My earliest memory is of lying. I pretended to be asleep. I knew that if the old lady taking care of me thought I hadn't actually napped, she would send me right back to the small, shadowy bedroom, and I would not get to eat the sweets in the kitchen. Lying awake, quiet, I could taste the honey in the air. This was in Greece, where even adults slept in the afternoon. Blinds shuttered against the farm heat, cicadas in the trees the very sound of sleeplessness, coffee bubbling on the stove, me on the old lady's knee. The flower tablecloth that smelled of boiled milk. I rubbed my eyes and yawned and convinced the old lady, who pulled the plate of pastry closer to us.

For most of my life, sleep has been hard but lying is easy: you just point with one hand while you hold the other behind your back.

I was thirty-five years old when I had the bike accident that resulted in my first concussion. This was when I was teaching in California as a visiting writer, my wife back in Philadelphia. I was going fast, my foot slipped off the pedal. I hit the asphalt and my head bounced—I remember this very clearly. The ground shot up against the part of my skull behind the left ear at the temporal bone, which is four times less thick than the occipital bone—that is, a softer part of the skull.

Until the moment my head hit the pavement, I believed I was wearing a helmet.

Dissembling requires holding on to multiple realities at once. Children learn to lie—their brains evolve to integrate deontic reasoning, which gives us the ability to recognize social rules and guess what might happen when those rules are transgressed. To lie, you must hold up what you want and at the same time imagine what someone else is thinking. By age three or four, the time of my first memory in Greece, a child begins to grasp that they know some things their parents do not; for the first time, they realize they can create a shadow self. We keep this second self long into adulthood, forget there was ever a time it was not with us. Like our actual shadow, it often goes before us, feeling out the path ahead.

After the bike accident, there is the second accident, the baby car seat that falls off a department store shelf. After the second, there is the third—all brain injuries, all within a year. At the hospital, a nurse takes in the full five feet of me and asks if I'm being abused by my husband. Her brown eyes: What aren't you telling me?

ooooo

A year into recovery, on a work trip to Amherst where I was teaching a graduate class, I went to meet a friend's new baby. Google Maps made the trek from my hotel seem easy, or maybe I just told myself this, wanting it to be true. Before my injuries, I never had to think of walking as strenuous, something I could fail at. But the upstate road meandered, drawing me away from houses, stores, sidewalks, twenty minutes across town turning into forty. A state trooper spotted me walking, offered a ride.

My friend with the baby answered the door shaking his head: Used to be I was the one getting dropped off by the cops, Parker said. He waved to the officer pulling out of the driveway.

I had spent so many lovely afternoons with these friends and was looking forward to this visit. In the pre-baby past, we had hung out by a bubbling creek at an old mill; in a dive bar; in Lisbon, where we ducked down a cobbled street and ate bright orange curry; drinking tiny beers; drinking bigger beers; drinking something much harder the night my friend and his students hid in the classroom with the lights off and the shades down, waiting to hear—as was I, in a building on the other side of campus—that they had found the gunman.

In their living room, I sipped water and ate stale Halloween candy. I watched Parker fuss over his new baby, who had not slept in days. Whenever she made a sound, he was at her side. He made me think of the KB Toy Store puppy dog that jumped and went in circles: I could already tell he was a beautiful, doting father. Years from now, I would learn that he had been with Mary Gaitskill in Russia when she fell and hit her head on a boat ride. But for the moment I was inside unintelligible, muffled words, somehow both close and far off. Parker's wife, Alina, a fiercely intelligent woman, was talking to me. She was clearly grateful to be face-to-face with an adult other than her husband. She spoke fluidly, while I was struggling to find any words at all. I fought to hang on to her story of the birth, to appear normal. Part of me was still trying to find my way to their house. My body was vibrating with weakness, a lasting symptom of concussion. I kept my coat on to hide how much I was sweating.

They asked if I wanted to hold the baby. Uh, no, I said. I added, a beat too late—I'm getting over a cold.

ooooo

In those days, lying was the binding that kept me from falling apart. It said I could go on work trips when I could not, it got me money I desperately needed, gigs I had to fake my way through. It was the reason I boarded a train to Amherst that set my teeth on edge. Even now, I do not wonder at the need to lie to these kind friends, good people who would have happily let me rest in a dark, quiet room. Every adult I've ever known treats their own pain as something to be masked, something that takes so long to earn that by the time you do, you're already dead. Growing up, the only professionals I knew were the teachers and principals at my school—all the other adults ran diners, made pizzas, or, like my father, did manual labor. Lying was the agreement I made with myself so I could imitate a life worthy of an immigrant daughter who was first-generation-to-college. It was the way that, as a queer person, I got to keep my chosen family; whatever happened between us, it would not be my illness that alienated them.

The researcher Pamela Meyer reminds us that lying is a social act. We prefer to forget this, but lying is cooperative, lying is collaborative. For my lie to work, you must join me in it. You want to be lied to. On any given day, you are lied to ten to two hundred times. You believe most of what you're told, because 25 percent of lies are meant to spare your feelings. If you have a partner, you lie to them in one out of every ten interactions. Lying prevents us from tearing each other apart.

The truth is, I waved down the state trooper. I could go no farther, felt the cars zipping by me, felt the sidewalk stretch forever. This is embarrassing to admit, my weakness and panic. Because I was a white woman possibly needing help, he pulled over. Still, the trooper seemed to ask, You really can't go a half mile? He threw glances my way—drugs, he thought, junkie. I countered with questions I thought a sober person might pose: Do you live nearby? Where can I get good coffee? Is that a fox? Anything to keep him from asking things of me.

His tires were spitting gravel before my friend opened the door.

ooooo

The Greek god of lies, Dolos, is a skilled craftsman. He is asked by Prometheus to sculpt a statue of Truth ("Aletheia") in order to trick people into thinking they are seeing the real thing. Dolos's fake is nearly flawless, every curve perfect, except when he gets to the feet he runs out of clay. When the two statues come out of the kiln, only one can walk. The lie just stands there, staring.

ooooo

Looking back—perhaps my friends saw through me, after all. Perhaps they were so exhausted from parenting an infant that my lie about the state trooper, the cold, my general state of wellness brought unique relief, excusing them from tending to yet another human need. Perhaps they could tell I was sweating. Perhaps they were secretly relieved that I did not hold their baby. Who could have blamed them.

In truth, the blindness was entirely mine.

What I'm about to tell you now, almost nobody knows. I've said it aloud only three times, to three people, one being my therapist, one my best friend. Virginia Woolf tried to warn us, "Illness is the great confessional," but I rarely listen. To be honest, I am afraid to write the words—because I have lived with the lie for so long. I have carried it the way some people carry heavy gear up a narrow mountain path. I suppose after a while I felt too light without it, like something would be missing if I put it down, there would be less of me, and too much of the person I never wanted to become. The lie protects something not only outward facing, but buried deep. It hints at partial truths that expose my denial, your complicity. There is the invisibility of the injury, and then there is the decision to remain invisible. Anyone who has had to hide their illness knows this feeling.

Men lie eight times more about themselves than they do other people, while women often lie to protect others. Extroverts lie more than introverts. In a 1996 study in the *Journal of Personality and Social Psychology*, Deborah Kashy and Bella DePaulo found that of the 150 people asked to keep a diary of lies they told in a single day, the biggest liars were people who worried about how they would be seen by others.

It's 1993. A man who will eventually be known by researchers as Mr. Pinocchio is a high-ranking official in Europe's economic community. But something strange is happening to him, something that hasn't happened in his fifty plus years. Anytime he tries to deceive the negotiators across the table, they catch him in the lie. Because every time he lies, he faints. The people who have been lied to by Mr. Pinocchio have to shake him awake. At the University Hospitals of Strasbourg, France, doctors find a tumor the size of a walnut pressing against the amygdala. Whenever Mr. Pinocchio's brain becomes excited by the untruths he is telling, he passes out. The surgeon removes the tumor, Mr. Pinocchio stops collapsing, can go back to lying for a living.

Like most children, I told all kinds of lies, and almost never got found out—and I was not even the biggest liar in my family. When we were six and seven years old, my sister and I collected used cigarette butts off the sidewalk with the boy next door and tried to smoke them. We hid them in an overturned bucket, and when we were caught and the kid's dad said what's in there? we said: a rabbit. And he said, Well let's see it, and my sister took off running. My first short story, written in junior high, was about a young girl who tries to tell her classmates about the tape worm living inside of her, but nobody believes her. I said I thought that kissing girls was gross. Once, I told someone's mother I was late to the sleepover because my grandmother was in the hospital. Then, when my grandmother was actually sick, I lied about hearing the bell, which she used to call out to my parents in the middle of the night. Bell ringing and ringing. The morning after, I merely replied, big eyes, Oh, I was sleeping. I think about that moment often, the thick cold sweat that covered my chest as I listened to someone I loved cry out and did nothing, telling myself I would go one minute from now, in one second I would be brave enough to walk down the dark hallway.

What you have to know is that in my post-concussive years, I survived on lies. I lied about being able to read. I lied about understanding what someone had said when in fact I was still trying to puzzle out their words. I lied about telling time. I lied about being stuck in traffic when in fact I had no choice but to pull over. I lied about being able to drink alcohol, and once, at an industry event, poured white wine into the soil of some poor plant so I could look like someone somebody might hire. You might be thinking, These aren't lies. But even when people aren't well, we expect them to tell us the story we want to hear, to cover over their sickness overtly or by omission. When someone is chronically ill, we wonder why they have broken the unspoken agreement of fictional wellness. The boss, toddler, coach, bus driver, cashier, colleague, interviewer demands our cooperation, our best self, even when that self is in deterioration. The lie preserves the liar, but mostly it protects the culture that prefers the lie. This is true especially of illness, which resists progress, which demands special treatment, exemption.

"The ill are the deserters, the refuseniks," writes Hermione Lee, admiring Virginia Woolf's audacity to own her unwellness. "They won't accept the 'cooperative' conventions . . . They won't go to work. They lie down. They waste time."

Mostly, I lied to my wife. I lied to her every day. I told myself that she still knew me if she knew everything about me except for my careful omissions. I was the car salesman who said whatever needed to be said so I wouldn't be left with a lot full of old cars. It wasn't hard to do. For nearly forty years, I had been protecting my loved ones from the real me. People want you to be okay. This is not always about dismissal, I have learned, but about intolerable hope. Your wife will look into your face, beyond the pain, and insist you are well. There is an eagerness, an emergency in such belief, when the alternative is unthinkable.

I knew how bad things between us were, and how much worse they would get. I saw it coming, just like the time she tied sixty birthday balloons onto a railing. I knew they'd disappear the moment we turned our attention elsewhere. I had seen such things happen as a child, when Mom ran a balloon shop called Cretan Creations. I was not surprised when we came back out to the deck and the balloons were gone. Not even a dot in the cloudless blue sky. S kept saying, Where did they go? Where could they possibly have gone? I understood there was no stopping something whose instinct was only to ever push outward.

What I'm trying to say is—

I told myself that the blank spaces between us could not be called lies.

ooooo

I look up, and it falls from the sky: stone, car, building, box, meteor. The third injury. I do not go to the doctor after this accident, which has happened because I am not yet healed enough to process danger when it's present or think an action through to its logical consequence. I tell no one that I am hurt again. I recall with scathing mortification the skeptical looks after the second concussion—*Did the box with the car seat really fall on you, was your back really turned so that it was entirely out of your periphery and you couldn't save yourself, did they really put such a heavy thing on the highest possible shelf, are you really descending into the netherworld that is concussion, or are you making it all up?* I lie to myself: you are not hurt, you will be fine. *No one saw it happen, there was no camera, you were in sweatpants.*

When the smell of salmon on my dinner plate sickens me, I tell my wife I'm not hungry. I have trouble with words on a page and leaves on trees. I can make sense of none of it. I begin to hear voices—ones that want me to finish the job, bludgeon myself, with something harder this time. This is not depression; it is the chemical reaction of head injury. I take one day off work and then, at the end of the week, as scheduled, I board a six-hour train to teach the graduate class in Massachusetts, telling myself I'll be fine.

This is not a new tactic. The night of my first head injury, I had gotten on a plane and returned to Philadelphia to help my wife move to a new apartment since ours had been sold by the landlord overnight. The dimmed lights of the cabin, the shuffling of people in their seats and out of their shoes, was both torture and comfort. In the morning, the flight attendant who had been charged to wake me every few hours lest I die in my sleep let her face crumple with relief. I tried to help my wife with the boxes, but the screech of the packing tape was like a car crash; the unplaceable smell of it, like burnt surfaces. Afterward I flew back to California and finished out my semester. Because I couldn't read, I hired a graduate student to read aloud to me, and because I couldn't handle the fifteen-minute walk to campus, I hired another graduate student to drive me. I told myself, as always, that this is what immigrants do: they keep going.

Less than an hour into the trip to Massachusetts, I get off the train because I am too sick to keep going. I am lucky that my wife's aunt lives nearby, and I call the university and tell them I can't make it. Admitting this, even years later, feels like failure. The very kind woman organizing the graduate workshop asks, What if we do it remotely? Such arrangements will be commonplace in a few years, but at the moment it is an accommodation that makes me squirm. I say yes, and agree to teach that night, though everything inside me says, no, please, no, I need rest. Rather than living on a single contortion, a lie exists in the habitual, in that which has remained unsaid many, many times. Once a lie is spoken, all those other invisible, iterative lies crawl out of hiding, too. Which is why, at the appointed time, I put on sunglasses, stare at the screen for three hours, and try to sound like I should be teaching. I stay up to celebrate S's birthday, which is coincidentally that same day, and which she had planned to spend with her aunt while I was in New England—but I take one bite of the cake and have to stop. Then I go to bed, where, because of the fresh injury, I am assaulted by the worst migraine of my life. Years later I will ask myself why I did not go to the hospital that night, at least to beg some relief. But I know why, have always known. I pretend—to myself, most of all—that I don't need to.

ooooo

Never marry a writer, they live two truths at once, both the story they tell and its revision. The lies of a writer, they arise much like her characters do, with you in mind. The lies are made to fit your body precisely as if you were a paper doll, the clothes that keep you from your own nakedness.

One night, during a brutal fight, S asks: What are you talking about? What third concussion?

You don't know? I say. I keep repeating—You don't know? I put the dining room table between me and her. She is saying, There were two concussions: the bike and the box. No, I say: not two, three. The bike, the box, and the third one. She walks toward me, but she can get no closer—her approaching, me backing away. Us circling the dining room table. I look at her like she is someone I have never met, someone who has broken into my house, while she talks to me softly, tenderly, a tone she uses on children and pets. All this time, I've been in the repetitive frequency, asking her over and over *why won't you believe me*, because she did not get it the first time, nor the second, nor any of the other times I did and did not try to speak aloud what happened. This is the moment when I realize that I have gotten so good at lying that, for over a year, without quite realizing it, I have kept the third injury from my own wife.

And she has let me.

Long before your own spouse fails to recognize you, you begin, at a creep, to lose yourself. This strangeness happens over a season—a death, a pregnancy, an illness—while you fabricate a version of yourself for others that remains unknown to you. You are alone. Not just for the day, or for the time being, but constantly. A lie might be the loneliest place to live.

In the morning, quiet in our contriteness, we stare at this truth together, a little blinded.

ooooo

But this was not the thing I meant to tell you. What I meant to say is this—

I knew what I was doing on my bike on that strip of road in California. I knew how fast I was going. I did not forget my helmet. I left the helmet at home, in fury or bewilderment. This was not about intentionality, but I wouldn't say it was about defeat, either. Only, there are those self-deceptions that follow you all your life, after you believe you've left them behind—they rear up when you are at your lowest to remind you how far you've traveled because this is the distance you'll always have to go. Then they devour you.

I may as well have been drunk, so sleep deprived I was, yet at no point did I not know what was going on. I knew. Still, it was a surprise when my foot slipped off the pedal. When I fell off my bike and hit the pavement, I understood what would happen to me—thought I did. I did not put my hands out. I did not try to catch myself when I crashed. I let go.

I could not tell my wife for a long time—for years, I could not say out loud what I had done to myself, to us. I could barely look at her when I confessed it, though we were in a beautiful place called, if you can believe it, Taberna Clandestina in Portugal. A little wine cask for a table, a plate of cheese, a candle. The words lodged in my throat, unwilling. She took my hand. She thought I was going to tell her I had had an affair in California. *Who is this stranger?* Three thousand miles from home, my wife could feel her sitting there alongside us, staring at us, asking her own questions: the other me, the shadow me.

Yes, I should have clarified—Yes, you're right, there is somebody else.

q&a with my wife #1/
false starts

We agree, let's do it someplace beautiful. Tropical but ▮▮▮▮ ▮▮▮▮▮▮▮▮▮▮▮. Somewhere that, years from now, will make us jealous of our younger, hotter selves. A whole new way of keeping time. Far enough away that work email can't get us.

YOU: Like a vacation?
ME: A vacation from ourselves. But we're the only ones invited.

So we return to Taberna Clandestina, the little yellow tapas bar in Portugal where I first told you the truth about ▮▮▮▮▮▮▮▮. The taberna, rustic and hip, sits above the ocean on a narrow street strung with tiny colored flags and packed with outdoor seating. The sun is setting yet it feels as if the day has only begun, blue sky bright as a marble, salt in the air. The place is busy, but not packed. You and I are seated by the window, except now it is a real table and not a barrel we have to squeeze our knees around. Copper mugs, pitchers of fresh basil. The strangers around us bring lightness into the room, as if they only make one another's lives better. Exactly the place I was picturing for such a conversation.

The agreement is you talk, I listen. Afterward, I will hand you the Q&A transcript and a black Sharpie and you can cross out anything you want. You can black out every line, the only thing we'll print is ████ ██.

Everything we've said or done, strike it from the record. Redact it for everyone—except YOU and ME.

ME: If you don't like a question, you just say pass.
YOU: Pass.
YOU laugh, I laugh.

We order a carafe of sangria, which I can drink if I don't push it. We play with the silverware. We smile at each other, out of joy and nervousness. I am supposed to be asking you questions about the blackest time in our relationship. But where to start. How do two people revisit an unknown known. What is left to say? What are the troubling thoughts that live beneath the surface of our days, even now? How does the partner of someone suffering suffer, too? Today, I want to find better words to ask than What was it like for you?

What happened to us?

*Can two people change so much they don't recognize themselves but
    somehow still know one another?*

What about regret?

Who will you be in five years? Who will I be?

I take a sip of the sangria, feeling it going to my head, and wake up my phone. I push the red record button.

ME: You ready?
YOU: To talk about my v█████?

You laugh, I laugh. It's like when I told you the title of this book was *Sex with a Brain Injury*, and you joked "Is it a picture book?"

ME: ███████████████████?

You don't respond.

ME, glancing at the phone. Once again, I ask: ███████████
████████████?
YOU: ███████████████████?
ME: ███████████████████?

The red button is blinking. The questions are piling up. But you are hesitant to answer, and I am, too. Who really wants to go back there? Things are better between us—lighter—and it's nice just to be here, isn't it? The cheeseboard with its thin, nutty Manchego, the little medallions of chorizo, honey dripping down the sides. The smell of charred peppers. We're sitting across from one another with an ease that we never again thought possible. Isn't that better than talking? Isn't it the entire *point* of talking? To never have to talk about it again?

How much of our lives are we meant to give over to regret?

ooooo

We have been here before—many times. The Talk. Sometimes there is screaming, sometimes a translator needs to be called in and paid an out-of-pocket rate, but every now and then there is a breakthrough so precious it could be a strange new life-form. Each time, we get closer to ██████████ ████████████ ██████████████
██████ ████████████████ yet, somehow, we still keep our

distance—the way you can run your finger through fire and not get burned.

We have the ████ in Asbury Park, the great gay Mecca of the Jersey Shore, the place that feels most like home.

We have the ████ in the furnished Philly apartment that the failed witch—our landlord—has slowly but surely been emptying of objects. We keep having it, even after the dining room table is gone.

We have the ████ in the car, where we can't get away from each other.

We ████ on the phone, where there is safety in the miles, and we miss each other a little.

We joke: For every right answer, ████████████████████████.

One day, you send me a Polaroid: no, I will not put it in the book.

Instead of ████████, we exchange emails, which at times is the safest, if coldest, form of point/counterpoint:

YOU: You went through something very ████████████
████ that most humans never go through. From the outside, you seemed too strong—hardly ever complaining. I thought, Who could go through this without some enduring pain?

ME: Do you mind vacuuming while I'm not home? Sorry— hurts my head a lot.

We ████████ at the therapist's office, walk home, and have a big laugh about it. We're doubled over in our laughter, hanging on to a chain-link fence. We could just have a baby. Isn't that what straight couples do to fix things? Picture it—you in labor, sweating and grimacing, pushing out Baby: and there I am, lying in the hospital bed next to yours having my own hysterical pregnancy. I push and push. Out comes a baby doll. We name it Heavy Baby.

ME: ███████. Bald. Big plastic ████████████.
YOU: Only ever wears a diaper.
ME: All through adulthood, he goes by "Heavy."

So small, so inconsequential, this joke we're sharing—but it's the first sign we might be saved.

Sometimes, though, we ████████ by not ████████ at all. We lie in the tent, dog huddled between us for warmth. The hoot of an owl, the baptismal smell of the campfire's dying embers. It is a very quiet ███████████, one that could be easily missed.
Every ████████ is the ████████ all over again.

ooooo

So let's begin: once more, in this beautiful little European café that suggests how easy life can be. Of course we both know it's not so simple. I see your fear, I am afraid, too. The red button continues to blink at us.

ME: ████████████████████████████?
YOU: ████████████████████████████████.
ME: ████████████████████████████??
YOU: No. ██████████████████████. Not here, it's too heavy. It's always with us. We never put it down.

I push the red button, the talking ends. Our knees touch beneath the table. You take my hand, or maybe I take yours, who can say.

Six months will pass before we ████████ again.

post-it/song on loop

The Song You Haven't Heard Since 2001 & Which Your Friends
Have Been Instructed to Never Play Nor Speak Of, But Plays On
Loop In Your Head Before You Even Open Your Eyes in the Morning

Lou Bega, "Mambo Number Five"

LeAnn Rimes, "Can't Stop the Moonlight"

Shania Twain, "That Don't Impress Me Much"

Haim Shaban and Shuki Levy, "Inspector Gadget Theme Song"

Chumbawamba, "Tubthumping"

Gloria Estefan, "Rhythm Is Gonna Get You"

Gloria Estefan, "Conga!"

Gilbert O'Sullivan, "Alone Again (Naturally)"

Whitney Houston, "Exhale (Shoop Shoop)"

Vanessa Williams, "Colors of the Wind"

Uncredited, "Head Shoulders Knees and Toes"

dancing in the dark

The two things we had in common: women and dancing. Mary in baggy jeans, sneakers, and a long black T-shirt; me in a baseball cap, a shirt with a collar, cleavage, rainbow beads on my wrist. She was excited to take me partying, to get me my first tattoo. Things she thought a mother should do for a daughter to prove that, even after years of absence, she had been there the whole time. My cousins came to the gay club that night, my friends, too. I sipped watered-down vodka from a plastic cup, thinking this is what legal vodka tasted like. I leaned against the cement column, hoping my posture suggested, No big deal, I am often surrounded by this many hot lesbians. In reality, I had only been to a couple of gay bars and, at twenty-two, I wasn't ready for tonight: the colored lights cutting the floor, the upholstery scent of clothing rubbing together, music rumbling up my spine, prowling women in the shadows, the building expectation of the crowd, the glint of gold teeth and cheap, low-hanging jewelry.

Mary and I had reconnected after years of estrangement. This place was her idea. She knew the bouncer, the bartender, the women posted at the bathroom doors who watched us come and go. Mary was a good dancer, had been a DJ (we both loved Madonna, rap, anything with a thumping beat), but she was not dancing with us. She hovered at the edge of the floor, sipping her Sprite, a big unmissable woman. She was looking, laughing. Her forehead glistened with sweat, her thick black hair glossy. I followed her gaze across the floor to us, to my friend. She was watching my friend, going: Damn, she's sexy. Damn, look at that girl move. My mother pinning my friend with her eyes, the way I had seen some men do to women from their car windows.

If I close my eyes, I can picture her in the spray of lights, nodding to the beat. The mole on her cheek. The way her big body shifts as if in permanent exile. She is Ursula the Sea Witch: short black hair, thick body, hard jaw, outrageous mouth. Her eyes have been known to scare children. Her mannishness to scare off men. She is a dyke, an addict at a time when people with substance abuse disorders have no place in America. She loses friends to AIDS in the eighties, loses friends to overdose in the nineties. She is in and out of rehab. She takes in young women when they have no place to go and then demands, with at least one of them, that they pay her in sex. She is lonely much of her life. She does not like to discuss what drugs she was on when she was pregnant with me. She left my father when I was two, my sister one, so she could finally have a life. I am a reminder of a time before she was free, and I am also what remains of the daughter she had to give up in order to claim herself.

She always wanted me more than I wanted her—that is, when she wanted me at all.

Me? My whole life, I want to be nothing like Mary.

When she dies, not yet sixty, I mistakenly believe I've escaped her.

ooooo

As a child, I knew why Mary was a dyke: she was an addict. And I knew why she was an addict: she was a dyke. This syllogism cast a long shadow that I still have not quite found the edge of. Sick in the head, the doctors in the family would say, not one of them actual doctors. Her erratic needs, her dark moods, emotional lability, selfishness, bouts of in-explicable rage, the way her emotions overwhelmed her like a detonated bomb. Mary's obesity, militancy, queerness, the reason she chose drugs and drinking over her own children—the adults in the room listed these and more with glee. I sometimes wonder if, down in the womb, I heard their talk, if I knew the poison my mother was pumping into her body, decided to get the hell out of there early.

ooooo

The hijacked brain is not the normal brain. Neurotoxicity interrupts normal networking, and physiological changes can occur in certain re-gions, such as the hippocampus, ventral tegmental area, nucleus accum-bens, prefrontal cortex. The result is often a severely impaired memory, altered behavior, unregulated emotions, impulsiveness, distortion. We have known about this pathology for a long time: it is addiction.

ooooo

The judge declared Mary an unfit mother. It is easy to criminalize a woman in America: just say she doesn't take care of her kids. This is particularly persuasive if she is a lesbian, an addict, a foreigner. My fa-ther understood why a man might leave everything and come to a new country to have a better life, but he did not understand how two crying babies fit into that, especially when there was no woman to hand them off to. My sister and I were sent to Greece to live on an island with my father's family until he could find another woman to take care of us. I might at times forget my address or bank card pin, but I will always re-member the day I returned to the States: my sister and I hiding behind our father, the unfamiliar cousins and adults gawking at us. I knew how to say one phrase in English ("I'm hung-u-ly") but was too afraid to speak. Our father introduced us to our new family. A new sister, one who, like me, was entering kindergarten. Another on the way. And most importantly, a new mother, "Mom," the woman who opened her home to two little Greek girls and told them women can be whatever they want, that they can even drive a car.

Soon enough, Mary heard her daughters were back. She began coming around. There were gifts of pink Barbie convertibles, a Barbie mansion. I watched Mom's face when I accepted gifts from Mary. I squirmed out of Mary's hugs. When I was seven or eight, Mary took us trick-or-treating. Because she had limited visitation, we could not go out on Halloween. Instead, we went on October 30. The yellow leaves threw a soft glow onto our sneakers, the brown curled ones crunched underfoot, the air smelled like wood and worms. Black and orange and purple decorations were strung up on the doors and windowsills, bats, ghouls, monsters. Not all of them lit up. I was a witch in an unfinished costume. I did not have a broom. I did not have the green face paint that would have made it obvious to these strangers what we were doing on their stoops. I was told, multiple times, to stop scraping my feet on the steps, to just walk, our hour together was almost up. We're just a little early, we had to explain to people over and over again. We're pretending it's Halloween but are hoping for real candy. Not everyone had treats to give. Someone gave crackers, little packets usually served with soup. Some people looked at us, at her, strangely but still dropped miniature chocolates and SweetTarts into our bags. I was ashamed of the way the adults received Mary, as if she were not an adult at all, or even a person. The thing to remember: what you're most afraid of happening has already happened. Are you from *The Little Mermaid*? one of them asked Mary from behind the screen door. Are you the witch from under the sea?

Mary was wild, liked to party-party, as my father would say. He warned: all addicts are lowlifes. His fingernails were black from welding, his work clothes all had burn holes. He wanted me to have a good life, a productive life. Not working in dirty shops like him, or sweating over an olive farm like his father who made it no farther than the fourth grade. I could hear the tremor in his voice when he said it: You are very smart, like your father, so be successful. The worst is to be anything like Mary. Eat that, you'll have an ass like Mary. Wear that, you'll look too much like Mary. Think that, and eventually you'll be exactly like a mother who gave up her own children. Do you want to be the one they all point at? Do you want to be the man of women? Will you be the reason that normal women look at you with resentment, since they have to deal with men all the time and you do not?

For years, I told myself I was not gay. I liked Nicky A, even after he accidentally stabbed me in the eye with a wooden sword on a sixth-grade trip to Medieval Times where we ate a thin potato soup and a tiny Cornish hen I got to dismantle with my bare hands. That wasn't gay, right? My sexual fantasy of being a logger come home to find my woman waiting by the fire? That did not make me gay. Neither did the one about being a soldier during the Civil War, come home to his almost-widow waiting by the fire. Or the one about Axl Rose where I am Axl Rose fucking Axl Rose. I couldn't be gay, because in each of these I was the man.

There is a photograph of Mary in 1996 with the actress Lea De-Laria, Mary leaning forward to lock eyes with the camera. DeLaria is in a white button-down and suspenders, her costume from *On the Town*, though she is probably best known for her role in *Orange Is the New Black* and telling that famous lesbian joke ("What does a dyke bring on a second date? A U-Haul"). The photograph with Mary was taken not too long after DeLaria appeared on *The Arsenio Hall Show*, the first gay person to out themselves on live TV. The adults around me said she shouldn't have used that word, shouldn't have called herself a dyke, though it is part of why DeLaria ultimately won the Equality Illinois Freedom Award for her "life's work to change people's perception of butch, queer, and LGBT." But in this photo, my mother out-butches the butch.

The girl who lived down the block and who sometimes saw Mary said, What's a "lesbo"? I tried to tell her but she kept saying what do you mean, what do you mean. I wrote it down, thinking that was the problem. I drew arrows to prove the point that would undermine heteronormativity. Her mother, doing the wash, found the sheet of folded notebook paper in her jeans. Her mother called up my house, said, We don't use those kinds of words. The words on the page were girl, girl, lesbian.

Years into adulthood, I assume the gender of "delicate man." I shoot for George Michael, end up looking more like one of my Greek uncles.

ooooo

When I was in junior high, Mary pulled up in a convertible after years of silence. Some children with parents like Mary are familiar with this pattern—the long absences, the abrupt and volatile appearances. I said yes to taking a ride because of the car, and because she wanted to impress me with it. The convertible had the hard glare of a candy apple and smelled like coconut ice cream, with the slightest whiff of boy deodorant. I thought, mistakenly, Maybe she bought it for me.

We drove to the next town. I wore the mood ring I had bought from Claire's, which on this day had a black face and a band that was turning my finger the same color as the little man-made lake we walked around. I could hear the gravel pulverizing beneath her boots. Me swatting away tiny flies that hung in the air, Mary a few steps behind the entire time, as if I were leading her on an invisible leash. Mary was not asking me to come live with her, but her need was all around us, like the insect larvae and the water lapping against the bank. She certainly did not know how to talk to a twelve-year-old. A black duck waddled nearby. It reminded me of her, this woman who walked in her own unmistakable wrong way and kept telling me she was my mother even though I had a mom at home. In the playground overlooking the lake, the kids had stopped swinging to stare at us. I recalled the last time Mary showed up like this. Jeffrey C, the shortest and meanest kid in my class, his mouth a jagged smile, announcing, Ooh, I like your dad. I tried with my mind to make the tiny man-made lake half its size so we could be done.

Anna, she said. Anna.

I turned around, finally said: That's not my name anymore.

She stopped walking, the gravel sound of chewing stopped, too. I gave you that name.

I shrugged.

You want me to use that baby American name? Don't you know it's their trick? To make you forget who you really are. Who you come from.

The trick, in fact, was forgetting who she was to me, after years of forgetting who I was to her—but I did not say this. Instead I said, I go by a new name now.

My mother looked slyly skyward, out at the blue that seemed intent to go on forever. Yeah, okay, Anna, Annie, Annie, Anna. I'll get it right one of these days.

It was still a year before Leslie Feinberg would publish *Stone Butch Blue*s, and another decade would pass before someone put it in my hands. It would be even longer before I'd recognize that the impulse not to bear children—the most androgynous part of my known self—was perhaps as strong for me as it had been for my mother. I did not want to be a girl, told my sixth-grade best friend that I wished I had been born a boy. My father, who came home every day desperately wishing his girls were boys, announced, You must stop this. I know what he meant—that that shadow part of me was Mary—so I smothered the feelings and tried to be like my sisters. That day at the lake, I did not understand why Mary would not just play her part, too—mother, woman. I had not yet realized that it is inherently false for someone queer—someone made into an outlier not because they fuck women but by consequence of sheer reclamation of the self—to play any part at all. A lifetime would pass before I would wonder what all this meant for Mary.

All the days at once. Mary pulling up in that red convertible, a trip to get cherry water ice, outings to the diner with enough plates of spanakopita and gyro for two more of us, nights at the club, a silver-tipped walking cane that she used anytime my sister, who eventually went to live with her, got out of hand. I hear Mary's anger rising over the phone, telling me a daughter should not want her mother to spend Christmas alone. I've been clean a long time, she said: What more do you want? Don't we have fun together?

ooooo

In 1984, Bruce Springsteen stays up all night writing "Dancing in the Dark," putting onto the page all his fury, his feelings of isolation after *The River*, his frustrations and desperation. The song spends four weeks at number two on the Billboard Hot 100, sells over a million singles, turning *Born in the USA* into the best-selling album of his career. A remix is released on my birthday, July 2. It is played in all the gay clubs. It is big in New Jersey.

You can't start a fire
Worryin' about your little world fallin' apart
This gun's for hire
Even if we're just dancin' in the dark

ooooo

Saturdays were for dancing. The adults got cleaned up and left us with a babysitter and didn't care how much popcorn, chips, candy, ice cream, cookies, gummies, powdered sugar we ate. If it was at the Greek agora, the men would cry a little ouzo, and the women would sweat through their dresses. More often than not, though, they headed to the bar down the street named for an old bitch everyone loved back in the day. On these nights, my father washed off the scent of burned metal, changed into one of his prized silk shirts, and put on a big gold ring fashioned from the drachma coin, larger than any jewelry I have ever seen up close on a man. He smelled like the cologne from a green bottle with a horse on it, a scent of chopped wood that would alarm me years later when I encountered it among strangers, him long dead. Mom blasted the radio. She and her friends put up blue eyeshadow, teased their blond bangs into a South Jersey frenzy, the hair spray sitting on them like a frost. Years into the future, we will joke that her tombstone will read "Went to a Pitbull concert on a rando Tuesday," though what we'd actually be marking is Mom's courageous joy. Claim every ounce of your life, because you won't get another.

The kitchen, as they walked out the door, smelled of perfume and alcohol. The vanity mirror, still lit up, lay forgotten, along with half-filled mugs of coffee or liquor. They drove off. This was what it meant to be free and grown-up in New Jersey—lit cigarette, shoes that tacked against vinyl tile, jingling keys, friends and *Koumbaros* greeting you with kisses on the cheek. Bodies revved to move, a break from the weekday drudgery, coming home "feeling good" but not coming home any time soon.

In the morning, their heavy adult jewelry lay in gold clumps on the dark wood of the bedside table. Inexplicably, within arm's reach, a ceramic breast held whatever had been in their pockets—loose change, a phone number, a receipt for a table of drinks. Their clothes, dropped onto the carpet, still heavy with sweat and makeup and the odors of the one a.m. scene. Children were never allowed in the parents' bedroom, and the proof of this was quiet that engulfed it the morning after, their underthings poking out of drawers, the groan they held in until they could go out and do it all over again next Saturday. I thought, back then, that such nights were about fun. Of course, yes, fun—but also, dancing kept the darkness at bay, a darkness that might have been about exhaustion but might have also been tied to mistakes, the unanswerable, not knowing where to turn.

I danced a lot as a kid. Two hours a day, at least, while my siblings watched *Kids Incorporated* downstairs. "Dancing" involved flinging myself across the room as if I had been shoved out of an elevator, plus punches, faux-karate kicks. Often in my dancing, there was someone to save: friends, teachers, the kids in school, Nicky A, Nicky A's mother, who everyone had a thing for because she looked like she belonged in Aerosmith videos. The bedroom walls crumbled like dry wedding cake when I slammed into them. Someone would knock a broom against the ceiling, but I kept at it. I didn't know what else to do with my body. I didn't want to do anything else.

When my youngest sister—seven years my junior—told me she was afraid to dance the agora, I replied, You can't be afraid to move. It's part of who we are.

When I die, I want to be reborn as the first three minutes and forty-eight seconds of Rosie Perez in the opening credits of *Do the Right Thing*, bucking against anyone who dares to confine her. On the dance floor, I don't care about being sexy: I want to be undeniable. We call such nights out "Church," when I am unleashed and make friends or enemies depending on how comfortable people are with women moving their bodies, hips, their plump asses for nobody but themselves. It is not uncommon for some stranger to whisper in my ear, You're flying, aren't you? Almost always, I am stone sober.

ooooo

Mary's parents didn't know what to do with her. Her hair was long and greasy, her voice husky, like a boy desperate to be a man, and she had a straggly look that no makeup could touch. They must have heard the bedroom doors opening after everyone had gone to sleep, must have known that the older cousin crept into their daughter's room at night, starting when Mary was twelve. Mary drank to forget. She broke into the neighbors' medicine cabinet and took whatever they gave old ladies. She was a Wild One who had gotten America into her veins by thinking she had a right to pleasure. They didn't know how to solve this problem, so they arranged a marriage with a family they knew back on the island. She was turning sixteen, my father twenty-two. He agreed to the marriage because it included a whole unexplored country of opportunity, whereas his own father wouldn't give him one measly piece of land for his dream of a trinket shop that would scam tourists. They married a handful of days after they met, with the whole village watching, returned to the United States as man and wife. He got a job in a welding shop, she got pregnant. He was too naive to understand what the doctor had been prescribing his wife until the doctor called to say he was cutting Mary off. He had never heard of any drug other than marijuana—it would be years before he knew about deodorant—and now the woman from the upstairs apartment who he thought was a friend to Mary was hiding all kinds of strange pills in his coffee table. In his mind, he put his wife on a plane, sent her back disgraced, sent himself back, too, so he could undo what was done and hold up the white nuptial sheets with no blood on them and shout to the entire village that she was not a virgin, he was not accepting a rotten fruit for breakfast. In reality, up until the very end, he begged Mary to be a mother to the two children. It was no use. Here he was, standing with two babies—girls, goddamn it—and he knew nothing about feeding them or changing their poop. But Mary was gone, Mary had left him for a woman.

When I was eighteen years old, I went looking for Mary myself. I'm not sure what I was seeking, except I suspected there was another story than the one I had been told. It started as any love affair, with letters that became calls. We went for lunch at a place where they knew Mary by her first name, got overstuffed cheese bread. She talked about my father, how the marriage had been a prison sentence, his cruelty, his naïveté. The baby before me that didn't make it. How, when she was in labor, she said to him, You did this to me, I'm going to kill you. I believed much of what she said. I had the feeling that this was not my mother, but a sibling or cousin, someone my age but somehow more susceptible, bruised. I said to myself there are a million miles between you and this woman. This impulse in me, one of cruel indifference, which for a long time I believed I was fully entitled to and could use against anyone who deserved it, even the woman who had been pushed into giving me life. I kept thinking a miracle might occur: I might rewrite my past with the past that had been deliberately kept from me, was being kept from me even now. Instead, she spoke of her therapist: I think she likes-me likes me, I'm definitely going to kiss her.

From a young age, there opened a great sinkhole in Mary, which nobody dared look into, not even her daughters, who were afraid that peering over the edge would make them fall in. She did not tell stories, did not have an acuity with words; nonetheless I am certain it's from her—looking out of the black—that I was given writing.

But this is not exactly what makes me like her, either.

ooooo

Once, an internationally famous writer was visiting the city I was living in, and I offered her a place to stay. I did not know her well, but that did not stop her from becoming a cyclone in the spare bedroom. I could hear the writer flinging herself around for hours, a kind of violent dancing. I wondered if it was out of need, rage, if she was taking advantage of my hospitality or if this was proof of unspoken trust between us. When she came out into the hall sweaty, unembarrassed, barely acknowledging me in my own home, a signal went off: within me, too, there was some dark matter yet to be reckoned with, which needed purging, through sweat, the throwing of the body.

ooooo

Neither my father nor Mary knew about my three brain injuries, or if they did, they behaved as if they didn't. For years, I felt like I was locked away in a room, dragging around someone else's body. My erratic needs, my dark moods, selfishness, bouts of unexplainable rage, the way my emotions overwhelmed me. I had never understood why someone would want to lose themselves in addiction, but now I was starting to. It is possible that, as a result of the blunt traumas, I was experiencing "slow-wave power"—according to Benjamin T. Dunkley and his study on mTBI—in the subcortical, temporal, and parietal regions of the brain, and that these low-frequency rhythms expressed on the alpha frequency band were correlating with anxiety and depression. That is, I lay in bed for hours with the blue scarf wrapped around my head. That is, I slipped away from public gatherings to sob in a bathroom stall, unable even to bare the metallic gleam of all that powder-coated steel. I had no idea where this new anger came from, these eruptions of a dark,

unhinged self, the discernment, at times, of a child, but I spotted, out of
the corner of my eye, a silver-tipped cane.

ooooo

My queer friends love Ursula the Sea Witch, call her big bitch of the
sea, our drag queen idol. I join in, though I understand—do they?—that
this is not the way it always was. These are the nostalgic fawnings of
adults who forget how giddy they once were for an obvious villain, a
dyke-y one. As children, we were repulsed by the sea witch. We thought
of her as a wet, thick eel, a warning of what we could become. The worst
kind of witch, one who refuses to overcome her own flawed, innate
nature.

Maybe if I had been shown other big dyke-y women, if I had had
texts to turn to—bell hooks, for instance—I might have seen a side of
Mary hidden to me. In my twenties, I'll tear through bell hooks's memoirs, stories about pigs that eat charcoal, a young queer child who hates
the red dress she's forced to wear to the pageant. I'll stumble on photos
of the writer where she is laughing: *joke's on you* but also *you're in on the
joke, come join me* hooks in her power. It's in her eyes, the ownership, the
challenge. "*Live consciously in a nation that lives in fantasies,*" she tells us.
"*Sometimes people try to destroy you precisely because they see your power—
not because they don't see it but because they see it and don't want it to exist.*"
In the series of sepia photos shot in quick succession, she wears a denim
jacket. Hands at her stomach, as if she might burst with joy and deliv-
erance, reminding us that love is a verb. Big, Black, queer, and beautiful.

No, I was nothing like my mother. Nothing like her when I was
harassed at work ("You like them soft like that, don't you?"), when I was
accosted at a subway turnstile (". . ."), when I marched in parades, when
I bought a purple dildo, when I could hardly picture what balls looked
like anymore except as a graffitied caricature on the side of a building,

when I forsook most family for queer family, when, the night after my wedding, my father said: What do I have to be proud of, when my whole family can see on Facebook what you are?

Queerness is not about wanting to have sex with women. It is refusing to be confined to a narrow, airless space. Queerness is consciousness, it is asking questions and creating something indefinite out of the crudely defined.

One day, after my shower, I take a sharp breath, because for the first time, I see it: I look like her, Mary. My hair is her hair, thick, brown, an unexpected curl to it in humidity. Shaved close on the sides, aiming for heaven up top. Other than my height and my nose—my ass—my hair is my most me feature. Essential to my queerness, proof that life has a life of its own. How high does your hair go? people sometimes ask. I reply, As high as God will take me and the Devil allows. My hair recalls for me who I am. But now her hair is my hair. Her butch is my butch.

I am nothing like my mother, yet no one had to teach me queerness. It is true all the way down to the marrow.

Earlier, when we were at the gay club, I said that Mary was leering at my friend. She wasn't. The woman she was eyeing was my cousin.

ooooo

In my fourth year of recovery, to celebrate having a body again, I go dancing with friends. In better days, they assigned me the nickname Cocaine Annie; tonight, they want her to come out. I'm feeling pretty good, I'm in yellow pants, leopard tank top, black eyeliner, yellow earplugs. We are right up front, close enough to the West Philadelphia Orchestra to follow the clarinet player's brown eyes. I hold a beer I can't drink just for the feeling of holding it. I sway. For years, I've had to back out of concerts even after we've gotten tickets because of noise and crowds, and because I could not risk even a light knock to the head. My friends and wife form a wall, protecting me from the drunk white couple throwing their stick limbs. I turn my face away from my friends so they don't see me tear up. I sweat through my clothes not because I am hot—I am not able to move like myself yet—but because, awash in music and people, I am in ecstasy. After long periods of bare existence—isolation, sickness—living takes on a new ferocious intensity that is both welcome and throttling. Ecstatic—to stand outside of. To be both yourself and something else.

Earlier I said Mary was eyeing my cousin. She wasn't. It was someone closer than that.

When Mary dies, I feel more pity than sadness, and some relief for us both.

ooooo

When the end came for my father, he would not allow me to visit him in the hospital. I believe I reminded him too much of Mary, what she looked like, what she had taken from him, what her existence—and mine—meant about his own.

After the funeral, I put on the yellow pants, went dancing. How many past lives one lives in a single lifetime. My silhouette, the way I moved, was Mary after she had freed herself from my father. I didn't stop dancing, not even when my friends took smoke breaks, not even when it was just me and strangers on the floor, pants sticking, socks hot and soaked, not even when I knew I'd pay for it later. I stayed on that dance floor for four hours. Everybody out there avoided me like a woman brought back from the grave.

ooooo

Really, we had nothing in common. Just look at her Facebook page, which serves now as a memorial. The posts are erratic. Angel statues, angel paintings, rants on corrupt America, rants on corrupt Greece, Mark Zuckerberg's "straight up Italian Jewish Nazi agenda." Plato, like most men, is a liar. The word "my" inexplicably and often appears as #my. She argues that excessive attention-seeking is not a flaw. She says that the Enslavement System is collapsing, and a new perception of time and space will follow. Get your shit together, preferably before the eclipse. She talks endlessly about #handle#your#responsibilities, never once mentioning her daughters. There is not a single clear photo of her, but many half-naked angelic women.

I still hold it against her: the addiction. Don't you think I want it, too, the oblivion? I demand an answer when there is no one left to demand it of.

After Mary and I stopped talking for the last time, I was alarmed by a post that said, "Someone talk to me quick before I light up!" But she was only referring to cigarettes, which she had recently quit. On April 2, 2017, she checked in at a McDonald's in Heraklion, Crete, to eat a quarter pounder. Unlike me, she did not let queerness and fear of rejection keep her from Greece, or from family. But a few weeks later, she was diagnosed with a severe lung infection, wanted to know "Thru all this . . . where the #fuck is my family??????? Not 1 fucking cousin . . . not 1 aunt . . . not one niece." What is the problem, girls?

Then, a few days later, her last post—a single red rose lying on pavement in the rain.

There was a lot I didn't know about Mary. That she ate Heinz ketchup on her scrambled eggs. That, like me, she mourned Whitney Houston. I did not know, until after she was gone, that she published a book two years after my novel came out. There is no title, no synopsis, no cover, no way to find out what she actually wrote, only the Facebook post announcing it. What I'm trying to say is, watching Mary all my life, it was not only her strangeness that frightened me, it was her courage, far bolder than my father's, far less apologetic than I could ever be. It was her subversive survival.

In fairness, I never showed her who I was, either.

ooooo

In the last decade, studies have emerged comparing the brain after a lifetime of head injury to the brain after years of addiction. We ask, Are there differences, or is damage damage? One study looked at 104 patients suffering from concussion and 104 inpatients enrolled in a substance-abuse program and assessed their cognitive and executive functions, determining that there existed "no apparent differences between the two groups." The effects of drug abuse "were shown to be similar to those of traumatic brain injury." Neurotoxicity interrupts normal networking; physiological changes can occur in certain regions. The result is often a severely impaired memory, altered behavior, unregulated emotions, impulsiveness, distortion. We are only just beginning to understand this condition: it is head injury.

That is, what is often disrupted in concussion—the neural networks that connect the prefrontal cortex to the basal ganglia—are the same areas tampered with by addiction. Emotional dysregulation likewise appears in the injured brain—lability, impulsivity, irritability, apathy. In a time when addiction is being reconsidered in the national consciousness, seen not as a moral lapse but as sickness, we're discovering that when it comes to the human brain, harm may be indistinguishable from harm.

In other words, my brain now looks a lot like my mother's. My depression, her depression. My anxiety, her anxiety. My rage, her rage. Her injury, my injury. My suffering, her suffering, her suffering.

When I realized what this really meant, I was on a busy city street, could not stop shaking.

We were alienated for so long and at best I handed my mother sympathy as one might an orphan. All it took was my frail body colliding with asphalt, all it took was hard contact with the ground to imagine what it might have been like to be her. These days, when I am caught between my silent drowning and the crowd, when I am raving alone in my apartment and the pets are hiding, I think of Mary. How many years she existed in isolation, self-loathing, the terrible primitive loneliness that plagued her. I know this is not how life works, and we could have never been friends, but might we have asked each other what it was like to nearly always feel out of control? To be dancing in the dark, bodies near enough to touch but nobody reaching out?

You can't start a fire/Worryin' about your little world fallin' apart

Is this what it's like for you? I might ask.

Even if we're just dancing in the dark.

drowning

woke most days wondering what would be taken away next. I lost both birth parents, said goodbye to my cat, suffered three head injuries, entered into conversations with my wife about divorce, had to learn to walk again after ACL surgery, got frozen shoulder, which never quite went away, and, because of the migraines, gave up coffee, chocolate, spicy food, and booze. I remember thinking, If I could just get myself into a quiet room. But I could not even do that. I was chased up some narrow steps by a drunk man yelling homophobic insults. I fell down my basement stairs carrying laundry. Black flies infested my kitchen. I was nearly hit by a car, multiple times, while out walking my dog. I was so afraid of a fourth concussion that I would sometimes turn around, wherever I was, and go home. Anytime I looked into the mirror, I was met with blanks, and yes, there were days I said to those blanks, Wait, did I actually die and nobody told me? After trauma, you walk around with the sense that you are ghostwritten into your own life. At the same time, you are terrified to stop moving, that the someone or something that has been after you will finally catch up.

ooooo

I was almost at a run—that was the first warning sign. The second was that I had forgotten water but if I stopped for some, I would miss the train out of Union Station. I had taken this trip to George Washington University a hundred times by now—three hours down, three hours back, twice a week; trolley, train, subway; Amtrak delays, near misses, the buffet energy of people anxious they'll be last to board, loud senators' calls, louder lobbyists. But today I was late, and the lateness made it feel like a new, harrowing journey. My mouth was paste, my backpack a hot seal against my jacket. I joined the line of passengers that snaked from Gate G to Gate K, from Starbucks to McDonald's, telling myself to hang in, only five more minutes until boarding. But my brain was acting up, the glitching had begun. The people started to move, I got a funny feeling, then realized I was at the wrong gate. My train to Philadelphia was back at D. I got out of line, went to D, only to realize, once the line started moving, that I had gotten it wrong again—my train was, in fact, back at K by McDonald's. Now they really were going to leave without me. Suddenly, the whole station came crashing down—the overhead lights, the people trying to be subtle about shoving each other forward, the distorted voice announcing departures. My head was a jammed flashlight. The blast of air coming out of the Starbucks had the faint whiff of roadkill. The Einstein Bagels sign glowed a sinister yellow. Around me, a swarm of bees. This is why people no longer like you. This is why they forget your birthday. I was drowning in details, in bits of data, in colors and regrets and the jostling of commuters, the music, all of it burrowing into my brain, into the place that set a trap for me—

There is a truth we hide from in our waking moments: calamity is the stranger at the door who will not be kept out forever. Remembering this is good, reminds us in our clumsy mortality that we must hold on to what's most precious, but constant exposure brings fear and then madness. This looks like rage but manifests as petrification. For instance, mice, two weeks out from induced concussion, hide in the corners of their cages. They vibrate. They no longer demonstrate "spontaneous exploratory behavior." After this exposure to repeated, meticulously recorded mild fluid percussion injuries, the hurt mice become cautious, afraid, overwhelmed, worn out. Any past trauma to the brain or body has the power to inflict PTSD.

What snapped me out of it, I suppose, was the threat of worse panic. I knew if I stayed glued to that spot any longer, I might not be able to get myself out of the station, that I would shut down completely. Such realizations do not always work, but this time, somehow, I got on the train. I spent the next few hours with the blue scarf wrapped around my eyes, trying not to gag on the cheap acid-smelling leather seats touched by so much human skin, aware of every person who brushed past me, every squeal of the tracks, until we entered 30th Street Station.

When my wife asked me about it, I left everything out except the part about having to run for the train.

ooooo

A neurologist (not mine, mine is terrible, mine says take these vitamins and don't forget the co-pay) explains that stimulus is like water, and the brain is a bucket with a hole in the bottom. In a healthy brain, the hole is big enough for the water to flow out, the bucket never overfills. In an injured brain, the hole is too small. The brain drowns in light, noise, sound, language, speech, balance, gravity, the body's circadian processes, movement, emotion. The brain, sensing stress, floods the body with overwhelm, migraine, anxiety, discouragement, defeat, fatigue, panic, tears.

Picture: a flower drowning in its pot. Picture: I get out of a hot shower and almost pass out from the steam.

ooooo

A joke—

Girl, did you fall out of heaven?

'Cause you're showing signs heavily suggestive of post-concussive syndrome.

ooooo

In the Edwin Smith Papyrus, the oldest known surgical treatise on trauma, forty-eight instances of treatment and injury are documented in ancient Egypt, the majority of them head injury. They occur at worksites, namely the building of the pyramids. While magic is sometimes noted as a cause of certain illnesses, the Egyptians have no need for it when evaluating brain injury. Twenty-seven instances of TBI are noted in the Egyptians' cursive hieroglyphic and discussed with astonishing sophistication. Egyptian physicians observe the gyri and sulci, characterizing the familiar folds and wrinkles of the brain as "those corrugations which form in molten copper." They recommend applying fresh meat on day one, thereafter wrapping the head in linen coated with grease and honey. Case #8 recognizes contrecoup injury, the brain rebounding after impact to hit the skull. Case #22, linking brain trauma to aphasia, or word loss, predates the famous work of Paul Broca in 1861 by thousands of years. What's apparent is that in 1600 BCE, the Egyptians knew the brain about as well as we do.

Physicians begin defining concussion as its own condition in the Middle Ages, starting with the Persian physician Abu Bakr Muhammad Ibn Zakariya al-Razi ("Rhazes") in the tenth century, continuing into the thirteenth century with Lanfrancus's description of it as brain "commotion." Arabic culture and medicine makes the greatest gains. Rhazes, who suffered his own trauma at the hand of his patron, is the first to use the word "concussion" in his manuscripts, stating that "Head injury is among the most devastating of all injuries." In Europe, Guy de Chauliac proposed a craniotomy to Pope Clement VI, who reigned during the Black Death and suffered from severe and constant headache.

A concussed person may have trouble: recollecting certain events, forming new memories, remembering what they were just doing, re-membering what they were just saying, retaining new information for long enough to act on it (remembering to remember), keeping track of time, remembering to carry or pack important items, remembering to do something important, recalling memories from the distant past and the distant-distant past, all the way back to the Middle Ages, to the ancients.

There is much still to learn about head trauma. There is also much we have learned and failed to hold on to.

ooooo

Camille U is a body worker and a healer. She is also a stroke survivor, a survivor of sexual assault, and at age twenty-four was paralyzed for a year after a long struggle with functional musicological disorder. But the months following her concussion, Camille says, were the worst of her life. A year ago, she was rear-ended by a careless driver (the young woman cried so much that it was Camille who hugged her), and Camille hasn't been the same.

"I'm really good at drowning," Camille says, "and no one can see it."

When the bucket overfills for Camille, she forgets the stove is on, where she's going, what she just said in a conversation—though not long ago she could have told you her childhood phone number and what shirt she was wearing when she first met her husband. There are other issues of discernment. An incident at Chipotle. A solo camping trip with no gear. Four months go by before she tells her husband she loves him, something he has to tell her about in a letter because she doesn't even realize it. She texts her landlord about an annoyance and it turns into a meltdown. Her co-worker, who is accidentally added to the chain, watches Camille unravel.

All the old joys are too much. Music, which Camille used to listen to eighteen to twenty hours a day; TV, the old black-and-white movies, which were the way she celebrated her father at Christmas after his passing. Even snow, which is magical for a Californian who moved to Seattle. Now she has to close the blinds. "We got eight inches, and I couldn't look at it," she says.

Injury, Joy Harjo tells us, takes you away from yourself.

For me, anytime the bucket overfills, I get hit with migraines. Before I was hurt I couldn't have told you what a migraine felt like. I had my associations, handed down through the ages: weakness, hysteria, frail compositions, womanly complaints. Migraine often arrives as a smell: vinegar, turning garbage. Tar is frequently mentioned in the colorful old accounts of the condition. Some people smell toast, others patchouli. I'll be walking the streets of Philadelphia and think I stepped through vomit, only to realize this is my warning sign, an attack is coming. A cough drop in a man's mouth will smell like spray paint. My own armpits will become overpowering and foreign. When "Mambo Number Five" gets stuck on repeat in my head, though I have avoided it for years (forever), I know I'm in big trouble. I get hit with anger hangovers, brain fog. The kind of exhaustion that comes when you're watching TV and think, I wish I were watching TV.

The first written incidence of migraine in Western medical literature appears in the seventeenth century, in late Medieval English accompanied by tags like "Vapours," "low spirits," and "The staggers." ("Hee is troubled with a perpetual *migrim*; at sea hee wisheth to bee on land, and on land at sea," 1631.) Anne, Countess of Conway, is the most celebrated "migraineur" of the era—a woman who suffered a continual headache for twenty years, by age twelve becoming "obnoxious to pains in the head." Of course, people have been getting migraines since the first stone was thrown. In 400 CE, Caelius Aurelianus in *De Capitis Passione* uses the word *crotophon*, meaning "pounding or hammering." In the eleventh, twelfth, and thirteenth centuries, migraine is described at length by Arab scholars, along with treatment involving bloodletting and heated irons pressed against the veins.

Katherine Foxhall, a social and medical historian and the author of *Migraine: A History*, writes: "In the eighteenth century, migraine came to be associated with nervousness, hysteria, and effeminacy, and began to be mocked, rather than taken seriously. By the nineteenth century, physicians talked of migraine as the affliction of female 'martyrs,' of mothers whose minds and bodies were weakened by childbearing, exhaustion, and anxiety. These narratives and assumptions about gender have been, and remain, central to the dismissal of migraine."

Treatments into the eighteenth century, particularly for women, included large doses of Valerian. My neuropsychologist orders a homeopathic drug. To make sure it is mild enough for me to take, he doses himself before prescribing it.

There is the pain that comes with the migraines, but there is a sense, too, of being haunted. A bat has broken through the attic window and can't figure out how to leave. Sometimes, when the migraine descends, it is like I am back in my parents' house, visited by the ghost of the woman whose ashes are buried beneath the evergreen in the front yard. Just like when I was a twelve-year-old, she slaps a sneaker against the plywood, where the floors are still unfinished. She wants us to know just how mad she is. The babysitter is so afraid, she gets out of bed and starts doing laundry.

Old Lady, I say to the haunts banging around my skull—What is it now?

⟡⟡⟡⟡⟡

Abraham Lincoln. You can almost see his suffering etched into the bronze statue in front of the civic building in Newark, New Jersey. Rumpled suit, iconic sadness, weight of a divided nation, the pain palpable. One head injury from a horse when he was a boy, another after being struck by a club in a fight while ferrying goods on a flatboat. Concussion for the sixteenth president means lifelong depression. There is much to be down about, of course. A mother who died of "milk sickness" when Abe was nine, the result of tremetol poisoning excreted by cattle that graze on white snakeroot. Being bound to a wife he will never truly love. The death of his son, eleven-year-old Willie, which occurs when the White House is lavishly entertaining guests in one of the parties that Lincoln forces himself to endure.

Head injuries cause the immune-system brain cells—microglia—to go on high alert. Later, when new challenges arise, they become overly inflammatory, a condition linked by scientific study at Ohio State's Department of Neuroscience to depressive complications long after recovery. Multiple concussions, like those that Abe incurred in his youth, and ones located in the prefrontal cortex where he was hit by the horse, make a person particularly vulnerable to suicidality.

Abe often weeps in public. He recites maudlin poetry. He is never happy on happy occasions. On the eve of his nomination, when everybody else is celebrating, he is accused by one attendant of being "one of the most diffident and worst plagued men I ever saw." He tells jokes no one laughs at, stories at the wrong times. Grief hangs like a heavy coat over his cartoonishly long limbs. He does not believe in racial equality, advocates for the resettlement of the slaves he intends to free. At the Corneau and Diller drugstore, he buys opiates, sarsaparilla on a charge account, an occasional fifty cents' worth of cocaine. He wanders the woods by himself with his gun. Friend Joshua Speed notes the winter they "had to remove razors from his room—take away all Knives and other such dangerous things—&—it was terrible."

In his mid-forties, Abraham Lincoln turns all he has endured into clarity and conviction, and guides the nation through its great split. He never forgets his suffering, wakes to it each morning, which is what allows him to empathize with a hurting nation. He knows what it means to be torn in half, to feel crazy, to be inside the darkness, and it brings him closer to the thirty million souls all hurting in their own way.

Thirty years into his career, he regrets opposing black suffrage as a young politician and delivers a speech that infuriates John Wilkes Booth. The man's plan changes from kidnap to murder. In his diary on April 14, he writes, "Something great and decisive must be done."

Here it comes, the derringer pistol at the back of Lincoln's head, the final, concussive blow—

ooooo

My sixty-five-year-old aunt is at a stop sign. A car rams into her, the driver distracted by her phone. Aunt Judy gets concussed. In the coming months, she has confusion, head pain, trouble following her own sentences. Judy is always up for an adventure, has "gone further for less," finds joy in places too often overlooked, makes friends with my neighbors, many of whom I haven't even met. She has always been the "cool aunt," and is one of the best mothers I know. She is my wife's aunt, mine by marriage, but I understand why we get each other when one day she describes her favorite childhood toy: a baby doll with ratty hair, a burlap dress, one clear tear, and a giant head.

Six months later, on a cold dark morning on her way to work, Aunt Judy slips on ice, hits her head. She is afraid she is going to die but is sent home from the hospital with paperwork and Tylenol. Aunt Judy has always taken care of us, so we do our best to take care of her. We pass her fresh ice packs, prepare her meals with veggies, take away her phone so she can rest. Most of the time she seems okay, but every few hours, she vacates her body. In the middle of speaking, the knowing drains from her face. Her skin is ashen, pinched, her eyes searching, her expression uncertain and embarrassed. When she returns, minutes later, I ask where she went.

She continues to work. She tends to her teenage daughter. But there are lapses. She forgets doctors' appointments. During one shift at the grocery store, she leaves the car running for hours. When we give her simple walking directions to her son's new apartment—go two blocks, turn left—panic rises in her eyes.

She tells me: "It's like being in a very crowded room with everyone talking over each other and I have no idea what's going on."

Clark Elliott, professor and scientist, is also rear-ended. He is sent home from the hospital because no one believes—or they do not understand—that something is very wrong with his brain. Someone left the tap on and now the whole floor is flooded. In *The Ghost in My Brain*, he talks about going all day with the feeling that something is off: then he looks down, realizes he's had his shoes on the wrong feet *the entire day*. People who are like him, he says—high-functioning, intelligent people, busy people, people with families—are "very good at masking such problems."

When you're standing on the shore, drowning rarely looks like drowning. People think that because the swimmer is not thrashing around, they must be okay, not realizing that, in trying to keep their mouth above water, the person has gone still.

∞∞∞

Waking up in a sweat in the middle of the night, not knowing your own bedroom.

Forgetting to put water into the pot; staring into the empty pot. Seven, eight minutes of this, wondering why the water still isn't boiling. Watching the oven mitt melt onto the pot.

My wife says, Pour me some OJ? Sure, I say. And though I am standing right next to the fridge, I walk away, forgetting she asked.

Dropping a blank sympathy card into the mail. No personalized message, no signature, but there is a stamped envelope and a return address.

I see a man wearing a beard of bees. Some of the bees falling to the ground, stunned if not dead, mad if not weakened. The man is perfectly fine.

At a party, standing among strangers and my best friend, I say something unkind. I believe I am joking. In reality, I am letting the darkness speak for me. I can see its reflection in the face of the woman whom I have recently befriended, and who will stop responding to my texts.

I break down, crying over things like a mother in a commercial expressing love for her fake children as she serves rolled-up pizza snacks, a man helping another man onto the bus, a blinking yellow walk sign.

Someone with a history of head trauma tells me how, once, she pumped gasoline into the back seat. A pool of it on the floor mat. Her children, who were buckled in, screaming at her to stop.

∞∞∞

A little bit of Monica in my life
A little bit of Erica by my side

ooooo

The poet I am introduced to at dinner shrinks from noise. When an ambulance screams by, she covers her ears. When she walks the streets of the city, she wears chunky construction headphones. Like me, she has suffered multiple concussions and is in collision with the world every day.

Me: Riding my bike in ninety-seven-degree heat on an errand, not thinking, not planning for the return. I am not in a place in my recovery to understand that such exertion can—will—flatten me. I get stuck on the part of Broad Street where there are no people or stores, unable to get home, unable to ride. Overcome with heat and sickness—of course, migraine. This is one of the memories that arises when Camille tells me the story of losing herself on a text thread. I realize for the first time that this is what people with brain injuries do: they find themselves in constant danger of their own making.

I've been dropped into somebody else's body, Camille tells me. This home didn't feel safe, she says, touching her chest. Nowhere felt safe.

There is a disquiet you must learn to live with—not the attacks, the attacks are the noise at the surface. It is an instinctual dread that pre-dates you, that will outlast your last memory, the mouse hiding in the corner even when there is no immediate threat.

ooooo

In 2016, Robert "Bob" Johnson, director of the Bluegrass Writers Studio, crashed his mountain bike going downhill along a ravine. His tire came out of the front forks. He broke his jaw, his wrist, woke up thinking he still lived in Oklahoma even though he had not lived in Oklahoma for eight years. It took weeks to recover, but his family—his wife, especially—people at work, his students, were patient with him, overjoyed at his return.

A few months after the accident, Bob was scheduled to fly to a conference in Lisbon, but when he showed up to the airport, his plane was gone. Somehow, Bob had missed all the emails telling him the departure time had changed. Now he'd miss the first four days of the conference, including the opening reception. This made him feel like even when he was very focused, he couldn't get things straight. On the plane, Bob looked around at all the calm people. He started to sweat. He began to cry, this capable, adventurous guy. He was afraid of going to another country even though he had been there before and had once known it well. He pictured the crowds on the cobblestone streets, the unlit corners, a set of marble stairs, what it would mean to slip on them. What it would mean to be away from home, unable to get back. How he would even navigate a map or the Portuguese language. Going for tiny walks in different directions, just to convince himself he could find his way back to the flat, one key in his pocket, a duplicate in his backpack, even if he was just going out for fruit. He had never thought about his brain before: he was aware of his brain all the time now. Despite the cabs, the available Ubers, he couldn't get himself out of the Lisbon airport. It was in his voice, if not his words. He felt so weak about the whole thing.

Would you like us to send somebody? the conference coordinator asked.

In 2016, weeks before my third concussion, when things really start to break down between S and me, my father-in-law gets his leg amputated in a medically necessary intervention that will protect his heart. This is a man who cannot bear to sit at home, who makes three days' worth of plans for an eight-hour excursion: brunch, airboat, beach, zoo, back to the beach for sunset photos. In the years following this procedure, he will come out of retirement and get a part-time job, more for the company than the money. Even at his age, he outsells the young slick salesmen. *Here is a man,* we like to say, *who can sell water to the fishes and sun to the sunburned.* In the coming years, he will have to replace his prosthesis six, seven times because it pains him to walk across a room. Despite his pain, he is full of love and enthusiasm. He leaves me voice mails in song form. Announces to the family, when we are overfed on the couch after Thanksgiving dinner and watching *American Ninja Warrior*, "Annie could be on that show." Even when I call him by his first name, you can hear the word "dad" in my voice.

We fly down, watch the Super Bowl on the eve of the surgery, eat chicken wings that my brother-in-law and I pick up from one of fifty-one Hooters in Florida because they're my father-in-law's favorite. After his leg is sawed off, they let us see him. He is drugged, moaning in pain, putting his fingers up to his lips as if to take a drag of a cigarette, which he quit exactly twenty-four hours ago. He has survived so much, worked so hard for his family, overcome demons through sheer willpower and strength—and yet his suffering demands to be named. My wife watches over him, never even blinking it seems.

The morning after the amputation, early hours, we go back to the hospital. I am moving fast, come up too short and bang my head against the car door. I try hard to steady my brain, but it's swelling. Already I'm drowning and cannot process all the bits of stimuli. We stand around the recovery bed, and dad shows us some stretches he's learning. The glare of the floor, the crackle of the loudspeaker, the smell of sweat on the bundle of bedsheets—it is to my great shame undoing me in front of this man who has just been through something unspeakable. I have to leave the room, breathing so erratically in the waiting room that a woman quietly draws her daughter away from me. And then at the last moment, she turns back, asks, Hey, you okay?

ᴼᴼᴼᴼᴼ

In *Mystery and Manners*, Flannery O'Connor famously pronounces that "violence is strangely capable of returning my characters to reality and preparing them to accept their moment of grace. Their heads are so hard that almost nothing else will do the work." I am the monkey sitting under the tree with the falling coconuts, and it takes one, two, three coconuts to the head before I get whatever it is I'm supposed to get. Probably, it will take more coconuts.

ᴼᴼᴼᴼᴼ

Convince the brain it is safe and, like a tiny mouse, it will come out again.

ᴼᴼᴼᴼᴼ

This is the invitation to unknowing.

There is no healing without letting go of what's come before. To reenter the world, I must engage in new ways. This starts with the fundamentals, such as staying in bed when I'm sick, relearning how to draw a clock, and figuring out, not for the first time in my life, how to remain an adult while angry. After the physical therapy, that's when the real work begins. Healing, for me, starts when I am finally paying attention. I have to stop the water from running into the bucket, yes, but I first have to see the water.

I discover that I have not been as empathic as I like to think. All this time, I've been misinterpreting my luck for strength, mistaking my tepid kindness toward others for compassion, thought I carried joy in me but see that what I've actually been doing is borrowing it. I could not fathom the pain and suffering of others until I was drowning myself. Like most people, I have been silently tallying and comparing myself against them. Camille, Aunt Judy, countless other women—yes, it's often a woman on the other side of my judgment. I have looked at them all with thin pity. "Sometimes," Rachel Cusk writes in *Outline*, "it has seemed to me . . . that one forges one's own destiny by what one doesn't notice or feel compassion for; that what you don't know and don't make the effort to understand will become the very thing you are forced into knowledge of." The poet closes her ears at the dinner table, the ambulance screeches, and I must reckon with my smallness. Ashamed as I am to admit it, my trouble makes theirs real. I am awed. They do not ask for awe. They just keep going. I look again, new planes of reality open up to me, other ways to perceive the world, no less real or true, far more human.

Once a month, Camille U escapes for four days to Orcas Island off the coast of Seattle, a place she says is located in a healing vortex, where she sometimes catches sight of whales on the horizon. When I'm on the island, Camille says, I don't have a head injury.

When I am on that island—my own version of it, the beach, the woods—I think of my father-in-law; in my mind I go back to that room with him. I am uninjured and able to be strong for him, for my wife. This time, I do not leave.

on anger

I am naked and shouting into the steamy bathroom mirror. The episode that started in the shower is full blown now. My mouth contorts, my face heats up, my cheeks are cutlets cooked to different temperatures. Tiny flecks of spit splatter onto the fogged glass. I pace between bedroom and bathroom, head dripping. The neighbor's dog, hearing me, throws himself against the fence.

The fury comes from nowhere and is directed toward whatever. An annoying student, the rental car company from a few months ago, the soap company that cheated me out of a free gift, dead father, dead mother, lying sister, the garbage truck, the neighbor's neglected pack of dogs, the woman at the grocery store who cut me off years ago, the stranger who delighted in my suffering, the family member who delighted in my suffering, the girl who plowed through the South Philly crosswalk and, when I yelled Yo!, got out of her car looking like she was going to punch my lights out. Some slights are so insignificant, they may as well not have happened, but others overwhelm me, take me back, ten years, twenty years. I call these Fixations. I'm gone half an hour—do not realize I am loud or even that I am angry—until the dogs are at it again. I end up in fights with people who are not there about things that have not happened.

This morning's episode is not special. Since the injuries, I am angry all the time. Impulsivity, rage, disinhibition: these are some of the primary characteristics of aggression following brain injury. I scream at my bathroom mirror for months before I realize the problem. It is the hot air—sucked in through the small vents and then pushed through nichrome wire coils. The blow dryer heating up my head is what sets me off.

ooooo

The limbic system is derived from the Latin *limbus*, for "edge" or "border." Key sensitive regions, part of the mesolimbic pathway, sit at the frontal lobe and operate as a set of structures that regulate pleasure, motivation, emotional regulation. Because of the way our skull is shaped—to protect our ears, for instance, so that we stay safe from predators—it is the orbital medial area that is at greatest risk, particularly the fragile bones of the eye socket and the orbitofrontal cortex, those structures vital to the mesolimbic pathway. A hard enough hit to the head and the neural networks that connect the prefrontal cortex to the midbrain, and suddenly you sound like somebody you never were. The most famous case of this is Phineas Gage who, in 1848, is impaled in the brain by an iron bar. He walks away from the injury, but Gage, formerly the model foreman of his crew, becomes "fitful, irreverent," utters "the grossest profanity." His outbursts ultimately cost him his job at the railroad construction company. He finds work driving coaches in Chile, dies just ten years later at thirty-six, becomes an old wives' tale of brain science.

The upper brain—the neocortex, prefrontal cortex, the logical brain—is responsible for higher-order thought processes such as cognition and language; it can act, through the employment of reason and logic, as a coolant to strong emotions. The reptilian brain at the heart of the central nervous system—the emotional brain—is much older, cruder, smaller, a kind of fist at the top of the spine that doesn't get enough credit for keeping us alive. Science journalist Ashley Abramson, drawing from neuroscientist R. Douglas Fields's *Why We Snap: Understanding the Rage Circuit in Your Brain* to talk about the physiology of a meltdown, describes "the amygdala as the brain's smoke detector and the hypothalamus as the someone deciding whether to put gasoline or water on the fire." After brain injury, there is some short-circuiting, the alarms are constantly going off, the blue stuff drips out. The brain swells just like any other bruised body part, but unlike the knee or the ankle, it has nowhere to go, it bumps up against the hard bone of the skull. This excessive neuroinflammation, which can damage neuronal circuitry, is sometimes expressed as irritation, anger, excessive aggression, raging at strangers, getting into fights, getting arrested—all the danger and reck- lessness of a teenager. Add to this an additional acute injury to particu- lar regions in the brain, and emotional dysregulation and hyper limbic activation are sure to follow. This is how we arrive at Phineas Gage's "grossest profanity."

ooooo

I can't sit under heat lamps at restaurants. Can't work under fluores- cents. Certain days, I have trouble in the sun. It's not just the headaches: my anger rises as my temperature does.

I walk the city, avoiding strewn garbage. One of my favorite pas- times is exploring Philadelphia on foot—down South Street, past the dress made out of hair in the display window just a few shops down from the window where it used to hang. The condom store, the famous cheesesteak shop that smells as much of Fabuloso cleaner as it does of meat, the kid asking if I want to buy H, the bar with the bumper cars where you can get pierogies and where I used to co-host a reading series. I have always enjoyed getting lost in my head on long walks—of being both on a particular street and in a place no one can map. Once, as a child, on the farm in Greece, I stepped on an inch-long rusty nail. I didn't see it in the orange dust, which the chickens and my own legs had kicked up. Only after an hour of looking at the delight and fear on my cousins' faces did I go to the adults and point out the hole in my sneaker and foot. I didn't want them to take away from me the freedom of wandering.

In South Philly, where I live, the blocks are all row houses and "workingman's houses," tight and hidden as fingers in a mitt. People are gruffly friendly, and the window displays are famous for being bonkers and sincere. Silk flowers, ceramic dogs, some kind of stuffed bird, photos, love notes to Obama or the pope. They aren't exactly competing against each other but, like Philadelphia itself, no one is backing down.

I walk my neighborhood and look at the houses and the singing fountain and try to think of nice things—try to set my thoughts free—but my mind goes right back to the rage, like a tongue to a sore. Today's target: my landlord. They are swindling us. They have been cheating the city, too, covering up code violations by dumping manure onto their own property. As if to prove my point, vultures have broken into their kitchen, left feces everywhere. They are on their university's ethics committee in New Jersey, yet they are sleeping with their graduate student, a blond man who looks exactly like their son will five years from now. They insist they are queer but only to people like me, they want everyone to know the most mundane details about them, their hair is not black but "raven," if I have something in my eye then so do they, they look like they flunked out of witch school, they believe they deserve greater happiness than most.

I think I am only ranting in my head, until I look up and see that people are crossing the street to get away from me. They will not even glance at my shadow. I am startled for a moment, that I am the person that strangers are avoiding, but also: I do not care.

ooooo

It is 1524. Most mornings, Henry doesn't rise until eight a.m., and even then, the fit and hunky king prefers to hunt or hawk than deal with matters of state. Nights are for gambling, dancing. Gifted with a shrewd memory, he makes quick work of England's ambassadors, secretaries, the thirty-thousand-word bestseller *Defense of the Seven Sacraments*, which he wrote and which names him "Defender of the Faith." He's an easy picture in those early days—lustrous reddish-gold hair, good skin, vigorous, generous, gentle, "more like a companion than a king" according to the Dutch scholar Erasmus.

Henry breathes in the grassy air at the field, watches armored horsemen storm at each other with wooden lances. He suits up in a harness of his own design, gear no one has ever seen before. Henry loves to joust, something his father forbid him from doing as a boy. Today, nobody realizes that he has failed to lower his visor. Henry charges, deaf to any cries of *Hold!* The counterblow lands just above the king's right eye, pushing the visor so far back that the headpiece is full of splinters. Henry will shake this off, put on a new helmet. But the accident leaves him with migraines that stoke his temper. His aides start to avoid him, whispering *the king is in a foul mood today*, no clue just how bloody his rage will become.

ooooo

The internet is full of people who are flooded by anger after brain injury. Rants at work, outbursts at home, confrontations in parking lots, explosions in the doctor's office. We all get Fixations. I wasn't like this before, one of them says. Somebody else posts, Try lavender, tub soaks, breathing exercises. Some days are just like that, sis, says another. Someone—a woman who suffered one collision after another—confides, The old me would have been quiet and apologetic . . . well, old me is gone.

As I'm walking past an outdoor café, a busboy passes me carrying a load of dishes, shouts, I wouldn't mess with you!

Greeks know anger. Lesbians know anger. Women who grow up in South Jersey have a mouth on them. People shake their heads. Poor thing has a trash mouth because she got brain damage. In reality, my relatives swear in four to five languages, and I have always run my mouth like this. I have seen adults wield anger when they're caged. Once, at a sleepover after a carnival, I watched a grown man beat the shit out of a little boy for embarrassing him. My sister, the coolest cucumber, tried to run a boyfriend over with her car during a fight. The gold Volvo with the broken horn that sounded like a whale because I punched it anytime I picked up a call from my father, cursing him out after we had hung up. Before S, I didn't even realize I was yelling, I just thought that this was how people proved their point in an argument. But after the injuries, fights get ugly again, with me having to return afterward to say, Sorry, sorry, I didn't mean that. Me having to call back, Sorry, sorry, I got over-whelmed walking through the crowd, it's so hot out. One particularly bad outburst in front of our apartment, tearing pieces of bark off an oak tree. I'm sorry, no, I don't hate you.

I can see it in her eyes: sorry is wearing thin.

The time our father threw the wooden pieces because we were "cheating" at Jenga. The canoe trip, which I was not present for and which you'd have to ask his ex-wife about. The night he spent in lockup. The evening, I swear, when he threw a large ceramic plate of spaghetti and it landed upside down on one of our heads—petals of translucent onion on the tile floor, red dots of sauce on the molding. (That one, we sisters still laugh about.) The night he punched holes into the walls because the "low-life addict mother" was back in our lives and he could not protect us. In an argument, he spit directly into one of our faces and made the others lie about it. You see what you make me do? one of his favorite things to say. You see how you make me angry?

But this anger: it is something else.

∞∞∞∞

Some months after Henry's jousting injury, there is a second blow to the head. He might have drowned in the ditch had someone not fished him out. Ten years later, another jousting tournament, a third accident— January 24, 1536, Greenwich Place. This one nearly kills him. Henry is thrown from his horse, and his horse, also clad in metal, falls atop him. He is unconscious for two hours. Anne Boleyn, terrified that he might never awaken, miscarries; in a few month's time, she will lose her head for it.

This third injury changes Henry—he is no longer Henry: he is Henry VIII. His depression, "self-pity and more than traces of gloom" confine him to Hampton Court. His multiple wives and mistresses secretly mock him for impotence. He suffers from explosive rage, insomnia, amnesia, sociopathy, trouble with impulse control, headaches, and his subjects suffer from far worse. His outbursts of paranoia turn increasingly brutal. It is in 1536 that "bloodletting of those close to the Crown" becomes frequent, estimates as high as fifty-seven thousand lives taken by the king, fifty of them his close advisors and friends. Blood, more blood, the king's raging brain demands.

∞∞∞∞

Fancy Babysitter, who sometimes took care of us, loved the word "twat." *Clean twat, dirty twat, put it in your twat.* In third grade, she taught me how to take on a bully by putting them in a headlock. She made amazing French toast. "Sharp" was one of the best compliments she could give you, whether it was talking about your smarts or your outfits. Fancy Babysitter was the thinnest, most fashionable person over forty I'd ever known—chunky brown glasses, sneakers whiter than on display. She was also in more pain than any other adult I have ever seen up close. As a younger woman, Fancy Babysitter had been beaten by her husband, sometimes passing out from the abuse and very likely suffering concussions—but this was something I would not understand for many years. There was an audible click in her jaw whenever she chewed. After she was done cooking breakfast, after the dishes were washed and there was nothing more to do, she'd sit at the table smoking, tissues tucked into her sleeve, and give into a crying jag. Fancy Babysitter would rage at the smallest infraction. She'd say: *Hee-yah! Queen of Sheba! Clean up this mess!* We'd scatter to find the specks of lint which did not exist. We'd try to be vacuums instead of children. We laugh about it now, anytime we recall being babysat. Once, at a family funeral, someone told about how a couple of teenagers cut off Fancy Babysitter in a parking lot at the mall and snatched up her spot. Fancy Babysitter pulled up behind them, grabbed the hammer from her trunk, and smashed in windows on all four sides of the car; the girls just sat there, staring straight ahead. She taught me how anger can make a woman far more dangerous than any man, how it can keep you alive even as it eats away at you. Sheer will and resilience, this was how she survived until she died, far too young.

After some time, the Fixations drop off—and I wonder if all the ranting was just me being hotheaded. Then I get into a fight with some light switches when I accidentally back into them, and am flooded with anger for weeks, the way I imagine Fancy Babysitter might have been. Yet again, I am going after people who are not there. Just me vs. me vs. me.

ooooo

It is a horrible, rainy day at Wayside School. All the children look over at the new boy, Sammy, and his dripping raincoat. One of the girls gets her name on the DISCIPLINE blackboard for saying he stinks. Well, you're ugly, Sammy replies. When Mrs. Jewls asks him to take off his raincoat, Sammy calls her a windbag. When the teacher helps him with his raincoat there is another coat beneath it, even dirtier and smellier than the first. Mrs. Jewls runs to the window for air, and he calls them all a bunch of pigs. Mrs. Jewls adds Sammy's name under DISCIPLINE. She removes another coat—four, five, six raincoats. He tells her, "Watch where you throw my good clothes!" She writes his name on the board. Eight, nine, ten coats, dirt under the teacher's nails. Sammy has a horrible laugh that scares the children. Hey, old windbag, Sammy says. If you take off one more of my coats, I'll bite your head off. At last, the final layer. There is no boy. There is only a dead rat. Mrs. Jewls picks it up, puts it in a plastic bag. Dead rats are always trying to sneak into the class.

I am not the dead rat. I am the many layers of stinking coat. I do not know how many more there are to go, or how I even got into this room. Trapped in my head, I call you all pigs, and some days are so consuming that I mean it—and, yes, I have yelled at my wife about where she puts my good clothes, or how many noodles she is cooking. A streak in me I have suspected but never seen surface before this. S, you deserve better, S, please don't walk away.

Please understand: I smell the dead rat before you do.

ooooo

"Mr. Zen" is what they call the butcher who cuts the perfect rib eye. He has thick, curly hair, tattoos, Jesus eyes, a deliberate way of speaking. He is the one the guys all go to for tips on weightlifting and how to keep a cool head. He shows me photos of his little girl anytime we share a shift at the meat counter.

Anger can be explosive, yes. But it can be private, too, and quiet. A solitary suffering after injury that looks less like rage, more like sadness, bitterness, defeat. One day, the kind butcher and I trade concussion stories, his the result of sports. He tells me he tried moving to Arizona, thinking sunshine would help, but it didn't and neither did the racism, so he came back.

He says to me: There are days I am full of spit. Okay, I can accept that: I am an angry person now. But how do I hide that from my daughter?

Bring anger and pride under your feet, says Rumi: Turn them into a ladder, climb higher.

ooooo

Historians, fascinated by the transformation of Henry VIII from bene-volent monarch to tyrant, have ascribed his personality shift to hypo-thyroidism, diabetes, psychosis, McLeod syndrome, sepsis, fistulating cellulitis in a leg that the wives complain about. Then, in 2015, a study published by Yale Memory Clinic reveals: Henry suffered from head trauma. According to research by a Yale University expert in cognitive neurology, "Henry suffered from many symptoms which can unambig-uously be attributed to traumatic brain injury."

Brain injuries back then must have been so suspicious. You are pos-sessed by head pain, angry fits, even the sun makes you flare. Not even the king is protected, not even if you can by a flick of your pinky order the death of a subject does it mean you are spared.

You cry out, It's her, it's the town witch! She's the one doing this!

The town burns you up instead.

In your next life, you come back as the fire.

living in the basement

In March 2019, twenty-three-year-old Olympic silver medalist Kelly Catlin took her own life in her college dorm. A month earlier—the day she was scheduled to meet the queen of Spain—she had tried and failed to kill herself by asphyxiation. Her family and coaches rushed in after the first attempt. She was referred to two sports psychologists, but neither could see her. She tried calling a suicide hotline multiple times, was once put on hold. Another time, no one answered.

Kelly was a member of the US cycling team, a three-time world champion in the four-rider group race called the team pursuit. She was earning a degree at Stanford University in computational math and engineering. She spoke Chinese fluently, was a natural athlete, a gifted classical violinist, had plans to be a data scientist. This all changed for her after a slick winter ride in December when, two months before her suicide, she suffered a head injury. Her family insists: "The concussion changed her."

I think about what it must have been like for Kelly in the weeks before her death, struggling through tough math problems and headaches, unable to withstand even a "coffee ride" with her coach. I imagine her putting her violin to her chin and grasping for Niccolò Paganini, touching only air. At one point, in four pages of frenetic journaling, she writes—*If I am not an athlete, I am nothing.*

"We didn't know about the racing thoughts and the obsessing," Kelly's sister Christine says.

In his paper on behavior analytical approaches, clinical psychologist Stephen M. Myles blames ruptures of identity after TBI on the "inconsistencies between her post-injury functioning and pre-injury conceptualized self." With a brain injury, even those we don't define as serious, there is the persistent sensation that you are not you. This is the Crisis of the Conceptualized Self. You look the same, therefore should be the same, and people react to you as if you are the person they remember. They talk to you as if you are still the silver medalist, even if your heart races after only moderate exertion. They do not know you are now somebody new—a secret person, a stranger to yourself—who researches and rents two cylinders of compressed helium for an exit plan, and in the end you are the body that your roommate finds in the dorm now filled with noxious gas. They expect you to be the same uninterrupted line you have always been. For a while—because identity is the natural formation that arises where we meet others—you fight to return to that person, too.

After my third concussion, I sit in the chair, wrestle with the empty page. I do this out of terror and habit. Nothing comes. This is not writer's block. I have lost the gift of sight—I can no longer look into that space ahead and conjure something out of the fictive world. It is less like blindness, more a body part gone numb. I forget how to imagine. I forget words entirely, how to set them alongside one another. It is as if someone has hidden language behind a curtain, and I can only see the shadow it makes on the blank wall. I'm able to hold on to certain pieces of the narrative if I concentrate, but I can't build much out of them.

Specifically, I am showing indication of low idea density and nonspecific language lacking detail (empty words—"anyone," "something"—keep creeping up). I try talking into a voice recorder, write entire chapters this way. When I play it back, it sounds like someone else's book, so I throw it out. Dear god, I pray, please make me whole if only on the page.

On my desk is a notebook, Post-its, a photo of Whitney Houston, a plastic pirate, a rubber octopus, some precious rocks, a puppet playing a lute, a very dramatically thirsty plant, a red daruma, and other writing talismans given to me by friends or found in the wild. On the bookshelf beside my desk, the sky-blue spines of my first novel stare back at me. The greatest kindness I ever felt from Mom was when she called me up and said, Of course I was going to read it, why would you think I wouldn't? and then, You can see why people like it, it's different. But I am very far from that book right now. I get the distinct feeling that the novel was written by someone else—another writer, someone I am outside of, somebody who could never recognize me. Overnight, my work has become no longer mine because I am not me anymore. I tell myself that writers always spurn their first books or else they would never write a second, and that every book written is many selves ago. I tell myself that, per neuroscientist Anil Seth, all reality is a "controlled hallucination." But then I look again at the blue spines. I turn the books so they face backwards, with the gray pages fanning out. Now the novel might have been written by anybody.

Kelly—and the whole Catlin clan—were overachievers. In third grade, Kelly started following The Code, strict guidelines to live by, which she wrote into a notebook and which included *no crying*. In eleventh grade, Kelly enrolled in classes at the University of Minnesota and got perfect SAT scores. She shut herself away for twelve-hour study sessions and went on sixty-mile bike rides. The only time she watched movies was on a stationary bike, and her $20 allowance was contingent on how much she had exercised that week. Her parents, who wanted to prepare their daughter for the future they believed she deserved, pushed her to excel. Her mother, Carolyn, after Kelly's death, said: "So many parents automatically just say, Good job. Their kids are successful getting a fork to their mouth: Good job!" Whatever Kelly did—origami, competitive shooting, riding, suicide note—it had to be perfect.

Her brother Colin says of Kelly, "She always wanted to basically be this monolithic, terrifying force of power."

ooooo

In Oliver Sacks's *An Anthropologist on Mars*, a painter goes color-blind after his concussion. Everything appears in black-and-white, like an old television. Everything looks misty, bleached. His abstract paintings, once full of intense color, are now gray to him, meaningless. His dinner plate is full of gray, dead food; when he closes his eyes and tries to picture a tomato, it's black. He sticks to black and white foods, olives and rice, coffee and yogurt. Flowers, museum paintings, are all wrong. He is depressed by rainbows. The flesh of his own wife looks to him "rat-colored." He dreams he is about to see color, and then he wakes up. In his sorrow, he sits for hours staring at his lawn, willing *green* to life. Sacks writes, "He knew all about color, externally, intellectually, but he had lost the remembrance, the inner knowledge, of it that had been part of his very being. He had had a lifetime of experience in color, but now this was only a historical fact." The color-blind painter tells himself, If I can't go on painting, I don't want to go on at all.

ooooo

After brain injury, we lose the words we once used to describe ourselves— strong, industrious, clever, creative, talented, resilient, imaginative. We are left with something unspeakable, a core self that can be frightening and exhilarating to meet, a stranger who wears our shoes and smells like us.

The me I used to know chose freedom over obedience and left home at seventeen. The me I once was graduated college at the top of the class, feeling herself behind everyone else but never showing it. The me I once was—but apparently no longer am—did not give into failure or fears of being an impostor, because scrappiness overcame almost any hurdle. I pushed and pushed.

A year after my first head injury, I travel south for a job interview, where I am asked to read and speak about my first book. I smile through it and deliver the jokes from page one. I sign copies of the book, as if I'm doing a favor for the real author. When I am offered the job, I can't help but feel like I've stolen someone else's work, that the nice people on this committee believe I'm somebody I'm not.

John Locke's idea of psychological continuity suggests that someone who comes through a struggle can still recognize herself on the other side if some idea of her continues to exist. Philosopher Carsten Korfmacher further explains this notion: "In order for a person X to survive a particular adventure, it is necessary and sufficient that there exists, at a time after the adventure, a person Y who psychologically evolved out of X." Yet, with brain injury, the shift is so abrupt, so decisive, that there is a cleaving—only the before and after, was and is, war and prisoner. After injury, who you were on Sunday is not who you are on Monday. After injury, the person giving the interview is not the person on the page.

I stop seeking out readings. When sales are down, I think, let it die, it's dead already. I accumulate pages toward a new novel, but deep down (I know it, my agent knows it), they are brittle. It is not just the words. I am locked out. My characters are at a party in the apartment next door, and all I can hear are their muffled conversations. It is slowly dawning on me that I am alienated not only from my body, from my brain, but also from my imagination. I cannot see into that distance where creation happens. My wife says, Don't worry you still have your voice. It takes years to figure out that what she actually means is I still have my soul.

Q: What do you call a writer who cannot write?
A:

The painter tries to paint in color again: it doesn't work. His friends, even his wife, tell him it's not a big deal—but the colorless colors are repulsive to him.

ooooo

Catlin Kelly is not the only female athlete to die by suicide after concussion.

A year before Kelly's suicide, Ellie Souter, the British snowboarder who won a bronze medal in snowboard cross, kills herself in a remote woodland on her eighteenth birthday. Seven concussions between 2013 and 2018, airlifts off mountains. No one suspects depression, her uncle describes her as "chirpy." Her father says: "I truly believe today that my daughter would be alive had I had any inkling, you know, even the smallest bit of information."

A year after Kelly's suicide, in 2020, Australian football player Jacinda Barclay kills herself. An autopsy reveals that there is significant degradation of the white matter in her brain, not unlike the CTE diagnosed posthumously in American football players.

In November 2018, a little over a month before her accident, three-time world champion Kelly stands at the podium at a World Cup track cycling race. She looks past the cheering fans, waving flags, all the way out to Tokyo 2020—where she's predicted to win gold. She sees the bright future she has been training for all her life, the one owed her.

"As far as we knew," Catlin's father says, "she was never a person that suffered from depression."

○○○○○

In his biography, first recorded in the late first century, Plutarch asks if we are still who we once were if those recognizable parts of us go missing. In the Theseus paradox, Theseus, hero of Athens, returns victorious from my home island of Crete, having slayed the Minotaur. The Athenians are so in awe, they decide to preserve his broken-down ship by replacing it plank for plank. Plutarch poses the question, If an object has had all of its components replaced, is it still fundamentally the same entity? If you replace all the boards on a ship, is it still the same ship? If someone takes those old boards and builds an entirely new ship, do you now have two ships? If this new Kelly Catlin can no longer race, sees in herself someone who is physically weak, without stamina, a person who fails after a lifetime of excellence, who might not be able to compete in Tokyo, who has unexpected dark, spinning thoughts, whose very body and brain are betraying her, is she the same Kelly Catlin?

With brain injury, there has been a disruption of borders: because a sequential self requires proximity to the past self for association to occur, the present unknown self is disquieting, mistrusted. The injured brain, unlike the ship that has been built back together from parts, is fractured. The split self arises from self-estrangement, the evaluation of deficits, enduring emotional distress. This is the untold legacy of head trauma. It is so common that it is described as being the sine qua non of brain injury. "Certain qualitative changes in a person's psychology or physiology may kill the person," Korfmacher says. "The question a criterion of personal identity answers is: what kind of changes does a person survive?"

"She was not the Kelly we knew . . . she spoke like a robot," Kelly's father, Mark, said. "We could get her to talk but we wondered, what has happened to our Kelly?" Yet even now, when Kelly Catlin is covered in the media, almost no one—outside her family—talks about the concussion.

About the time that Kelly Catlin falls off her bike, I attend the Mind Your Brain Conference in Philadelphia. The keynote speaker is a snowboarder whose professional career was cut short by a bad ride—an Olympian, like Kelly, an athlete to rival Shaun White. In the audience are medical professionals, students of neurology, but mostly, the attendees are people with brain injuries. There is a free lunch. I tell myself I'm here to conduct research for a new novel since, little by little, over five years' recovery, I have been regaining the ability to write—not just put down mangled words, but to see true shapes. I show up late to the conference, I'm jittery and don't know why. The back of my neck prickles. I can't shake the uncanniness, as if this is all an elaborate set with hired actors whose job it is to fold me into their ranks. People sitting on plush chairs, eating apples. People flipping through the schedule. A woman with blond curls sauntering up to a table for free swag. Then I realize my unease—the hundreds of people wandering the booths and finding their seats are entirely unremarkable. They look just like me. What were you expecting? I ask myself. Limping? Dark glasses? Someone helping them down the stairs? Eye patches? We look mostly the same.

I sit in on Dr. Ann Marie McLaughlin's astounding presentation on emotional health, entitled "I Am Not Me," and learn just how many of the walking wounded are troubled by a divided self. This comes as a revelation, because all this time I think I've just been coping badly. And it turns out, I have. Apparently, overachievers with perfectionist tendencies—Kelly Catlin, Annie Liontas—have the worst time adjusting to cognitive disruption. Dr. McLaughlin compares us to homes in a Class 3 hurricane. We have not all suffered the same damage. This house over here is okay. This second house is a mess, foundation gone, insurance wants to know if the symptoms correlate with the accident or if it was always a run-down house whose owners are now trying to scam the system. This house way out here is narcissistic and grandiose and is bound not to know itself after the storm tears down its walls.

Suicide, she tells us, is at three times the population norm. We are seeking to understand the relationship between white matter changes in the brain and suicidality.

Then Dr. McLaughlin pulls up a slide called "Living in the Base-ment." The Basement, Dr. McLaughlin explains, is where a lot of peo-ple with brain injuries end up. This is not a metaphor. Thousands of survivors can no longer live upstairs: 20 to 30 percent are wracked by vestibular symptoms, another 19 percent suffer from vision problems and headache, all are in "psychic distress or withdraw."

I know the Basement. Despite my childhood avoidance of base-ments (the philosopher Gaston Bachelard calls it the dark, subterranean, irrational entity of the house, the place from which fear springs), I have been living in one. My Basement is the blue scarf I've kept wrapped around my face for the greater part of four years. It is the separation I have felt from people even when we're in the same room. My Basement has no staircase, it is just one long step down. It is at this very moment that I realize I've sensed my old self missing, I just haven't understood where she'd gone.

I look at all the people sitting around me—the people too sick to even make it here today, Kelly Catlin who is only beginning to suffer—me with my snotty nose, all these people in their own dark basements but all of us somehow together. Somebody in the next row sees this is too much for me, passes a napkin that smells like a ham sandwich, and this feels like a great kindness.

I tell myself that the brain injury did not take away a self, rather it revealed many other selves heretofore unknown to me.

Mark Doty writes, "That is a relief, is it not, to acknowledge that we do not after all know what a self is? A corrective to human arrogance, to the numbing certainty that puts a soul to sleep." He goes on, in *The Art of Description*, to say, "Consciousness can't be taken for granted when there are, plainly, varieties of awareness."

I rewrite the book until it is a different book; then I rewrite it until I am a different writer.

ooooo

One morning, as the painter is driving, he sees the sun coming up over the highway, the reds all blacks. "The sun rose like a bomb, like some enormous nuclear explosion," he says. He starts working again, abstracts as before in a series called *Nuclear Sunrise*, with one big difference: he paints in black and white. He never gets green back, but he sees black/white in an entirely new light.

There is a philosophy experiment that is even better known than Theseus's ship, and that is "People Who Divide Like an Amoeba." In this puzzle, philosopher Derek Parfit asks you to imagine that your brain is sawed in half and placed into two different bodies. Both brains survive, both go on to live different lives. Parfit, who most of all does not want people to suffer (the idea of anyone in pain, even Hitler, makes him want to cry) wants us to remember that even the divided self can never fully be divided. "They can be different people and yet be me, just in the way the Pope's three crowns are one crown." I can be both the writer and the non-writer. The artist can see in color, and also see no color.

Kelly's parents beg her to quit school, quit everything. Come home, forget classes, heal, be somebody else for a while. Her sister sends her articles on a little Italian town where Stradivarius violins are made by hand. Wouldn't it be nice to go there? Maybe Kelly considers the possibility, briefly. Maybe she can almost reach out and touch that other life of Kelly Catlin, before it disappears for good.

In her final words, she writes, "I was dancing before the end. Just so you know. I woke up, danced a dance, played my fiddle, and died." After her death, still seeking answers, her family donates her brain to concussion research at Boston University's CTE Center.

The colorblind painter who paints in black and white is a night person now. He drives to random cities, Boston, Baltimore, pulling up at dusk, wandering the streets for much of the night. He is drawn to diners. He says, "Everything in diners is different at night, at least if it has windows. The darkness comes into the place, and no amount of light can change it. They are transformed into night places."

The basement is still dark, but little by little you get used to it, and then you realize—

there is something to be found in the darkness.

the big sleep

In the womb—which is tucked so far inside my mother's body it is hidden even from her—I cannot sleep. I am wide awake. This is when sleeplessness first arrives for me: before I am me. It is all this speed coursing through our veins, me and the woman about to give birth to me. She has been sneaking the drugs from neighbors, plus procuring them legally from her doctor, who prescribes opioids. The drugs are my twin, for she has made space for each of us inside her body. She has carried me only seven months, but my twin has been with her for years, and my mother would ache if she lost either of us. She knows I am coming soon, too soon—because of the drugs. There is desperation to keep me with her and also to push me out. But I cannot be lulled or rocked back to sleep. I am wide, wide awake. Our bodies convulse—and here I come, two months early, dancing myself right out of the womb. It is 1981. Everyone is alarmed. I am only three pounds, my lungs not yet lungs, my eyes not yet ready for light, my leg the size of a man's thumb, my father's thumb in fact. He drives to the hospital cursing to himself. I recognize his voice as soon as I hear it, heavy like lava cooling but also bright in spots. How surprised he is to find his he is me. How strange, she looks like a bird that fell out of the nest, she is thin and glassy, you can hardly hear her cry, all she wants is to sleep, this preemie baby, twenty-two hours a day.

My whole life, I yearn for the Big Sleep: a sleep to end all sleeps.

ooooo

A year later, after my sister is born, my mother leaves. My father does not know what to do with two needful infant girls. He begs her to take the children and he will send her money, but his wife says no. She is done with being stuck inside with babies, she wants to go out and live her life. This makes no sense to him; he keeps trying to put one and one together but there is no logic to her. When has anyone cared what a lesbian has to say? Such is the ongoing conflict that embroils them.

My sister and I are sent to Greece to live with an uncle, and when that ends abruptly—because he has been pocketing the money my father sent and feeding us coffee and bread—we are split up. One to a grandmother, one to a kind old lady who smells like butter. Most days are spent on the farm, surrounded by insects that wake up screeching as if they've overslept. Pictures show days at the beach, rolling in sea-foam in orange swimmies. I will, at odd points in my life—at a work meeting, on an escalator—be hit by the inexplicable smell of warm goat's milk, a sign that my island is still within me. We will not return to our father or America for almost four years. Our father, who has cried certain nights because he has missed his little girls, will wonder who are these children who have suddenly appeared on his doorstep to eat all his food. Sometimes I will catch him looking wistfully past me when a door opens, thinking that his little *koukla* has finally, finally returned to look up at him with eyes that see nobody else.

There is a photograph of me getting ready to come to America. I am maybe four, five. (Time is slippery when you are sent away only to return.) Someone has hung a miniature purse on my shoulder. I am wearing a blue-and-white-flower dress, looking as if I do not quite know who I belong to. I am little—not frail, but as if I am made of tiny pieces that can be boxed up and slid onto a shelf. What is most noticeable are the dark wells beneath my eyes, the swollen lids. It is the sleeplessness that started in the womb, and which has only worsened in Greece. Whatever country I'm in, it seems that sleep slips away just before I arrive, so that when I come to the United States believing I will finally get to sleep—haven't I been promised that this is the land of bounty?—sleep is off again, to places I can't even imagine.

ooooo

As a child, I believe that if I can make my thoughts small enough, I'll be able to fit inside a matchbox. This would be the perfect place for the Big Sleep—dark, smelling like a fire that's died down. You wouldn't need a thing, just someone to slide the lid closed behind you.

ooooo

I tell people it was a bike accident that caused the first head injury. I rarely talk about how the night before I got only forty minutes of sleep, for a total of four hours of sleep in three days. This was when I was thirty-five and so rankled by insomnia that I dreaded coming home to the apartment I was subletting. The edges of the furniture, the beige carpet, the smudged windows, all a piece of why I was sleeping an average of two hours some nights, mere minutes others. Nothing I tried worked—melatonin, Benadryl, meditation, warm milk. Insomnia is seasickness, madness. It is fretting that you forgot to lock the door when in fact you've left it wide open. I would stay awake all day, push my heart rate up to 180 with the hope that physical exhaustion might override whatever was keeping me up at night. There was a banging in my head, a portent of what was to come, and it would not let me sleep. My body, unable to rest, would not regulate. Most people spend seven years of a single lifetime trying to fall asleep, while an insomniac can spend four, five times that, can lose eight, ten billion light-years. I lay there wide awake night after night, desperate to return to the illusion of safety that adulthood brings, to get distance from the past, when even the philosophers know that such distance cannot exist in sleeplessness. Insomnia is duplicity, insomnia manipulates the mind, and I had not slept in so long. Six weeks of this, and I crashed my bike. I was not wearing a helmet. I was pedaling fast, hard, and my foot slipped and I slammed onto the asphalt. At the hospital, the doctor's irritation turned even his pale beard a reddish pique when I told him about my insomnia. *Why did you let it get this bad?*

∞∞∞

Sleep and death, remember, are twins. In Greek mythology, Thanatos, the god of death, and his brother Hypnos, god of sleep, live together in a cave in the underworld. Hypnos has a bed made of ebony. Poppies and other soporific plants grow at the entrance of his cave. No light enters, no sound. But Hypnos is gentle, kind when he invites us in. He can afford to be, he owns half our lives. If we live to age seventy-nine, we give up twenty-six years to Hypnos. We will do almost anything for his oblivion. Sleeps, the tiny, tiny deaths we grant ourselves to escape the agonies of living. Little gifts for the weary, the promise of restoration through annihilation.

∞∞∞

Most nights, my father would lie in his gray recliner, still wearing his welding uniform scarred by burns and holes. He smoked one Saratoga after another and flipped between the weather channel and his beloved westerns. I would listen for the faint sound of horses and gunshots and the creaking of the old gray recliner as my father tried to get out of his own head. In the morning, he heaved himself out of the recliner, having gotten maybe a few hours of rest. His mother, our *yia yia*, had done the same in Greece, staying up to watch lousy English films interrupted by commercials that ran twenty minutes at a stretch, barely able to read the subtitles because she had had almost no schooling, preferring this to her cold bed. I was surrounded by adults who never rested, though I never connected their staring at the television with what I did, the hours of looking up at the ceiling in wait. The story of loneliness at night is far older than the story of a waking life, it reaches all the way back to the earliest humans huddled around a fire, alert to danger and eager for morning to come.

Leave it to Shirley Jackson to write, "No live organism can continue for long to exist sanely under conditions of absolute reality; even larks and katydids are supposed, by some, to dream."

Sleep, when it will not arrive, becomes fantasy, a world just beyond our reach. Big fluffy cloud bed, sheets so cool. The sky an indigo blue nearly gone black, the prickle of starlight. There is the faintest smell of cinnamon, clove, cardamom. There is a conductor driving all of us lucky sleepers through the night sky, the light rocking of the sleep car, everybody smiling. No one gets thirsty. No one has to pee. No bad dreams of blood or looking into a pot and seeing the last little drop of delicious soup and being told, I'm sorry, it's not for you. Oh yes, the Best, Biggest Sleep.

ᴏᴏᴏᴏᴏ

The poet Airea D. Matthews asks, "How do you confess without admitting?" In her poem "Rebel Opera," a conversation between a mother and daughter happens inside the father's mouth. Is it the mother who confesses, the daughter who admits? Or do I have that backward? Does the mother, actually, in saying very little speak the unsayable?

In the poem, Mother tells us: *We inherit the cause, not the illness.*

∞∞∞

Growing up, I am afraid of everything: I am frightened by a can of hair spray if it stands the wrong way. Alone in the dreaded bathtub after the sun has set, I sing the ABCs at the top of my lungs so Freddy Krueger doesn't come up the drain. When I hit Z, I go back to A, start again. Mom sits in the kitchen with her friends and coffee cups, occasionally joining in the bathtub ABCs from downstairs while my sisters sneak in to play with the lights. Mom—the woman who took me aside when I was little and said, with tears in her eyes, "She's your mother but I'll always be mom," the woman I grow to resemble despite having no genetic connection, the person who was always Room Mother—does not always know what to do with my fear. When she is bit by a spider in her sleep, her whole face blows up—now I'm scared of spiders—and until she heals, I can't recognize her except when she laughs.

At night, I sleep with the door cracked. I get up to cover up the plaster head I myself sculpted in art class. I get up to make sure nothing is lurking in the closet. Or I stay in bed, petrified. The house we've moved into is being gutted and the old lady's ghost comes back, shows up angry the night we forget to snuff out a candle. The walls are gone in places, open beams and plywood for flooring. In other places, patches of animal hair stick out of the lime plaster, old newsprint between the boards. There is thick gray dust everywhere, even in the tissue after you blow your nose. On the day my sisters and I have to clean out the meat freezer, which has gone off with the power and leaked rotting blood onto the cellar floor, I am terrified that I have let demons into our house that are more powerful than Clorox. This keeps me awake for years.

Night is arrhythmic, unfamiliar. Noises are not sounds, rather they are inhabitants of this strange in-between, demanding to be heard. Ticking, traffic, the whir of fan blades, cats fighting, Pop Rocks, television, a man urinating, the air conditioner, a stranger's voice, the sound of a ship's horn though there isn't a body of water for miles.

At seventeen, I go away to college without the financial support of my family, unsure what college even is since no one I know has a degree, constantly anxious that I'll be kicked out for unpaid tuition bills, warming up cans of red beans when the scholarship money runs dry. At twenty-five, I tell my father what he has been dreading, and when I introduce him to my future wife he replies, If we let two women be together, what's to stop someone from marrying his dogs? At thirty, I teach a young queer graduate student who confides in me that her parents will not accept her or her trans partner. For her final project, the student creates an exquisite artifact of her life, a kind of handmade book. Some months later, I receive a tearful call. The young woman who made the beautiful portfolio has killed herself. Count the reasons that you are wide awake.

ooooo

An insomniac almost always knows when she is closest to sleep. She experiences its approach as sheer joy. It is like seeing, along the desert's shimmering edge, a thousand horses. A jolt—the joy too great—and then the near-sleeper is denied. She is wide awake, again.

In *Insomnia*, Marina Benjamin writes, "To be without sleep is to want and be found wanting."

The Big Sleep Hotline. Someone answers, but no one has to say anything. The Big Sleep App: every user shows up as a point in a constellation, and you look out and see a whole galaxy of insomniacs and know you are not alone. Big Sleep! The Gameshow, where the prize for guessing the exact minute you'll fall asleep is the sleep of a hundred baby lambs. The Big Sleep Truck, which rides around at night playing its lullaby jingle, which never gets stuck in your head. The Big Sleep Podcast, where you listen over and over to Gogol's "The Overcoat." The Big Sleep voice mail, sounding like somebody's mother but nothing like your mother. The recording says, gently—How infinitesimal you are, as fine and granulose as a speck of sand, how nice is that?

○○○○○

It is night, again. I am in bed. The wide, wide awake. My own heartbeat, a basketball echoing through a gym. The bed against the wrong wall. The discomfort of the pillow. My wife has moved to the couch again though I have not asked this of her. She wants to help, offer me a little relief. I stare at the ceiling darkness. I listen to the calm voice on the meditation app and visualize: lights going off down long concrete corridors, shutters closing on corner shops, shades being drawn, a street emptying of cars. Still, my brain goes to crazy places, like landfills, which are full of New Year's paraphernalia and selfie sticks. At this landfill, I hold a rusty shovel taken from my parents' garage (which sat atop the little sloping hill with the fat carpenter bees, hiding away the green GM that no longer ran but which my father refused to sell). I dig up my favorite childhood toys—some toy cars, a Glo Worm. My Pet Monster, with his blue hair and big honking nose and soft rubber teeth shaped like inverted mountains. When he hears me coming, My Pet Monster breaks out of his orange handcuffs and climbs upward through thirty years of undegraded plastic, and we are reunited. Then, because I still can't sleep, I redo every other minute of my life, deciding what else to keep, what to throw away, knowing that actually nothing is ever truly gone, just buried a little or buried a lot.

Careful now, says the doctor who treats me after the first head injury—
You don't want to forget how to sleep.

Can we really forget, when the living body conspires toward sleep? The
digestion of food, the production of enzymes, the growth of muscle tissue,
our very chemical and neuronal oscillations, our slowing heartbeat, the
subliminal connection to seasonal and climatic changes, all in reciprocity
with circadian cycles. Insomnia overpowers all this. Insomnia, to protect
the body, starves it of an essential nutrient. The brain remains diligent,
alert for danger. The brain saying, Not yet, not yet, you cannot relax just yet.

Every now and then, when I am stranded awake like this, I get a
stabbing image—this is the only way to describe it. Me back in Greece,
little. My uncle has left the bedroom door open; it swings wide behind
him. From the hallway, a candle flickers, or maybe it is just the white
flag of his shirt. My uncle's daughter bites her hooked finger and stares
into my face: hush. Be quiet, say nothing. Later, my father will remove
us from this house, angry that the money he has been sending for for-
mula has been spent elsewhere, that there have been things that my
father has failed to see. Years will pass before we meet this uncle again.
He will have fewer teeth, a beaten expression, and skulk around the
property's edges. I will avoid him.

ooooo

I tell people it was a bike accident: in actuality, it was insomnia. I tell
myself it was insomnia: in truth, it was much darker, the disquiet that
hounds the sleeplessness. These thoughts you have, explains Dr. G, my
therapist—they are as old as you are. This is preverbal, this is fight or
flight, this is not knowing if you will be able to take your next breath.
Death, the closest thing you knew to being born. Perhaps this is precisely why you claw your way back each time.

In the womb, in the seconds that my mother's body is pushing me out, I must understand something that, upon the moment of birth, I immediately forget. I will not remember it again for a long, long time—until my fortieth birthday. The primal knowledge I carry with me—the thing I forget, though it will keep me awake for most of my life: the world has not prepared a place for me. I must, like so many others, make one for myself.

A body recognizes another body who cannot sleep, even when they're worlds apart. It is the breathing: we can hear each other breathing.

ooooo

In the *Iliad*, Chiron is abandoned by his mother, who is disgusted and ashamed that she has given birth to something that is half animal. Chiron is taken in by Apollo and taught the healing arts, music, prophesy, and Apollo's twin Artemis teaches Chiron archery and hunting. Chiron becomes a medic—Homer names him the "wisest and justest of all the centaurs." In battle, he is hit by an arrow dipped in poison. For all his knowledge and skill, Chiron cannot heal his festering wound, but neither—because he is immortal—can Chiron die. And though he suffers, though he never tastes that beautiful, prized eternal sleep, he spends his days teaching others, healing what he can.

ooooo

Why don't we sleep? Because we must, must stay awake.

ooooo

Long before the bike accident, I had the strangest dream.

In the dream, where I could swear I'm awake, I take out $200 and follow two men into a field. I am there to buy a gun. I have a plan. I'll go to the parking lot of a police station so that no one I know will see me, stuff a towel against the windshield. No child will find me, that is very important. No dog walker or skateboarding kid. I will sit in the front seat of my white Geo Metro, a tiny thing itself—easy to miss, not even taking up a whole parking spot. I'll run the heat to fog the windows, turn the radio on low, Mary J. Blige on the station, my own fear booming up to the very end. What happens next should be as easy as flipping the sign to "Closed." In this dream, I am young, lost, do not consider that sooner or later *someone* will look through the window and that what they see might keep them awake for nights. I do not yet understand that I have not met all the people in my lifetime who will love me through my faults. But the plan fails. The men in the field run off with the money.

In the dream, the next gun I get my hands on is given to me by a man I've just met, who keeps coaxing me toward his bed. I pull away from his endless mouth and look over at the gun on his bureau—the only reason I am here—and then I see his sheets. They are the exact color of quicksand, ask any third grader, ask third-grade me.

But on this last minute of this last night of my life, the gun doesn't go off, and then there is not enough money in my bank account to try again.

So what do I do, I go to a party on a boat. I arrive at the precise moment the sky turns inky blue, no, battered blue, no—actually, in my sleepwalking, I can't make out what color it is, only that there are two, three stars coming through, and then night arrives very quickly. My boss sits on the deck in a low lounger, his breath smelling like carcinogens, a silhouette against the horizon except for the cherry of his cigarette. He flicks a dead lighter, click click, it sounds just like the gun that failed; the boat dips up, down, down. There is cheap beer on the boat. There are many Eastern European women, aged only in the eyes and being circled by four sharks pretending to be men, one of them crossing his legs at the ankles. They are talking, laughing, as if a woman's body is the funniest joke in the world. These coarse men I have known for lifetimes. The girls laugh, too, slipping into their pockets the "tips" that smell like low tide. I turn my face so that the wet kiss from my boss's friend lands on my cheek. Years later, I'll realize they are throwing me a goodbye party. I had quit my job—at least I did so in my head, did so on the time sheets— believing I had just one shift left, one final task before I could punch out for good. But a gun cannot tell the future, only temperature, only cold. No idea yet, how many selves live dormant inside me, or that the wind rocking the boat is ancient, that it will be the same wind blowing my hair into knots many years from now. The universe has more to say, I have to keep listening. So maybe a gun can tell time after all. Hours pass, somehow I end up in the hull playing strip poker with the others, girls vs. boys (this is how I'll describe them later, how I'll describe me to myself when I look back—children at sea). Miraculously, I win. I keep winning all night long, though I have never played a hand in my life. I get so many flushes or royals or whatever that the boys' nude bodies glow like streetlights against the waves—but I get to keep my clothes on. The girls and I pass secret looks, as if one of us holds the card to beat. I forget all about the gun. I think about the moon, which in the dream is so much bigger and more yellow than anyone ever said. I am on a boat winning, I am on open water, not realizing that we ever set sail, hoping the boss isn't so drunk that we ram into something and drown. Funny thought. It rises up in me, like soda fizz. The words rise up, too—so faint, yet I can hear them even now. Stay just a little longer, Gwendolyn Brooks says. "Sit down," she writes. "Inhale. Exhale." She says, "The gun will wait. The lake will wait. The tall gall in the small seductive vial/will wait will wait."

Green is your color, the poet says. Remember that? All the colors are your color, if you look again.

ooooo

The Big, Big, Big Sleep. Can you not picture it? I did, in the split second when I was flying off my bike. One moment upright, my foot coming down hard on the pedal, and the next—it wasn't. When I fell forward, it was as if I were hoping to catch something that had been running from me for years. I was so tired—years of fighting the inevitable—and I said: No more. Sleep as black as asphalt, as suffocating as satin. Sleep as ongoing as the darkness behind eyelids. Sleep so big, there's no room for anything else. Sleep in the shadow of everyone who's ever lived.

But you cannot have such sleep in this life. You merely wait for it night after night, you and all the other orphans in slippers and socks— only to be surprised in the morning when the sun touches your face.

post-it/beware!

Falling objects
Bass from a car stereo
Candles on a table
The slanted opening credits to Star Wars
Gifs
Tacos
Ping-Pong
People who talk with their hands, so your whole family
Silence
Pillows
Light switches
Exclamation Points
Blind spots
Weird smells
Passwords
Sprinting
Anything that bounces, shakes, or goes wavy
Too many things going on at once.
Shirts with many colors. Shirts with many patterns.
Spontaneity
Night drives

Trolleys

Elbows

Liquor, wine, beer

Loud music

Names of friends' kids

Names of friends

Horsing around

Paintings hanging on a wall

Shelves, walls, car doors

Aeschylus, the father of Greek tragedy, died when an eagle threw a turtle onto his bald head, fulfilling a prophesy that he was to die by head injury by some falling object dropped out of the sky. Add turtles to the list.

Drunken sex

Average sex

Crying after sex

Bonks, donks, hits, knocks

The periphery

Alone

Anything that might be coming from behind

Anything you can't see

Anything Anything Anything

me vs. the bear

My wife and I planned to meet at the train station—her by subway, me by Amtrak—and then walk home together. It was crisp
autumn, early nightfall. We loved Ferry Street at dusk, the string lights
above restaurant parking lots, the Portuguese bakeries with their golden
custard desserts. I was thinking that if we hurried, we could get a *pastel
de nata* and some barbeque and eat it on the couch. I was not far from
Newark-Penn Station when she called.

Hello, S said—Babe?

Right away, something was off, something was happening. What's
wrong? I asked. In my family, except for the men, we have learned to
drain all emotion from our words when a crisis hits.

My wife did not say anything.

I said, Where are you?

Waiting for the train, S said. Her voice thin, as if she were trying to
slide a note under a door.

Terror, what overtakes us when we're under threat; horror, what we
feel when others are in danger and we're powerless to protect them. The
train's darkening window showed nothing, only buildings, one falling
away after another: how were we still so far out? My ignorance wasting

precious seconds. An older white lady in front of me turned around, peeved, said, Would you please stop kicking my chair. I lifted my shoe from the leather seatback as if it were stuck in tar.

S was telling me that the subway was delayed; she was waiting on the platform three, four stops away.

Are you alone? I asked.

No, she said.

Is it a man?

Yes.

Is there anyone else there? My voice low, like hers.

Silence.

Can you walk to the next stop?

Silence.

She whispered, He's locking the gate.

Get out, I said, my voice climbing. Go, now.

He's coming, she said. He's—

Then: a scream, and the phone cut out.

The longest ten minutes of my life, waiting for the train to pull in. I sprinted the two levels down to the subway entrance. I kept dialing, failing to get through to S. Instead, I ran into police officers surrounding a man, too drunk to stand on his own.

I found S shaken but unhurt. The man demanded money, but when S took out her wallet he refused it. He had not actually locked the gate at the top of the stairs, only closed it—that was what S heard when he rattled the chains. He pretended to have a knife, and then, hearing the subway approaching, he pushed her. This was when she screamed and dropped the phone. The subway pulled up, she got on, shaking, crying. The man got on, too—S could see him through the window, in the other subway car.

I could see the man, swaying against the wall—laughing, resigned, desperate. It was not clear that he even remembered what he had done.

There is a reason that S called me when she felt unsafe even though I was miles away and could not get to her, a reason that I was able to intuit she was in danger. It has nothing to do with how much we love each other and, evolutionarily speaking, everything to do with it. This attunement between S and me is not unique, rather it is apparent across our entire species.

In *The Body Keeps the Score*, Bessel van Der Kolk explains that S, alert in the dark subway, had only a handful of choices available to her. One was flight (but the man had locked them in—or so she thought). One was fight (he had a knife, or so she thought). One was freeze (once, not yet knowing her rule about not being chased and running behind her down a motel hallway, I watched her drop an ice bucket and sink to the floor in brief but total paralysis). The fourth choice—which van Der Kolk argues is actually the most instinctively human one, and the one we go to first whenever we can—is to reach out to others. "We call out for help, support, and comfort from the people around us," he writes over and over, in one form or another, throughout the four-hundred-page book. "Human beings are astoundingly attuned to subtle emotional shifts in the people (and animals) around them." There is the slightest quiver of the mouth, the intake of breath, the eyes that widen, the unmistakable tremble of your wife's voice from the darkness as she says, Babe?

Imagine swerving for a deer, then crashing into a ditch. The car is totaled. If someone drove by right now, they would pull over to check on you. No one is driving by. There is no cell service. Your family, your friends have no idea where you are. This is a remote area, no one can see that you've had to climb out of the ditch, that you're injured, that the sun is extreme and indifferent, that you're out of water and can't possibly walk all the way back to civilization. What would preserve you is being found by others, but no one knows how to reach you, or even that they should be worried. You send out a flare, but nobody catches it. That flash of light could be anything—heat lightning, the tail of a jet. Darkness starts to set in. The invisibility starts to make you a little paranoid: am I even still here?

This is sometimes what a brain injury feels like.

The really crazy thing is, even when you get a faint signal, you don't make the call.

After the third concussion, I dialed my best friend.

At the time, warming a can of soup was almost as trying as swallowing it. Talking on the phone was brutal. My brain was in constant revolt. I was nauseous, moody, unable to properly dress, wishing I could find a black box and lie inside it. Cate was four hours away. She was managing a restaurant in upstate New York and described her job as "salads." She did not have children, and would have accepted a train ticket had I offered it. I told myself, this is what a best friend is for.

But all I said when she picked up was I wish you didn't have work.

That was the closest I got to begging her to come see me.

Cate a.k.a. Huck Finn is an Irishman and carnivore. When we first met, she challenged me to a duel of arm wrestling: I lost in seconds flat. She used to have long hair, has always worn boat shoes. When she drinks from a glass, it sounds like water is walking downstairs. She loves car washes and hates wearing shoes (has left the house without them and had to turn back). She insists Massachusetts is the best state in the union. Her blue eyes are the way I picture a New England sky, but warm. Like me, Cate knows chronic illness, is writing work that resists silence and erasure, i.e., she wants to hang herself daily, i.e., she is writing nonfiction that stresses her out. She operates out of sincere kindness and a utilitarian, generalized friendliness that bubbles over, and which people always misinterpret to be about their own exceptionality. In reality it is Cate who is special. Years ago we promised to protect each other and mistakenly believe this means saving each other from the darkest parts of ourselves.

Maybe this is just a fantasy about friendship, but I could picture Cate boarding the train with her duffel, telling her boss to toss his own salads, showing up at my doorway and using her dyke muscles to wrestle me into recovery. Any sign of dismissal or refusal, and she would cut me off—"But it's your brain!" As if my brain were a baby for everybody to love. She would be as constant as Julia Stephen, author of *Notes from Sick Rooms* and mother to Virginia Woolf. Closing the blinds ("When a light is required, it should be skillfully shaded"), quieting the rattling ("There should be no bustle or noise in the sick room"), fixing the bedding ("Some people think that the whole comfort of a bed depends on its pillows, and I am not sure that they are not right"), becoming, with every thoughtful act, as radical a caretaker as Nurse Stephen. She would make soup.

It is possible that I could have asked and Cate would have said, Sorry, no. Money was tight, the salads were important salads, her girlfriend needed her, she'd like to but, no. Even if she could have done none of this, Cate would at least not have asked me to prove my pain. Ever the Irishman, she might simply have insisted *Despair is the only sin*, and then, despite being a fan of pizza in the bedsheets, would have echoed Nurse Stephen on crumbs: "The torment of crumbs should be stamped out of the sick bed as if it were the Colorado beetle in a potato field."

I wasn't trying to keep Cate—or my wife, or my sister, or my chosen family, or anybody else—in the dark. Rather, fortitude was what I understood was required of me, because this is what had always been required. If you want to heal you have to deal, is how the saying goes in my head. I blame such misunderstanding and personal failure on the invisibility of the concussions, but also on misogyny, personal mythologies, America, the immigrant tradition, Greek culture, George Michael lyrics, Buffy the Vampire Slayer, My Pet Monster, perfectionism, queerness. That is, who told me otherwise? The universe, ever comically unfolding, laid out an unsolvable knot designed especially for me—as it does for us all—born of my self-imposed aloneness.

This was Me vs. The Bear.

You may know this Bear—for you it may be addiction, disordered eating, chronic pain, depression, suicide ideation, PTSD, an abusive partner. Just when you think you know the Bear, it changes on you, and you realize you've been fighting the wrong fight all along. The Bear attacks, and then, as you are catching your breath, the Bear attacks again. It smells your sweat, your dank hesitation, becomes all your fears combined. It does not matter how fast you run, how high you climb, the Bear sinks its claws into your back and drags you down. The Bear is the injury, but it is more than this—it is the hot breath, the stinking pelt that trails you even in sleep, the aggression, the promise that the moment you yield you will be mauled. It is the fight you mistakenly believe you must go alone. The Bear may not kill you, but that doesn't mean you will survive.

When the Bear comes back a third time, I think: I'm going to die alone out here.

How do you escape a Bear?

You play dead.

How do you play dead?

There is no playing dead: there is only being dead.

It has taken me this long—decades—to reckon with the probability that the self is a myth. There have always been pyramids to pharaohs, ballads to heroes, Beyoncé, the idolization of self-made millionaires, the arrogant assurance of American moralism. It was not even until 1992 that we discovered—by accident in an Italian science lab—the existence of mirror neurons, those specialized cells in the cortex responsible for sympathy and much of our socialization, and why one baby crying gets them all crying in the maternity ward.

I can admit, since it's obvious, that there is in me a strain of self-reliance and stubbornness that goes way back—to my father, my father's father, my father's mother. When I was seventeen years old, my parents said our way or the highway, so I took the Jersey Turnpike up to New Brunswick, wrangled together four years of higher education and then tacked on one more year for a master's. Then my father said, You can't be gay, so I cut my hair and paid for my own wedding. Deep into adulthood, whenever I left the house, I played a game: with the clothes on my back, with just the money on my person, how long could I survive in the world?

Self-reliance is useful. Without it we wouldn't have camping or Vermonters, but at times—especially these years I am writing about—self-reliance can become an existential threat. After my third head injury, the day after I should have gone to the hospital, I closed my eyes the whole two-hour drive home. I did not complain about the nausea, the onslaught of headlights, the tires against the road that were causing vibrations in my head and traveled down to my teeth—I just went quiet. The family friend who had joined us for the ride said, Aw, she tired? I pretended to be sleepy.

In Laurence Gonzales's *Surviving Survival*, two hikers set off on a chilly morning in 1983 for the Crypt Lake Trail at Waterton-Glacier International Peace Park. The woman, Patricia, ignores her gut feeling—turn back, now!—and follows her husband, Trevor, as he bounds ahead. They see fewer and fewer people, and there is an awful smell just beneath their conscious awareness. An alarm goes off for Patricia, and then

a flash of darkness, a roar. She can make no sense of what's happening—
"a tremendous blond shape, a concave face, the humped back, moving
improbably fast." Patricia claws her way up a tree, watches the bear man-
gle her husband until he goes still, and then the bear charges *up the tree*,
coming for her.

Wife and husband survive. But Patricia, after torturous surgeries,
never quite heals. They have to remove her eye. She is afraid of night-
time. Her husband, who more quickly recovered from his injuries, goes
back out on hikes. Patricia splits into two selves, a before and after.
Though they went through the bear attack together, Patricia now lives
with the Bear on her own.

Patricia gets pregnant. She's sure it's twins, though the technician
insists she's wrong. Patricia knows it is the world that is insane, not her.
Patricia—awake in her sharp instincts—is finally listening to herself
when no one else seems to be. She is right: about everything. About the
bad feeling that first alerted her to the predator, the sensations of twin-
ness, her ongoing caution, the unseen dangers. She is connected acutely
to a core self that promises truth, thus safety. But this brings no relief for
Patricia. No comfort, no escape. She cannot push through to the Non-
Bear self. Twenty-two years of living with the Bear, of publishing a book
entitled *The Bear's Embrace*, of being heralded by *National Geographic* and
the BBC, of raising four children, Patricia, who has faced this all on her
own, can do no more. She checks into a hotel room and takes her own life.

All trauma is pre-verbal, says van der Kolk. Trauma is the experi-
ence of "This will last forever." Trauma is the past invading the future.
The tree's shadow turning into the Bear turning into the shadow of the
Bear that follows you even when it's not there.

I try to draw a bear; it's impossible. No one in the history of the world
has ever drawn a bear, because a bear has no shape. A bear lumbers. As it

shifts its weight, its relationship to darkness changes. It walks, its claws sinking into soft earth, but there is no separating it from the black mud below, from its own shadow. The fur on the haunches fanning, the massive muscles quaking. Its bulk never diminishes, its danger only grows.

At some point into my recovery, I started ignoring calls, went silent on social media. In this breezy way I lost most of my friends. I scrolled through my phone and realized just how many. Which ones did I miss the most? Tequila, wine, gin, I like to joke. But in actuality, losing my friends—especially my queer community—was hard. It was like looking at a place where a grove of trees had once grown and seeing stumps.

I had always made and kept friends easily, because people enjoy being listened to. I am good enough in casual crises (terrible boyfriends, money woes, colossal boredom, bridal parties). I helped a friend through a breakdown, served as a witness at a secret wedding for another, stood by a third as she got herself out of an abusive relationship. My friends and I had great times talking, cooking, going to movies. Often I was a recipient of sudden and at times outrageous generosity—for instance, when friends threw me a surprise engagement party and we cracked open the piggy bank and there was more money in there than anyone had ever given me in my life. But now that I was facing a crisis I wasn't sure I could overcome, I was looking for something "more"—what van der Kolk describes as being "held in someone else's mind and heart." I believed this "more" would simply appear. I did not understand the trap I had set for myself, having given friendship freely for so long, never asking for anything in return. When a friend talked only about herself, I let her. If someone, out of politeness or genuine interest, asked how I was doing, my answer, no matter the day, was, Better, Busy. Swamped, Let's get a drink soon. (They didn't know I couldn't drink; I didn't tell them.) This was a far more comfortable place for me, someone accustomed to independence. But now I was asking for more, and it was creating discomfort.

After years of being stuck at home, I went to a party. I had forgotten how to hide my eagerness, and everyone nonchalantly moved away from me, looks pinging between them, as if I were the source of a bad smell. I was asking the wrong questions, trying out the wrong jokes. Isolation had turned me clumsy. I found myself fumbling around one woman—tall, quiet, the center of the room even when she was in the corner. I kept bracing myself, worrying about every word. This is because you admire her, I told myself, but that was not quite right. In becoming someone who preferred not to be seen, I had become someone that people would rather not see.

When we are in trauma, we are outside of the human experience, waiting to be let back in. To be let in—to return to the group—we must resist our natural impulse for constant vigilance. Remembering this might have saved Patricia from the Bear. It is aloneness that brings about a hypervigilance to potential threat, and hypervigilance makes us even more alone, unreachable. This is akin to madness, if you're human. "Everything about us—our brains, our minds, and our bodies—is geared toward collaboration in social systems. This is our most powerful survival strategy," van Der Kolk says.

The story I've told myself since childhood is that there were shadows everywhere. But what if all this time it was me who shrank from the light?

The only way to survive the Bear: stop fighting it with your bare hands.

It would take almost the entire timeline of my recovery to understand this. What I had been missing, what I was now seeking, was reciprocity. We learn reciprocity from a young age, only we spell it H-E-L-P—but after all these years, I wasn't really even sure what reciprocity looked like. I had created rules for others to follow that I now wanted them to break—and more than this, I wanted them to intuit that the expectations had changed without me having to say it. But reciprocity is not unlike a prayer or a raise: you don't get what you don't ask for. Reciprocity exists only to those who are open and receptive to it, who in humility welcome all the generous and startling sensations it brings. Reciprocity asks us to join. In this way, it is like falling in love. The great cost of closing yourself off is not having to white knuckle it through life, it is missing out on a mysterious gift.

Twelve families of spiders in Texas spin a web that stretches two hundred yards so that no one goes hungry.

Dolphins link up to make one giant wave that pushes fish to shore.

Orcas teach other Orcas tricks to snatch birds out of the air.

Bees keep each other warm, bees keep each other cool, they clean the honey off the ones whose wings are sticking together. Nurse bees often take care of the sick.

Rats save their friends from drowning, even if it means losing out on chocolate. (This happens consistently unless they are on antianxiety medication, which can blunt receptors.)

"The brain is a cultural organ," van der Kolk maintains.

I am invited to a writing retreat. The women have minds like furnaces, I can feel them churning day and night, and I know I am out of my depth. I decide to go for a walk. Someone—a brilliant and kind writer—asks if I want company. We are both a little grimy at the end of the hike, but neither of us wants to part ways for a shower just yet. I feel a flutter in my chest: maybe I have made a friend. But what does an adult friend look like? If I send her a message on Monday and then another one on Tuesday, will that scare her off? Is that one too many LOLs on my side of the text chain? Months later, when my father dies, I text her, because I know she knows what it's like to have a dead father. My new friend (!) sends me a care package of books on grief. After she gets a book deal, I send her a kit of homemade chai. So this is how you do it? I think.

Cate and I take a trip. On our cross-country flight together, Cate gives up the aisle seat, and I accept. For the entire five hours Cate keeps an eye on the young, frazzled mother who keeps rummaging in the overhead bin for baby supplies, and I accept her watchfulness.

In 1964, it was discovered that rhesus monkeys starve themselves to protect each other. The monkey who pulls the chain to get the food will not pull the chain if it means his friend gets an electric shock. (He will not pull the chain for twelve days of the experiment.)

When a female mule deer goes out to graze, she leaves her babies with the other females. If they are attacked, the female mule deer protects all the fawns, not just her own, not even ones belonging only to her species, and charges the wolf.

A baby wails in distress when it hears another baby wailing: Help us! Helps us!

If I had asked—if I had really asked: if I had let the fear into my voice, the uncertainty, if I had not performed strength on the phone, if I had let Cate know how bad I was—she would have come. Instead, what jumped to mind was the fare for the train, the weight of the duffel, the buying and cooking of soup. I counted up the corrections, the adjusting of pillows and blinds, the dimming of lights—all such small, delicate gestures that I did not yet know how to receive.

Emperor penguins keep each other warm by huddling, moving as a single body two to four inches in one direction, then two to four inches the other way, getting their blood flowing, leaving nobody out, eliminating the spaces that let in the cold air.

Elephants speak in tones not captured by the human ear. They say, Alert! I'm lost. Their messages travel at super low frequencies over miles of forest or sand. The other elephants answer, Come this way, we're here. You are not alone.

Consciousness not as individual impulse and perception, but a sense far more cooperative, more connected. A shared experience so essential and intimate, we realize that, all this time, we've been wrong about ourselves. The self is in fact many selves joining together.

This, of course, is how queers have always survived.

The Bear is never the Bear you think it is. It never comes from where you expect. It is not until my head injuries that I recognize in myself the streak of isolationism that places me in continual peril, threatening my connections to those who love me. If survival is necessarily collaborative, then self-reliance is not resilience, it is egocentric. Van Der Kolk reminds us, "Our brains are built to help us function as members of a tribe. We are part of that tribe even when we are by ourselves, whether listening to music (that other people created), watching a basketball game on television (our own muscles tensing as the players run and jump), or preparing a spreadsheet for a sales meeting (anticipating the boss's reactions) . . . Our culture teaches us to focus on personal uniqueness, but at a deeper level we barely exist as individual organisms."

This is me trying to be more like the elephant, calling to you, reaching out across the distance.

How do you scare a Bear?

Noise.

What makes the most noise? Me making myself real big, getting real loud?

No. Us, getting real loud.

I once housesat for a researcher in California who studies the lekking rituals of grouse in their ancient mating grounds. She and her graduate student build a grouse robot and introduce it to the bevy to track their reproductive habits. One of the big male grouse (this guy fuuuuu) mates over a hundred times, a clear win for Survival of the Fittest, a vote for separating from the pack. But wait for it! Listen! There, in the sage-brush, the sound of popping corks, the throat action, the strut, the big fantails—and then a dozen male grouse are dancing for the attention of the discerning hens. They are not competing, they are collaborating, they are each other's wingman. They are eyeing up the guy everyone hates and still liking their odds together more than their odds of going solo. They are dancing as one, have been doing so for eons, as if their lives depend on it.

q&a with my wife #2/ horse or boat

Imagine two paths, one by boat, one by horse. You choose sea, thinking you don't want to ride a horse, not only because you are not good at it but because—the eyes. This is the gaze of a creature that has lived many lives, and you are not sure you can handle that. So you get on the boat— the other choice, the faster option—all because of a feeling. The boat sinks. You live, but everything you had—gone. Your clothes, your wooden chest, your money, your little locket, sunk. Your wife, swept away. You stand there, ruined, thinking how you should have taken the horse and stayed on dry, firm ground. It would have been a joy—an entirely new experience, you now realize, maybe even an adventure—to feel beneath you the thunder of muscle, the swift creature's heavy, almost spiritual breathing. How horse and rider become something more when they join like this, a transmogrification. The journey would have only taken a little bit longer, been a tad bit arduous, but at least you and the horse would have arrived, and your wife, well . . . Instead, you chose the fickle, timeless sea, which everyone—including you, now—knows to be the darkest hole. It sours your stomach, all you should-have-would-have, and for the rest of your life you replay over and over what might have been.

Philosophers call this retrospective regret. It arises from a neg-ative comparative concept (boat vs. horse) after a decision has been made and there's nothing you can do about it. There is no way to take the horse anymore, yet what you think about is taking the horse. It is not just that the final outcome would have been sweeter. In this fantasy of better choices, you are holding on to a counterfactual, ide-alized self—the self that does not exist, the self who wisely picked horse over boat. You are convinced, "That me is the better me I would now be had I been them." The loss, then, is twofold: you have less, you are less.

Such fixations can result in preemptive regret in the future, where you anticipate disaster regardless of what path you take. That is, you regret who you are before you've even begun.

For instance, I wonder what my relationship is to the me who was of-fered a job in New Orleans at an acute point in my recovery, but who turned it down because it would have destroyed my marriage. How much do I grieve that me who never was? In this regret multiverse, do I live in an airy Southern apartment with long white curtains and plants I can keep alive? Do I make cool friends? Start writing climate fiction? Simply by moving to a location with warmer days—someplace not gritty-friendly like Philly, but hyperbolically welcoming—do I come out of the cave of my injuries to experience joy, thus get healthier quicker? Increase both the quality and quantity of my years? Are there fewer bad days? Even if it is the result of divorce and dissolution, do I uncover a more adventurous, more exciting self? Do I get to be the person who rejects the very conceit of limitations, the me who knew me when?

If I go to New Orleans, what becomes of S in this other, maybe better existence? Is S happy on her own? Happier?

ooooo

ME: Who were you in a past life?
YOU: Happy turtle in a little pond.
ME: Describe heaven if it exists.
YOU: Dogs. Animals. Sunlight. Us. No screens. No hits to the
    head.

ooooo

The red light is blinking again. I am supposed to be leading this Q&A between ME and YOU, but it is mostly background noise and the dog whining. We are not at the Taberna Clandestina; we cannot smell the sea. Nothing even close to a vacation. It is a snowless winter, six months later, and we are surrounded by chores, dishes, a rabbit that becomes a little devil if it's not given love, an unending to-do list that we have been promised will someday bring personal fulfillment. I am trying to fight off actual and counterfactual selves.

Before me, a stack of questions demand to be asked. Instead, I say—

ME: Remember our wedding day? How you were up till three
    a.m. writing your vows?
YOU: I really procrastinated. I didn't even have them written
    the morning of ███████████.
ME: Very unlike you.
YOU: Normally I would have done it a day or two in advance.
    I was in complete denial. I don't know what I was think-
    ing. I was panicking. I was so consumed by all the activity.
    I barely slept. I couldn't face it and once I faced it I couldn't

██████████████████   ████████████████████
██████████. I couldn't believe ███████████. I didn't have it.

ME: I look back at those two young people and think they have no idea. What would you say to the you back then who was up all night? What would you tell her?

YOU: Really hard things are coming. What you've been through is nothing compared to what's coming. When things get really, really hard, trust that you'll come back to the power of the bond you have. You'll be tested. And you know nothing.

ME: You know nothing?

YOU: Back then, it felt more like an adventure, not the inevitability of catastrophe or big, painful trials that would come close to ending us. It's naïveté. You don't know how you're actually going to handle true strife or how your own shit is going to come up against it.

ME: What do you regret?

Of course, I don't actually ask this. Such a question can only reveal an imbalance or, worse, wounds that will never heal. What if what you regret—or what you *don't* regret—only brings us farther apart, one on a horse, one on a boat.

∞∞∞

Nonetheless, there is a strong moral argument for regret. Those tough feelings—sadness, disappointment, repentance—reflect back to us what we care about, how we've failed to protect it so that in the future we can save something even more precious. It means that having blown up one relationship to change our behaviors for the next—choose horse, not boat. Or, more radically, we stay in the boat, change our words, our actions. And maybe our partner does, too. And maybe the boat makes it after all.

In his article "Regret, Remorse, and the Twilight Perspective," Christopher Cowley, philosophy professor at University College Dublin, suggests that regret is often a result of ambivalence surrounding our choices—most of the time, we don't know really what we want. Add to this the fact that mortality makes each decision matter, even when we aren't consciously aware of it. (How long to stay in a job, whether or not to have a child; how many books are on your bookshelf, and which ones will you never get to because there are only a finite number of books to read before you die, and which should you read tonight? Is it this one? Which should you skip? Is it this one?) We struggle with what psychologists call affective forecasting. Brett Pelham, professor of psychology at Montgomery College, Maryland, adds, "Miswanting refers to the fact that people sometimes make mistakes about how much they will like something in the future. That is, people often mispredict the duration of their good and bad feelings."

ME: Was there ever something you thought you wanted but it turns out you didn't?

In Tolstoy's *The Death of Ivan Ilych*, Ilych forsakes his family for an envied career as a high-court justice, spending time with his card-playing buddies and making big gaudy purchases of curtains and antique clocks. Then Ilych gets sick—a mysterious, ruthless illness that causes him to scream in pain for three days (which, if Tolstoyan lore is to be believed, may have happened to the man Ilych is loosely based on). While bedridden, Ilych laments his poor choices—that he prized ambition over his wife and children, that he is only forty-five and out of time. Suddenly, this is not about illness and recovery but life and death. There are no more counterfactual selves. Soon enough: "The dead man lay, as dead men always lie, in a specially heavy way." We think: poor Ivan Ilych, if only you had chosen better.

But maybe we're wrong about Ilych. Up to the end, Ilych doesn't quite know what he regrets about his life, nor does he ever feel sorry for what he's put his family through—only, he concludes that he should have done things *differently*. Cowley argues that we might have a false understanding of Ilych's last laments, that his thinking is too loose and ill-defined to sound a clear moral edict. "I find the short story problematic as a cautionary tale," Cowley writes. "One should beware of falling into a twilight where one comes to reject *all* one's previous life." The danger Cowley is naming: if we wallow in regret, we lose all perspective, we risk sinking into self-pity and going down with the boat. More than this, we risk forsaking all we've created and everything we've become.

I can't help but think of Ivan Ilych in his mourning and penitence at the end, and yet, I can't forget how much he loved bridge with his friends, that selfish pastime that took him from his family but brought him "pleasure that beamed like a ray of light." We cannot possibly understand Ilych—he would not recognize himself—without those indulgences. Maybe, by considering only the binary—family or ambition, wife or gambling buddies, halls of justice or exquisite red drapes—we reduce the man and the book to a fable. In doing so, we risk reducing our own complex selves.

It is Tolstoy, after all, who tells us that "All the beauty of life is made up of light and shadow."

Thinking about Ilych, watching the red light blink even when it's not there, I wonder: Is there something radical about refusing regret? Is there some agency, some power, in reclaiming the imperfect self? The life unfulfilled. The troubled marriage. The years we did not know and often did not like each other. Is there some secret, deeper connection that, in failing and in accepting we've failed, we uphold? Is rejecting regret, in fact, an act of higher love? What is the gift we give ourselves if we refuse to lament all the ways we might have gone. Is it grace? Is it breath? If we let go of the ideal self, the "ought" self, which is the tighter belt loop on our moral and spiritual selves that tells us we are still not the right configuration—do we become better for our faults?

And what if in the end my pain allows you to become the person you believe you are, the one you were always meant to be?

ME: How can denying regret be self-revelatory? How can we find our highest self by refusing to disown earlier, flawed versions of ME/YOU?

Any anchor, if too big, too heavy, will drown you. Forget regret. It is a selfish act that annihilates the self. Instead, give way to remorse, which recognizes that there is a wronged person on the other side of the act, the one who, all this time, has been in the room with you. The wife on the boat. The widow of the Russian judge, now tending to the children alone. The person across the table in the taberna. Remorse is specific, it is demanding, it relies not on counterfactuals but actual selves, says: "I did this to you, and I'm sorry. Please forgive me."

Nonetheless, the questions chase me—

    ME: What do you forgive me for?
    ME: What can't you forgive?

The red light keeps blinking at us.

professor x and the trauma justice league by annie liontas & marchell taylor

It is a glowing summer afternoon at the Governor's Mansion in Colorado, just days after Independence Day. Marchell Taylor is in a vest and button-down shirt, purple tie, shaved head, light stubble. He stands at the governor's side as he signs into law the bill that Marchell himself wrote while in prison. Afterward he walks out with Dr. Kim Gorgens, whose research made this all possible. Laughing, both of them saying Can't believe we just did that shit. They take a selfie to celebrate, squinting into the sun Marchell rarely saw from his one-foot-by-one-foot window—sometimes no window at all—during his twenty-year sentence. Marchell takes a second photo with what he calls the Trauma Justice League, allies who have known him since he was an inmate: "Wonder Woman" Dr. Gorgens of the University of Denver, "Superman" State Senator James Coleman, the Department of Corrections, the Colorado Criminal Justice Reform Coalition, and "Morpheus" Corey Shively, Marchell's business partner and the bill's co-author. It was Marchell who brought all these people together. Marchell, of course, is Professor X. What he brings is wisdom and knowing, which rarely come without suffering.

Before they ever step into a cell, a prisoner is seven times more likely to have suffered a traumatic brain injury. Of the two million men and women housed in the criminal justice system, 50 to 80 percent, like Marchell, have experienced at least one TBI, compared to the rest of the population at 5 to 9 percent. Such numbers are so staggering as to suggest that we have been doing something very wrong—a reminder that we have long been incarcerating sick people—and insist on a radical approach to prison reform. And that is exactly what Marchell is after. Now, thanks to Marchell and Corey and the Trauma Justice League—after forty letters to a news channel and talks with senators and nonprofits—Colorado will offer neuropsychological screenings to defendants suffering from TBI. It is the first state in the union to do so, legally recognizing the role of brain trauma in repeat offenders and recidivism. A task force is formed to steward the initiative. Marchell—Denver businessman, ex-inmate—is on it.

It has taken decades, a reimagining of justice, for Marchell to save himself—and then to reach back and help others.

ooooo

We presume that a prisoner who has a head injury must have gotten it during lockup: penitentiaries are dark, violent places no one ever imagines for themselves or their child. In actuality, most brain injuries happen years before the first arrest, before even the first crime: a sports injury, a driving accident, an abusive parent. For Marchell, his came when he was nine years old, in a car accident—mom hit a brick wall going 35 mph. Marchell was in the front, pulling his seat belt across his chest. They were on their way to a funeral, his brothers in the back, ages ten and eleven. Little Marchell woke up, saw his mother with blood on her face. He needed nine stitches. Years later, neuropsychological screenings would show that the car accident changed Marchell. Prefrontal cortex damage, here we go. The inability to rationalize. A brain stuck in survival mode, doing anything to survive.

Proximity to violence during childhood or adolescence—whether at school, at home, in the neighborhood, or at the hands of authorities—is a strong predictor of incarceration. An eight-year study of ninth graders in Flint, Michigan—Marchell's hometown—found that young people with brain injuries are more likely to engage in violent acts as adults. Head trauma can spur behaviors that tend to be criminalized—aggression, disinhibition, emotional dysregulation—which means that many individuals with TBI have early encounters with law enforcement and enter prison at a younger age. Marchell was a little guy growing up on Dayton Street. His mother was an overworked case manager at Front Community Mental Health. She taught Marchell how to take care of himself: "If anybody messes with you, if anybody comes at you, you pick up the biggest thing and you hit them." But after the car accident, Marchell became particularly violent. Older kids would tease him and Marchell would grab hockey sticks, pipes, a brick, a glass bottle, whatever he could get his hands on.

What Marchell would give today to say how sorry he is for what he did to that boy.

There was a new darkness inside of Marchell. By age ten, Marchell was addicted to weed and alcohol, having been taught at age six by his father, a Vietnam veteran self-medicating with heroin, to steal by putting things down his pants. Age thirteen, he was breaking into houses to fund his cocaine habit. At fourteen, staying with his dad in Denver, he robbed a 7-Eleven on Downing and Seventeenth. Trauma and substance abuse were exacerbating Marchell's injury, undermining his recovery. The teachers were throwing their hands up, Mom was coming home to calls from the police. Then, when Marchell was seventeen, his mother died of cancer on New Year's Day. Weeks later, his father was imprisoned for robbery. Marchell was homeless and alone. The TBI and compounding traumas had rewired his brain, and he was no longer able to discern what was safe, what was threatening. After years of "adverse childhood experiences," street violence, brain injury, racism, Marchell's neuroception was altered. He stole and used and got coached, through the age of twenty-four, by "some pretty good criminals" on how not to get caught.

Then, in 1994, he got picked up for robbery and sentenced to three years.

ooooo

Marchell and Annie chat over text and Zoom. They share a love for X-Men, football, loud talking. They laugh through most of their calls. Marchell says that none of the Greek fathers on his block let the black kids near their daughters; Annie confirms that Greek fathers from the East Coast aren't much different. Marchell looks deeply into the camera as if making actual eye contact, proof of the warmth he carries into any room. He talks about his granddaughter—her name is Annie, too. He is full of ideas and plans, this thing is going big, we are going to be the most trauma-conscious state in the country. They discuss Annie's work with Pen City, the writing program created by Deb Olin Unferth for incarcerated men at the Connally Unit, a maximum-security prison in Karnes County, Texas. It might be part of why Marchell lets her in at all. Marchell looks at Annie, gets serious—sizing up how she moves through the world, her privilege and access, her profession and all of the other unseen circumstances: You're a writer. There are doors you can get in that I can't. When you told me we were doing this, I was like nothing happens on this day, we are going to get this story out. They are going to listen to us.

It was "Wonder Woman" Dr. Kim Gorgens who first put Marchell and Annie in touch. She said, I think you'll really get each other. When she describes Marchell, she uses the words "charismatic," "devoted," and "passionate." She says, "He has never wavered . . . I know him better now, know him to be earnest and committed and truly altruistic."

Marchell pushes Annie to speak about her own brain injuries, even when Annie doesn't want to. The nickname this earns her is Rogue of Novelism. ("Be careful of who you touch, you absorb everything.") She shows him the little index card that sits on her desk, which reads: "What would someone in solitary confinement want to see?" She picked it up during Eastern State Penitentiary's exhibit on "Photo Requests from Solitary," an innovative campaign that takes photo requests from those in solitary confinement and asks the public to fulfill them. On the back of the card that sits on Annie's desk, and which she shares with students, someone has asked for a photograph of "Anything in motion like a waterfall or traffic at night with trails of light."

When Marchell gets the job he's been hoping for, he lets Annie know. When Annie finally sells her book, Marchell is one of the first people she calls; he is so exuberant, she's convinced he's more excited about it than she is. He tells her about the five forensic psychology interns who are now assigned to help him with outreach, sends photos of packed boardrooms captioned, "Transforming probation departments." Annie texts about buying her first house, Marchell announces he's getting married next year. He goes on his first big vacation and calls Annie to say how blue the water is, but you can keep the helicopter rides, he's better off staying on the ground. Over time, his beard grows in a snowy gray, he strays from the script he's made for them. Their laughter changes—now quieter—less of a line to pull in a big fish, more a line between two distant points. The friends share, but to a different degree. Whenever Annie asks how Marchell is doing—how he's really doing— he always replies with a cheeriness too neat to be entirely true. It is not clear if this inflection is how Marchell keeps himself from slipping into the dark past, or if it is a necessary performance in his new life, when he must convince every person he meets not to give in to their worst suspicions about a man who has spent much of his life behind bars.

He does say, in one of his softer moments, Sometimes I get stressed just trying to pick out clothes in the morning. Then he cracks a joke about how his fiancée tells him what to wear, since apparently he doesn't know how people match colors.

In these moments, Annie wonders, What would it have taken to protect young Marchell after that car accident? What would it have taken to make sure he got well at age nine, kept him out of trouble? Saved him from his own snowballing aggression and impulsiveness? What protects Annie, even with the three head injuries—even with her own trauma—what invisible forces go on protecting her? What other differences separate the friends, many of them as invisible as their injuries? Across such distance, how can they excavate the story beneath the story?

Annie asks herself what it means to feel connected to this person. Had she never gotten hurt, she and Marchell would not be friends. She would know of Marchell only abstractly, as one of many Black men wrung by the system, a stranger she had nothing in common with and could only vaguely wish well. Instead, she finds herself thinking of Marchell often, wondering what he would say in a given moment, tries to emulate that. They trade words like "the darkness," "the crazy," knowing that even as they are speaking a common language, the words cannot possibly signify the same thing to each of them. Still, no matter what mistakes she might make, it is worse to admit only her own experiences with head trauma. She thinks of Trinh T. Minh-ha in her film *Reassemblage*, critiquing the genre of documentary and declaring, "I do not intend to speak about; just speak nearby." Annie tries to listen better to her friend, make the words on the page serve his story, amplify Marchell's voice, recede from this part of the work.

This is not a profile. It is asking what goes unseen and why. The interviews have become a collaboration. One day she says, What if we did this together? Tell it our own way? Wow, Marchell says. Wow, we really are about to change the conversation.

ooooo

Thinking of those early years, Marchell shakes his head: I'll be damned if I see a kid out here—a kid like young Marchell, who turns to Olde English and whatever else he gets his hands on to deal with pain—and I'm not going to recognize that there is something wrong with this child.

It's 1994: in for three years on the robbery charge, out for three months. Back in for two and a half years on a drug case. Out three months again and then, in 1998, back for fourteen and a half years for aggravated robbery of a bank. Marchell's not getting any help. Society is ostracizing him and criminalizing his brain damage. They are looking at his behavior and not what's beneath it. Marchell's aggravated robbery landed him in a Level 4 maximum security facility in close custody, with limited access to people. Double-perimeter fencing, razor wire with sensor detection, continuous patrol, towers, bars on all the cell's openings, sliding doors that locked on command. Sometimes it was a relief not to be out there in the yard with the other men, many of them also dealing with head injury. Once, Marchell watched a man push two of his fingers into another man's eye. Marchell and his celly walked away speechless. They turned to each other and said, That was absolutely barbaric. This was trauma on top of trauma.

What Annie wants to know is, How does head trauma affect the most vulnerable people—such as the men Marchell is talking about—but also: How does it push them to the fringes? How does it make them unrecognizable to themselves? How can we understand trauma as a powerful agent while acknowledging that a person exercises their own agency? How do we look at Marchell's crimes as choices Marchell made, while considering how those choices have, for decades, been shaped by brain injury and untreated trauma too often inflicted by a racist and inequitable system? What is the social contract, in such cases, and who honors it?

Marchell: Can you imagine a bunch of disordered boys masquerading as men living with just the reptilian brain functioning, the most primitive part of the brain?

Even when mild, TBI shares overlapping symptoms with PTSD. Both are marked by depression, anxiety, migraine, difficulty concentrating, hypervigilance, insomnia, nightmares, destructive behavior. More than this, because TBI changes the brain, specifically the volume of the amygdala—that almond-shaped cluster of nuclei that emerged with the mammals to enlist fear conditioning—head trauma makes the brain more susceptible to PTSD. The brain revolts, the individual becomes erratic, an unpredictable hostage to their own pain and panic. The two populations most vulnerable to the convergence of TBI and PTSD? Those facing military combat—such as Marchell's father—and people like Marchell, who have gone through the criminal justice system. People who don't even know they've had a brain injury, have only been told they had their bell rung.

Marchell would tell his good friend Corey Shively, Something is wrong with me!, and Corey would reply, You're good! Do some pushups! But admittedly Corey, who met Marchell in 2007 when they were both serving sentences at Colorado's Delta Correctional Center, also began noticing that his mentor very often thought and acted like Corey's young children. Corey would ask, What's wrong with you? And Marchell would answer, I just don't know. Turns out he was a highly educated parolee suffering through TBI and mental illness and did not even know it.

In her interview with *Prism,* the publication for abolition and reform, Dr. Gorgens explains that "brain injury is oftentimes part of a really complicated soup of comorbidities. We coined the term the 'superfecta' because trifecta wasn't enough to reflect the overlap between someone with a history in criminal justice, with a brain injury history, who also has significant long-term severe mental illness and long-term substance misuse or abuse disorder, cognitive impairment, and a history of suicide attempts." Whatever the prior or concurrent conditions—ADHD, anxiety, issues of anger management, PTSD—TBI enflames them. Because of this, it is messy, nearly impossible, to separate head trauma from all the other damage. Yet because TBI is invisible, it is also rarely identified as a primary culprit.

Annie: If Marchell had started smoking at age nine, wouldn't we point to cigarettes as an obvious cause of lung cancer?

ooooo

In 2012, after spending nearly twenty years in state institutions, Marchell was released. He had done his time for the 1998 armed robbery. He was determined now to get right, keep his freedom. A new start. On his birthday, he was accepted to a halfway house in the Stapleton neighborhood in Denver, got cleaned up, went on to his godmother's house. He got a job with Marriott Hotels. But at forty-seven years old, it was aggravating to work so hard for so little pay. Here was an ambitious, self-educated businessman, yet, They had me cleaning an elevator for ten dollars an hour. He was struggling to pay bills, logging seventeen-, eighteen-hour days. If he wasn't working in laundry, he was in banquets, and if he wasn't in banquets he was in the kitchen. At the same time, he was trying to get his marketing company off the ground, which his partner Corey had been fighting to keep alive these last few years. They launched a campaign called Eternal Life, a fundraiser to honor both their mothers, whom they had each lost to breast cancer. At the end of one of his shifts in 2013, preparing the meal for the hotel's catering director Brian Lenfestey, Marchell asked if Marriott might back the fundraiser. If the Marriott had Marchell on his knees with a toothbrush, he was going to get them to back him! When they met again, Lenfestey, having looked over the proposal, said, Not only will I give you the meeting space, I'll give you a prize for the raffle. Marchell landed similar support from the American Cancer Society, the Colorado Cancer Coalition, Buick, and others, totaling nearly a million-dollar contract for the campaign.

But the contract was never signed. In 2016, Marchell robbed a pizza place.

"I walk into the Papa Johns. A lady is in there. I don't want to be doing what I'm doing, but I've gone for over thirty years without the right treatment, without being given the right tools to deal with my injuries and my trauma. The pressure is getting to me. I need to get high and I need some money. I don't have a knife, didn't have a gun on me. I tell her, you could just give me the money, I won't hurt you. She was getting ready to push a button. Myra was her name. I strong-arm her. It was two hundred and fifty bucks I walked out of there with. You see what I mean? How unclear I was? How dark a place I was in? The police had to put spit bags on me.

"I wish I could tell her today—

"It wasn't that I wanted to rob a pizza shop, I just didn't know what to do."

Another aggravated robbery, plus a second-degree kidnapping charge. Marchell had already lost two decades, and now they were stretching him over a twenty-five-year sentence.

∞∞∞

What Professor X hopes to teach people: TBI is both a predictor and a consequence of incarceration.

Once in prison, the injuries pile up. The two most frequent causes of head trauma in prisons are conflicts among incarcerated individuals and use of force by jail staff. Those newly admitted to prison are 20 percent more likely to suffer subsequent TBIs in fights—initiations like "pumpkinhead," whose purpose is to induce brain swelling—or at the hands of guards. Within three months of a TBI, many individuals become more violent, and those in the criminal justice system have few resources available to help with recovery or protection. Add to this the additional risk of self-inflicted trauma, the knocking of heads against bars or concrete floors, particularly among people in "seg"—long-term stretches of solitary confinement often employed extra-legally by facilities to manage inmates—and incidences rise exponentially.

Yet underreporting of head trauma across demographics in prison is flagrant. This is both because of institutional policy or neglect, and an inability to recognize symptoms—even in oneself. When *Prism* looked at brain injury in New York City jails, it found that rates among the incarcerated were fifty times higher than estimates from surrounding communities. Though Black men disproportionately comprise a large majority of the prison population at 38 percent, new research from Dr. Gorgens suggests that there is "only a slight overrepresentation of racial minorities" with TBI in the criminal justice system. The issue is violence, how close you are to it—whether the state is sanctioned to use it against your mind and body, and who in the criminal justice system might be especially vulnerable.

The question is, What becomes of a nation that is complicit in refusing to interrogate such practices, having long conflated injury, illness, and mental health with criminality?

The first five years of his sentence, Marchell spent much of his time in the hole. An eight-by-eight room. He used to lie there thinking, dang, Shaq is seven foot one. Four months in the hole, five months in the hole. Once, a seven-month stretch. It felt like being in a casket. He would sit there and pray and breathe and pray. One time he started kicking the door, hard: I can't breathe, I can't breathe. Moments like this, when he got panicky, he would get heavy into his books, law statutes, business. He won't lie, sometimes on an odd day the hole was a comfort, a way to escape the violence and the officers, because threat was constant. Once, during a period of racial tensions that culminated in riots, he was ambushed and nearly went over the second-floor railing.

The question is, Is there or is there not a perpetuation between head injury and trauma and drug addiction and violence and self-destruction?

Annie, recalling that Muhammad Ali once said that he probably took 29,000 hits over his career, wonders what hundreds of violent encounters after serving twenty years in prison might do to a person's brain.

Marchell: Imagine the hundreds of thousands of individuals who suffered just like I did. It's irrefutable, the cycle of TBI and criminality and back to prison.

After the Papa Johns, the attorney came to Marchell and said, Man you're looking at over 296 years, bro. The DA was saying he should never set foot on land again. The lawyer said, What happened, Marchell, wow. You've been doing time since '94? He said, I've gotten five cases like this, where people get out and go right back. He said, I can tell you, this is mental health all the way. You're worth saving. But in the county jail, facing another two decades in prison after the Papa Johns robbery, Marchell took enough Elavil to put him to sleep for five days. He was hearing voices, could not make sense of the world. Corey, who visited him after he regained consciousness, pleaded, You are valuable to our family, please don't do this. They transferred Marchell into the Men's Transition Unit, one of the only trauma and mental health units of its kind in the United States criminal justice system. It was there that the Brain Injury Alliance of Colorado and Dr. Gorgens's team from the University of Denver screened Marchell for brain injury. They determined Marchell had been suffering for years from untreated TBI and PTSD and invited him to participate in the Colorado TBI Model, where he would learn about his own brain and be given tools toward recovery.

No one was promising Marchell wasn't going to get a life sentence, only treatment. But help was finally here, and Marchell was going to help himself. Interventions included substance abuse classes, as well as mindful meditation, one-on-one counseling ("EMDR changed my life"). Marchell learned to regulate his emotions and control his impulses. He became zealous about his own brain and how to repair it, would jump in front of the class to teach the other participants whenever the doctors arrived late. When it came time to appear in court, Marchell and his doctors brought Dr. Kim Gorgens's research with them. His doctors, including Dr. Nina Minagawa, director of psychology at the Denver Sheriff Department—in an unprecedented show of support—testified on his behalf.

Judge, we've been going about this the wrong way. We're incarcerating the brain, the body, and the mind. We've been criminalizing the behaviors, but we haven't been dealing with the underlying traumatic brain injuries nor psychological modalities.

We're going to shed light, and we're going to see if they will incarcerate a sick Black man. It's a thin line. We let him back out on the streets, he may commit another crime. Or we side with all these professionals behind him and see who he is, and who he can become.

Marchell didn't get life for the Papa Johns robbery. Instead, Judge Brian Whitney told him to pay it forward. He gave Marchell a sixteen-year suspended sentence—a judicially appointed alternative to serving time in prison, providing strict conditions are met—and eight years mental-health probation.

As long as Marchell stayed out of trouble, he got to keep his freedom.

ooooo

But Marchell didn't just want to get out of prison, he wanted to set others free, too.

He recalled his friend Corey saying, Trauma is the only thing that we let get to a stage four before we start to treat it, and the treatment is prison. So Marchell ran out his last eleven months from the '98 case, the result of a parole violation he committed after Papa Johns ("had to kill my number"), and served out the unfinished time, and he used the opportunity to educate and inspire others in the system. From behind institutional walls, with Corey he launched Rebuild Your Mind, a non-profit that advocates for prisoners suffering from TBI and PTSD.

Encouraged by Marchell, the men in the MTU sent letters to Kyle Clark on 9NEWS. They started writing their judges about their diagnoses and experiences with trauma (an inmate's grandmother provided stamps). They got Deputy Mike Jackson, president of the Fraternal Order of Police Denver Sheriff's Lodge 27, to join them in recording the first digital testimony. They challenged their parole officers. They challenged the mayor. Quit incarcerating sickness! The judges and the news anchors were like, Who are these inmates? Word was out.

Marchell: How often do you get a man inside, he takes this scientist's info, uses it to get himself free, exposes the knowledge in the criminal justice system while within the criminal justice system, and then comes home and works directly side by side with the scientists and activists?

Terri Hurst, the former policy coordinator at the Colorado Criminal Justice Reform Coalition (CCJRC) who was essential to moving

SB21-138 through a gridlocked political system during COVID, wants you to know that she was as likely as Marchell to end up in the criminal justice system. "Everything was partying, what are we doing to get high tonight," she says. For years, Hurst has been fighting to eliminate the overuse of incarceration through parole reform, sentence reform, lobbying and legislation, and directing money into communities overly impacted by the system. But, twenty-five years ago, Hurst suffered from her own serious TBI. Back then, a hairdresser at twenty-one years old, Terri was "ripping and running." An injury in a car accident crushed her fourth vertebrae and forced her to learn to walk again. She recalls that even reading became difficult ("the words would swirl on the page") and her temper would flare at loud noises or the TV. She has learned how to control her reactions but has "certainly relied on alcohol and drugs" as a way to cope and even sleep. We need to change the way we think about injury and incarceration, she says.

A month after his release, Marchell was invited to speak to District Attorney Beth McCann's advisory council. People like Beth McCann were seeing that people like Marchell can talk to people on her side of the table to find real solutions to mental health problems. They see the power of legally enforced neuropsychological screenings to change lives. Sometimes you have to listen to those who suffered through it.

Marchell: I look around and think, are these people really supporting me? Is this real?

Annie thinks, They're depending on you now, Professor X.

ooooo

There are people who would question Marchell's remorse—is he even sorry for the crimes he committed? Does he talk about the bad things he's done? Does he ever wake up in the middle of the night thinking about those poor people at the Papa Johns? Surely, many of them still think about that day, dealing with their own trauma of wrong place, wrong time. Some might say, Even if Marchell brings light to mental health after brain injury, does it warrant his freedom? Where is his own responsibility in all this? Where is the atonement? An injured, guilty man has been released from prison, serving not a single day of a sentence for his crime. What role does doubt play in credibility?

Annie wonders: What does such stark awareness of Marchell's own culpability suggest about justice and punishment? But in actuality, this is not her big worry. What Annie wants to know is, What if he does it again? She knows some days how hard it can be for her to keep going, and she is not even facing all the pressures Marchell is, or wrestling with his history—so what does that mean for Marchell's open-ended future, for his bad days? There is darkness they may never get to in their conversations, won't talk about, the shadow of trauma that no degree of treatment can cure. But what if even the success is too much for him. Ten years from now, where is Marchell?

It is a question full of promise and fear.

Marchell would say, There is a difference between Marchell Now and Marchell Then. Life skills versus survival skills. I didn't know how to stop and breathe. That's what it takes if you want people to change, give them the tools when they get out. Marchell Now has the ability to reason and to understand that everyday stresses are not trauma. Marchell Now went through years of treatment for head injury and PTSD. He is a trained practitioner, he surrounds himself with wise counsel. That keeps Marchell grounded. It keeps him from going back to those dark, dark places.

Marchell Now: I still go through grief and loss, I still hurt. I just don't allow myself to get lost in it anymore. I have command of my own emotions, I can regulate. Criminalize the behavior, not the disorder. If anyone proves that, it's me.

Why does Annie get to ask these questions of him when they both know he will never put such questions to her?

If Marchell were not always playing defense—if he had the privilege that Annie has—might he ask, Who did *you* hurt after your injury? What price did *you* pay for it? And when he hears the answer, which is nowhere near twenty years' hard time, how might he feel? Marchell might sit awake at night, a longtime habit, his mind jumping over puddles, trying to puzzle out how suicide sickness in a white woman is treated with pity, while in a Black man it is viewed as innate aggression. Why is your self-destructive behavior forgivable, when mine is not? Is there no culpability in that? Look at you, a thirty-some-years-old white woman with a couple head injuries and all those tools to cope, and then look at me, a nine-year-old Black kid without any idea of what's happened to me or how to keep from drowning in it. A leads to B leads to C, but we never think past C in this country. What in you has yet to be criminalized that in me has been locked away? Who keeps you, cares for you at home and at work and in societal institutions, so that all is forgiven?

But Marchell does not see it that way at all. He just keeps asking questions about what Annie's suffering is like, because this is what he does with people. I want you to tell me how it affected *you*. You hide your stuff behind your degrees, but we know it's there. His eyes light up when he realizes that there is a whole population of women "on the business side" recovering from head injury. Wouldn't it be powerful to get their stories out, too.

ooooo

Perhaps most troubling of all the data: though women account for only 7 percent of all prisoners, they are twice as likely to have experienced brain injury. Nearly all repeat female offenders have a history of head trauma—97 percent, Dr. Gorgens's research tells us—and it usually occurs at the hands of a partner or family member and *in the very year* preceding incarceration.

Data surrounding brain injuries among survivors of domestic violence is nearly nonexistent, since most TBI studies focus on men, and almost no research has been done on head trauma in women in the criminal justice system. Eve M. Valera, associate professor of psychiatry at Harvard University and a leading researcher on TBI among women who have suffered domestic violence, believes that while hundreds of concussions occur in the NFL and thousands in the military, survivors of domestic abuse who suffer from head trauma might be as high as 1.6 million. Valera, who volunteered at a shelter when she was at graduate school in the mid-1990s, "heard about women whose heads were pummeled with baseball bats and work boots. There's no way these women aren't sustaining traumatic brain injuries, she thought." Yet not even the United Nations, which recognizes vulnerabilities in women in prison, particularly those with a history of domestic abuse, considers the role of TBI in women's incarceration.

In light of such findings, the state of Colorado has selected La Vista Correctional Facility, a medium-security prison sized to hold 560 women, as the site of their new pilot program for neuropsychological screenings. The penitentiary is located in the city of Pueblo, where women from the prison can volunteer to farm the nearby fields for $9.60 an hour (of which they keep a small percentage). Its Honor House, in existence since August 2021, houses thirty women with the mission of promoting "successful reintegration into society" by offering specific rewards and responsibilities that mirror the real world—including more freedom of movement, access to gym and laundry facilities, more comfortable furniture, and the privilege of ordering from Walmart or Amazon twice a month. Public information officer Annie Skinner says of

La Vista, "The old-school way of operating prisons was to make them harsh and punishing environments, but what corrections officials across the world have grown to understand is that the best way to reduce recidivism is to provide opportunities for incarcerated individuals to make positive changes while they are incarcerated, to work toward achieving additional privileges . . . and to support them in preparing to transition from prison back into a home environment."

To serve those with TBI among the four hundred of La Vista's residents, the DOC is partnering with Denver University, MIND-SOURCE Brain Injury Network, and the Brain Injury Alliance of Colorado (BIAC). Dr. Chris Estep, the pilot's correctional/forensic psychologist, has met with 180 women since the pilot launched in 2022. Estep administers neuropsychological screenings using the Ohio State University Traumatic Brain Injury Identification Method (OSU TBI-ID) for those coming to La Vista from the Denver Women's Prison—where, Dr. Estep suggests, the numbers positive for TBI are likely much higher. Questions include "Were you ever injured and should have received medical attention but didn't?" Participants additionally conduct a self-screen, and ongoing neurocognitive assessments to determine further treatments and accommodations. Forty-three of the women that Dr. Estep screened were invited to participate in a psychoeducational group, and sessions seem to be going well. ("Fridays are a good day.") Using the A.H.E.A.D. curriculum (Achieving Healing through Education, Accountability, and Determination), the group moves through seven modules focused on teaching coping strategies regarding memory loss, memory impairment, disinhibition/impulsivity, attention issues, mental flexibility, physical and sensorimotor difficulties, organization, language, and emotional regulation skills.

"Brain injury amplifies experiences, whether that's language or memory or just getting through the day," says Dr. Estep. "We do work together around assertiveness, emotional regulation, understanding the basics of TBI, and grief and loss. We talk about being a survivor of your experience and having those philosophical and physiological aspects of a TBI." One La Vista client with a long history of abuse suffers from seizures, but now that she and her family are connected to BIAC, they have a better understanding of the impact of the brain injuries. Another woman at La Vista who in the past had been sent to solitary confinement—the practice was eliminated at the institution in 2017—told Dr. Estep, "This is helping me to stay out of the hole." She has "really come out of her shell," he emphasizes. A third, whose mother recently had a stroke, connected with BIAC so that when she returns home, they will both have support. Women at La Vista who aren't in the group but have heard about the program are reaching out to get more support from DOC. One resident, writing to BIAC, states that she has not had medical attention for complaints such as "concentrating, thinking, understanding," and that she has "seizures," "shooting pain" down her neck, and "tingling" in her head.

Jaime Horsfall, vice president of professional programs at BIAC, the community-based agency that serves survivors across the state, is working with Dr. Estep to conduct capacity building for La Vista staff. In October, they trained eighty-four staff members in TBI awareness, and a second training is planned for August. The trainings are part of the Correctional Endurance Mindset program, which, Dr. Estep explains, "provides education for staff around burnout and compassion fatigue and teaches them how to navigate the stress that comes from prison." Future outreach will involve parole so that the pilot can develop continuative service for those returning home. As of this date, BIAC has not yet received referrals of women exiting the prison and returning to their communities.

The pilot has additionally appointed a program evaluator to oversee and gather data, and to administer quarterly reviews. Two volunteer peer educators who have themselves come through the program are helping to mentor participants, and make suggestions to Dr. Estep about what might get participants further involved. And a contract with DU means that specialists will be able to conduct more in-depth neuropsychological screenings using the Colorado Brain Injury Model, which Dr. Gorgens, as the pilot's research expert, helped introduce to the state, and to a dozen others. Upon completion, the two-year pilot at La Vista will yield recommendations to the legislature about how to expand the program to the entire Colorado justice system. Scaling the program will require training district attorneys and public defenders, many of whom have long been correctly identifying individuals for the pilot based solely on patterns of behavior. We've known all along, even when we didn't, they say.

Dr. Estep, who has been with DOC for ten years—working at the Centennial and San Carlos Correction Facilities, and as a diagnostician for the Residential Treatment Program—was drawn to the SB21-138 pilot not only as a practitioner, but as a survivor. A few years ago, putting some miles on his motorcycle to celebrate a recent promotion, he had a stroke. His clinical awareness of his new neuropsychological condition made recovery difficult at times ("my insides were not great"). "It was rough to understand I was in bad shape. I just really wanted to get back to work. But my passion came out of that—to help people. I got to learn about the TBI model from a civilian perspective." He returned to serve as the DOC's mental health administrator, and had worked for a few years at a sex-offender program when he applied for his current role in the pilot. "Not only am I a facilitator, but I know what my clients are going through."

Marchell knows, too. He hopes that the pilot program at La Vista will help save women's lives.

Marchell: May it shed light on their injury and connect them to treatment before they come home.

ooooo

Marchell is still getting used to freedom. There were no cell phones when he went to prison, no automatic checkout at the grocery store ("That's stealing! You go first and then I'll go!"). When he looks at a woman on the street, there's that same old jolt of anxiety that he'll get written up by guards.

There are great losses to reckon with—not just the years in the system. Marchell lost two sons, even after getting one of them into treatment with the very doctor Marchell credits with saving his own life. His oldest son, in 2012, at age twenty-five, was found in a bathroom, dead of a fentanyl overdose. His youngest, Marcius, in 2018, three months before Marchell came home from prison, at age twenty-eight, was also found in a bathroom, dead from a fentanyl overdose. Marchell grieves his sons. He can't get through to his big brother. He can wish him well but he can't will him well. There is pain in that.

Marchell: It hurts my heart when I can't do anything about it.

Annie wonders, All this trauma across generations. How to escape it? How to keep from forgetting so that we don't keep passing it on?

Marchell: My kids were anybody's kids. It could have been your kids.

Now Marchell advocates on behalf of injured people facing serious time. He sits with the families of those incarcerated, talks with them for hours about trauma. He speaks to Dr. Gorgens's students at

hit like a girl

for Connie

My first job had me walking the dim event hall in a white button-down shirt and ponytail, the trays of Swedish meatballs only recently pulled from the freezer. Men hung on the open bar, paunchy in their wash-and-wear suits, their wedding dates dragging them onto the parquet dance floor for "Unchained Melody." There was no such thing as a gay wedding in this place, or really any place in 1995—it would be a long time before I dared to think of marrying a woman anywhere—and I was struck by how the adults around me were eager, perhaps relieved, to fit themselves into obvious shapes. I recall thinking that when I got rich enough to never have to work in a place like this again, I would be nicest to the people carrying the appetizer trays. One night, D, my family through marriage but my sister for life, found a hundred-dollar bill on the carpet; we bought pints of ice cream and bags of sunflower seeds at the Wawa. We talked about that found money for years.

At the end of the shift, I lined up with the other teenage girls to receive the weekend's pay in cash. You had to kiss the damp cheek of the big man propped up on a little stool—his property, like everything else in The

Riviera—and if you kissed both cheeks, he peeled another bill off the wad stashed in his pocket. This was not required of the teenage boys, nor the workers who scrubbed pots and hauled the trash. I was fourteen. I recall, at some point, asking to be switched into the dish room where there was no chance of finding drunk-people money. I could disappear by pushing stacks of wineglasses through a machine until they were scratched clean. I kept my head down, worked hard, and at the end of those nights, when I smelled of stale champagne and creamed potatoes—when I looked like a much older version of myself pushing a mop around—the boss slid extra bills across the counter without looking at me.

A few years later, I got a job at The Grace Cafe. An evangelical bistro and coffeehouse, The Grace Cafe was a hangout for Christian teens. Religious music played on repeat, the most memorable song being about how Scooby Doo says "hallelujah." I had applied thinking that Grace was a woman's name. Mike, a very large man who saw himself as having an even bigger heart, greeted customers from his own little stool. He was the kind of Christian who would let you borrow his new truck and then forgave you when you sideswiped it and lied about it. He was also the kind of Christian who repeatedly asked if you were the one who trashed his truck, but it turned out it was the woman who babysat their little girls who did it. I had been taken in by Mike and his family for a time when I had nowhere else to go; I was also cautioned during the "highly encouraged" "Christian therapy sessions" facilitated by the woman everyone called "Mama" to beware any "dangerous feelings" I might have toward women.

Mike had done time for finance fraud, was repenting a life of drugs, idolatry. The Grace Cafe was his dream, and he desperately wanted it to be my dream, too. After we worked together over a few years, he begged me to drop out of school, come manage the place full-time.

One New Year's Eve, he and I single-handedly served a crowd of over thirty worshippers—some men drinking three, four mochas, splashing chocolate-flavored milk onto the tables and floors—in what would turn out to be a last-ditch effort to save the bistro. Soon after, The Grace Cafe folded. At the back of my filing cabinet, I still keep the pay owed me from a time when I could not make rent, two checks totaling $1,200, which were never any good but which had Mike's signature on them.

On nights and weekends, after my shift at The Grace Cafe, to make ends meet, I'd go wait tables at an Italian restaurant a few blocks away. The proprietor was more gristle than man, the opposite of Mike in every way. He, too, sat on a stool behind his office door, which we were never to knock upon. He hired young women from Eastern Europe to tend his tables for obscenely low rates and had them stick around late at night to entertain his friends. Everyone tried to please him except Melissa, the young manager who had pushed him to hire me. Don't worry, she said, I know how to handle the old guy. We got close in the way that women working temporary jobs do. A few times, she brought me back to the trailer she moved into after her mom's boyfriend tried to come into her room at night; she offered me H and did not judge me when I said no thanks, nodding that she got it, her mother was an addict, too. On my last night she threw me a going-away party whose parting gift was a male stripper, and whom I gladly gave back to Melissa for the remaining fifty-eight minutes. I watched her hair whipping around as she sat astride him in the dining room, teaching him a thing or two.

I was one of those young people who always had a job. I staffed my family's welding shop, operated a cash register, served in a cafeteria, wrote articles for a bilingual magazine whose primary audience was Korean mothers, counted a hundred-thousand transistors in a physics lab as part of an annual inventory, most of the devices the size of a needle, and blew up balloons in my family's pop-up shop. At thirteen, Mom dressed me like a clown. She put me in a rainbow wig and used lipstick for rosy cheeks, foundation for the white clay mask, and sent me to sell balloons at the church's carnival. Paul, a cute boy, bought one from me—it turned out he liked me more as the clown.

I often take on two, three jobs at a time, slinging meat at a meat counter, tutoring neurodivergent learners, teaching in city schools, taking care of other people's children. Even when I sit down to write, I "clock in," paying myself twenty-five cents per hour and dropping the coins into a jar on my desk.

Work was what I was taught early and often by the man propped up on the stool, whoever that man was, even when that man was my own father: labor proves your worth. It says you have earned your place, that you deserve to be here, and it makes an implicit promise to keep you alive if only through your own sweat. Work was the gift taught to me by my immigrant family, my welder father who scrambled atop buildings with little more than his blowtorch and the cigarette sticking out of his mouth. He slept many nights at the place we called the Shop, on the couch in the small kitchen that smelled of burning chemicals, with its grim bathroom and harsh soap. Thanks to his work ethic, I wake most mornings asking what needs to be completed or achieved. It's also why I'm attracted both to people who are compelled to make something out of every moment—my wife—and the wanderers—my best friend—who think that maybe they'll spend the day training the crow that lives above the parking lot. Immigrants work, women work. For a long time, I conformed to such expectation, even after I started identifying as a feminist, even when I knew intellectually that women are paid less than men—particularly Black women, immigrant women, indigenous women—and that even when they're paid the same or close to the same, they work longer, harder hours, that the free labor expected of women is not only childcare or mentorship or committee work but the very coddling of men's dreams and ambitions.

Then I got three concussions, and it was nearly impossible to work. I started to suspect that I had been wrong all this time about how much pride I took in what I gave, and gave, and gave. I did not take sick days or cancel classes. I was an adjunct: I needed to be asked back next semester. I wilted under fluorescents, so I taught with the lights off, wore special sunglasses. Mondays were migraine day. So often did I get hit with one, my students and I joked about which flavor Frappuccino I should hold against my head. A friend, someone who struggles with periodic disability, recommended an ear device to mute excess noise. I requested accommodations at the universities—there are usually multiple when you adjunct—including my six-month stint in California, three different colleges in Pennsylvania, a semester when I went each week from a class that ended at ten p.m. in Philadelphia to the grad class I was teaching in Massachusetts. I apologized anytime I showed a doctor's note or asked for a different room—fearing that I was a hassle, that this could mean losing the gig. I developed a sixth sense for who not to tell. My temporary colleagues and supervisors were sympathetic, but still they looked at me out of the corner of their eye. I started thinking of these workplace exchanges as the mirror that helps get the lipstick off my teeth, being unfamiliar with both lipstick and such looks.

We assume that most people, when sick or injured, just stay home. In fact, there is a growing trend of sickness presence in Japan, Germany, Belgium, Sweden, and the United States, where unlike other industrialized nations, we have no national standards for sick leave or paid family leave. With sickness presence, people—women—come to work on days when they can't or shouldn't, leading to more productivity loss than sickness absence, and increasing the risk of further illness. Leavism, first coined in 2014 by Dr. Ian Hesketh at University of Manchester, describes the phenomenon of employees—women—who then use their vacation days to catch up on work they were unable to complete when unwell, even if they were physically on-site at the job, because they cannot appear to employers to be falling behind. The cost is high: overload, burnout, stress, an inability to truly heal, a cascade of serious health issues, hopelessness. The trends, since the pandemic, have only increased, and it's not just workers who are feeling it.

The juggling and scraping of adjuncting went on for about three more years—and then I hit the jackpot with an interview at George Washington University. The position came with a heavy teaching load, thesis duties, committee work, and a biweekly three-hour commute each way. For an unwell temporary employee, it was a dream—steady work, brilliant and kind colleagues—but also a terrifying test, one that I was bound to fail in my vulnerable state. All I had to do was prove I deserved the job out of a sea of applicants who equally deserved it.

The day required stamina: an interview with the English Department chair, a talk for the department, a conference with the dean, lunch with senior colleagues, a workshop teaching demo, a meeting with the director of Creative Writing, chats with strangers down every corridor. Everyone welcoming, excited to see what I had to offer. But I was only halfway through the teaching demo, and I was barely holding it together.

The lights were doing their damage. I kept retreating to the corner of the room where one of the fluorescents had gone out, hoping the adults in the back taking notes wouldn't notice me giving these three students extra attention. The demo ended. I touched the cool wood of the desks, the pen in my hands, anything to stay grounded while people approached me with questions. I tried to be charming, knowing that being charming was part of the work. I was too weak to walk to the restaurant but went anyway, trying to appear sure-footed and curious about the program and the neighborhood. The two people seated across the table from me were seniors in the department, pioneers in their field, and enlisted to catalogue my every move. We made small talk about DC. I hoped my nodding and smiling was making up for my thickheadedness. To prepare for this part of the interview—the lunch part—I had read up on each of their bios and watched episodes of *Lifestyles of the Rich and Famous* so that I, a first-generation learner who was always playing catch-up, had something to say about the Scottish castle that featured prominently in the professor's scholarly work. Despite myself, I liked these people very much, was finding that I wanted the job not only out of necessity, but because I could see myself among them. But it had been too long a morning, I was struggling to hang on to the thread of the conversation, I was sweating and overwhelmed by hunger. I thought of the scene in *Gattaca* where Ethan Hawke's character rips the electrodes off his chest—insisting he's fine when the technician questions him—and then he convulses alone in the locker room, gasping for breath. I debated sneaking into the women's room to shove a granola bar into my mouth, as I had done in previous university interviews. At last, the appetizer arrived, the one they had been talking up. Save me, pretzel bread! I thought. But it just sat there, two brown humps with thick salt, a golden buttery crust. Out of politeness, no one was breaking into it, and I understood that part of the test of getting this job—any job—seemed to be about how long I could hold out, how long I could refuse my own bodily state to appear strong, stable, sure, resilient, composed, a far healthier version than the me in that room.

Somehow, they made me an offer. Ninety-nine percent of me celebrated. The razor-thin 1 percent, invisible to all but me, suspected some sort of self-betrayal. That part kept asking, What if you can't do it?

ooooo

A healthy person, on average, might have ten *usable hours* a day. Most people are productive for only 50 percent of that, according to Alex Soojung-Kim Pang, founder of the Silicon Valley consultancy Strategy and Rest. You might think of these hours as spending cash—say, $10 a day. Every act costs something—taking a bus might be fifty cents, going to the grocery store might be $2, dealing with a neighbor might be $3. A healthy person might go over by $1, $2, and say, Whew that was a day! And maybe they take it easy the next day or build in a nap or use a substance to help them keep going, because this is America after all. By comparison, a person with a chronic illness, particularly a head injury, has maybe $4 to spend. This is because there is a decrease in blood flow to the brain, a leaking of neurochemicals, damage not only to neurons but also mitochondria, those power plants of the cell that give us energy so we can give our energy to others. According to the Concussion Alliance, concussion weakens the brain, biologic processes are diverted to aid in recovery. Less energy to devote to thinking, moving, caretaking, working.

Let's say, after her injury, that our person in question has $5 to spend. Let's call her X. If she is a cis-woman, she may be more susceptible to concussion and have worse and more prolonged symptoms than her male counterparts (though we aren't sure why, since we've only begun to study the female brain, with only 1 percent of studies written since 1967 looking at female concussions). Different hormones coursing through her brain, different neuron architecture.

Let's say X is a mother of two children, has a career, is in a good-enough maybe not-great marriage. Let's say X has three meetings back-to-back, has to miss lunch. Let's say X leaves the car running accidentally and the battery dies and the kids are crying/fighting in the back seat. Let's say X has to take the car to the shop where there is loud drilling, and let's say today is also the day X checks in on her own mother, and X has to run to the post office where the lights are more poltergeist-y than usual. There is the job, the children, the aging parents, the pets, the neurologist, the neuropsychologist, vestibular therapy, video games with the eye doctor, the pharmacy, the rage, the call with the lawyer, the dog poop, the migraines, the tinnitus, the fatigue, the ongoing to-do list. If X started with $5 but has spent $9, what does $4 in the hole look like? But suppose X's boss, and all the other people she encounters at work, think, I spend over $10 a day, and she's only giving up $9? X knows she is *being seen* to give less. And if X is a woman of color, there is far more scrutiny, perhaps significant hostility and judgment. So let's say X says to herself: You just have to do it. Puts out not only $10, but $11, $12. X gives this much of herself to the man on the little stool, the workplace that may or may not be toxic, the industry that likely undervalues her or at the very least expects a great deal of invisible labor, the society that for decades used only crash test dummies modeled on the bodies of men, the result being that women are more likely to suffer debilitating injuries or die, a public that does not believe—though it is statistically valid—that the rate of recurrent concussion is higher in girls' sports than in boys', and a medical industry that has historically and myopically studied and therefore advanced the health of men and doubts, in general, a woman's suffering. And because we have a fascination with sweetness, but only in girls and women, X should do it all with a smile. Now X is $7 in the hole. If X does this every night for a week, every night for a month, every single day for a year, if X does this even when she is in agony, how deep is the hole?

ooooo

Sometimes, I dream of asking someone on Etsy to fashion me a replica of the 1925 Isolator featured on the cover of *Science and Invention* magazine, a hood that blocks out all light and noise, allowing me to see only the page or task in front of me. Total sensory isolation, improved concentration, and there is even an oxygen tube attached. I could live in that kind of darkness for a while, I could be the kind of worker they need me to be.

On some of my worst days, I think of Melissa, the manager from the Italian restaurant. What Melissa would have done—how she would have gotten by—how she would have kept herself safe, alive. I think of people who have it far worse than I do, who cannot work at all anymore, some because they aren't physically able, others because they are exhausted by all that would be required to make work possible.

∞∞∞∞

In the workplace, TBI fatality disproportionately affects men, who are more likely to work machinery or operate vehicles or work in law enforcement. But rates of work-related TBI (wrTBI), which are head injuries that occur in the workplace, are higher among women, doubling among those ages sixty to sixty-nine. Women are also more likely to have been victims of assault-precipitated wrTBI and work in healthcare, social services, and education. Following their wrTBI, women are less likely to return to work, or are forced to reduce their hours, despite often feeling guilty for not working through recovery. Treatment, when it exists, is mostly for self-selecting patients and tends to respond to cognitive gaps, such as trouble with focus, rather than secondary symptoms like depression. We expect a woman's work from a woman.

The National Institutes of Health in Canada and Europe concede that all medical research and treatment—not just inquiry on brain injury—is dominated by findings on cis-men, and there is almost no holistic inquiry into the health and well-being of trans or nonbinary people. Until 1993, women were not required in clinical studies; until 2016, only male mice were used in medical research. Women are, on average, diagnosed four years later than men across nearly a thousand diseases. They are 30 percent more likely to die when operated on by a male surgeon than a female one. A review of medical research determined that men who suffer from chronic pain are often described as "brave" or "stoic," whereas women are called "emotional" or "hysterical."

To no woman's surprise, there is "insufficient data" to respond to or treat women in all areas of medicine, including TBI, and nearly no data inclusive of trans women. The gendered experience of head injury goes unseen. We have no idea why, for instance, in a study of eighty thousand soccer players across American high schools, female players were nearly twice as likely to suffer concussions as male players. Despite such findings, a 2021 study that examined the most influential medical journals revealed that only 6 percent of studies focus on cis-women, while 31 percent focus solely on cis-men.

The UNITE Brain Bank in Boston—the largest facility of its kind in the world—holds thirteen hundred brains, but only 3 percent belong to women.

Though mild TBI (mTBI) is a discrete injury with a metabolic cascade, including altered cerebral blood flow and impaired axonal function, among others, concussions bring difficult-to-explain symptoms; frustratingly, mTBI cannot be simply classified as a less severe form of TBI, and it is women who most often pay for this. Women—in sports but also the workplace—are more likely to report a concussion than men. One recent study asserts that "women consistently report greater symptom severity," especially in the early stages of recovery, and women demonstrate higher rates of post-concussive syndrome. They more often complain of headache, nausea, fatigue, with headache emerging as the "biggest" indicator of a long recovery. Because women also tend to shoulder much of the emotional labor at home, recovery tends to be prolonged. There are medical hypotheses to explain the discrepancy between genders, mediating factors including an "anxiety sensitivity," which can result in a more "nuanced" experience of injury and may be legitimate or may be the most recent evolution of the diagnosis "hysteria." Add to this that much of our research on head trauma comes from the Department of Defense and from athletics, with subjects being primarily male, and that the effects of biological sex and gender are particularly underreported and underappreciated, it is no wonder that women suffering from head trauma, a nearly invisible condition, feel dismissed.

As with most medical conditions, gender-based perceptions inform treatment of mTBI. So can sex differences. In the case of mTBI, this might include difference in skull thickness, brain size, metabolism, hormone levels. But because our clinical tools for evaluating mTBI are still quite crude (nothing shows up on imaging, and neuropsychological screenings often catch cognitive but not psychological consequences of injury), we must rely on our more subjective assessments. These include perceiving, extrapolating, determining, evaluating, and—if we are a doctor, if we are running a concussion clinic—ultimately making a conclusive judgment about the patient standing in front of us. Of course, anytime human beings employ these softer tools, they also bring into the room social and cultural perceptions, assumptions, judgments, and these include racism, sexism, able-ism, transphobia. That is, a doctor does their assessment, concludes: This isn't clinically real, it's just X being X.

Believe women becomes a call that extends into all areas of a woman's life, including her wellness.

ooooo

Mel Bailey was twenty-two, recently graduated, living on their own for the first time in an apartment in New York City, had gotten an internship as a teaching assistant at a writing camp. When they were asked, during the ice breaker, to act like a little kid, Mel leaned way back in the roll-y chair, and the full weight of their body came bearing down on the top of their head. Mel did not black out. A manager brought Mel an ice pack. Their colleagues were worried, and then an hour or so passed and everyone went back to work. Mel's headache was bad now, but they still managed a full day, stopped at the library, went out for drinks with friends. The next day was much worse, the ones after that worse still.

The question Mel was faced with every time they went to the doctor was, Are you better?, as in, Why aren't you better yet? Mel wanted to be better. Mel felt pressure to please the doctors and the bosses. Mel, who at the time was female-presenting, understood the expectation was to get over it. That was what men did, and men were the standard in treatment. With the doctors, "there was a tendency to assume that I was exaggerating." So Mel started to respond, "Yes, I'm better," even when they weren't. Instead of talking about depression, they spoke only to tangible symptoms (cognition, blurred vision). At work, especially because the accident had happened there, they felt pressure to conceal their injury. Even when their colleagues offered sincere sympathy, which dried up pretty fast, as it would in most workplaces, it did nothing to solve workplace pressure. "The desire to help someone female-presenting out of their pain is engrained, but it doesn't translate to head trauma," Mel says of their experience. "The expectation is that you continue in your role once you return to work." Anyone who doesn't is suspect.

Two months into treatment, Mel had to fill out a form. Was this a workplace-related accident, yes or no? Mel checked yes. "It would have been better for us both if I had said no," because now it was the employer's insurance paying out. The boss said, You didn't have to declare it as a workplace thing. Mel found themselves having to defend their wrTBI, not only to managers but to colleagues who had watched them fall out of the chair. Mel quit the internship. "It ended badly." They stopped teaching. They stopped writing. Then came the depression, the panic. Who were they, they wondered, without their work?

ooooo

A workplace culture lives or dies by its office manager. But there has only been one Connie, and I was lucky she was ours.

Connie started in the English Department at George Washington University in the 1970s, a work-study student who went back for a second degree in French and then stayed on to run things until she retired. She was a big woman with a lilting Southern accent, soft brown eyes, irreverently funny. As a child, she had disobeyed her grandfather when he told her to keep out of a certain pen with a certain bull named Otto, and somehow charmed her way out of being gored. Connie was a people collector, not out of some desire for accumulation but because she had enough love to give—minus the fools. She was very good at her job, came to work even on snow days. She knew every institutional procedure and piece of paper, and the deans often asked her to train managers of other departments. She was, like any great office manager, a historian of the institution, which is a way of saying she loved gossip. A person—Connie was known to say—should be measured by the enemies they make. Prickly, stubborn, loving and kind, a natural storyteller, Connie asked prying questions and made edgy jokes and still gained everybody's trust. She liked passing on what she heard in the DC loop, how warm Hillary was in meetings, how Hillary knew every assistant's name, how on a bad day Hillary would request chocolate mocha cake. She had a long memory, never forgot a name or act of racial bias, a spate of which had been directed at her over the years. She was famous for wearing baggy T-shirts and sweatpants, for her knowledge of wine. Like me, she had a troubled understanding of her own birthday. I learned, after joining GWU, that Connie was the invisible member of the hiring committee. She joked that I was her adoptive daughter. At work parties, I beelined for her, in my head called her Auntie Connie. I wish now that I had called her that out loud.

After I got the job, Connie took care of me. This is the only way to say it. All I had to do was tell her about my vulnerabilities, my phono- and photosensitivity, and she moved the immovable institution of higher education to recognize me as a full and integrated self, not merely a worker. That is, she fought like hell to get me what I needed. She asked questions, solved problems, sent me a list of classrooms with big windows, and then visited every one of those rooms herself, to make sure I got the best pick. She would have done it for any of us.

"I do have another office I might be able to move you to that is brighter," Connie wrote in an early email. "The office is currently being held by the Provost's Office for high-ranked administrators." Later, "How many bookshelves do you need? I was thinking of moving one or two out to make room for your sofa. Oh yes—I have a nice leather couch I am moving from one of our vacated offices. No idea where it originally came from, but it is ours now." I had a place to nap between classes if I needed. She believed in naps, especially at work. "Also, I am going to pick out a new lamp. The ones they have in storage are pretty crappy."

As a thank-you, I bought Connie wine and some fancy soap. She said she almost tasted the soap, thinking it looked like candy someone had once given her. "Don't worry; I didn't eat it," she wrote. "I'm laughing hard now."

Sickness and healing connects us with certainty and humility to all who have come before us: those who stood, stumbled, suffered, got back up, went back to work, died. "Everyone who is born holds dual citizenship, in the kingdom of the well and in the kingdom of the sick," Susan Sontag tells us—but at work, we pretend otherwise. When we see illness among us, especially in the workplace, how scathing we are, how we refuse any part of it. I will always be grateful that Connie rejected this nonsense. With her generosity—not the couch, the couch is not the point—she showed that there could be another way.

Connie retired after a quarter century at GWU. (Joke's on you, she said when she left us, I barely did any work for the last twenty years.) Her dream was to travel, especially to her beloved Maine. There are photos of her on a dock, another beside her husband, Jim, wineglass in hand. She passed away only a few months later, quickly, unexpectedly, breaking our hearts. In the department fridge, we keep a bottle of wine. For Connie, who was one of us, the best and baddest, we all say.

ooooo

My teaching job at George Washington University is contractual, three courses a semester, four preps a year. My colleagues ask after me, my students are patient. Yet when I am at the head of the classroom, fighting to be worthy of my students, what is required remains unseen and unknown. The only way to do my job is to place myself on a strict schedule. Same oats, same jar; same #138 train, same walk up same stairs; same mini-lecture perfected over many years, same tone, same thoughts delivered aloud to students from the typed feedback before me. Everything accounted for, even spontaneity. Doing this means I'm less likely to mess up or get so overwhelmed that I can't deliver, or worse, that I fumble my way into another accident.

Every few years at the university, as with most institutions, there is a re-view process wherein I am asked to build a forty-page dossier that proves I should be hired again: here is the stuff I do in class, here is evidence that students like me, here is my added value to the department. I do not add in the annual report how hard it was to get back on the train after the third concussion (still can't sit on the left side), or how migraines can make walking down the stairwell from my office feel precarious, every step down as wavy and strange as the air over a hot grill. I do not know how to answer the question "Do you have a disability?" in the employee portal, even when the university lists my particular condition beneath the banner that reads, "We are required to measure our progress toward having at least 7% of our workforce be individuals with disabilities." Or how, after reinjuring myself—backing into a light switch—I end up on the late train home after a ten-hour workday. For some reason, the conductor, Joe, takes pity on me—maybe it's my pinched face, or the fact that he perceives me to be a white woman. Though he has been on his feet, tending to passengers for who knows how many miles, he helps me into the quiet car. He stows my bag and coat and umbrella ("don't want to forget that") and dims the lights. He dims them again when he sees I'm still in trouble, throwing the whole cabin into merciful darkness. Later, I go to the website for the company that employs Joe, write him a thank-you letter.

I know how lucky I am. What a privilege it is, to make this living, to receive this reasonable salary, to get the costly treatments, like craniosacral therapy, that so many cannot afford, so I might have a more normal-seeming life. How many cannot. The reality of this hits me every time I encounter a person paid beneath their talents, going through the drudgery of an inadequate, necessary job. Sometimes, you feel the weight pulling at them, that they have clocked in today not for one shift, but for many.

There is always the fear—the possibility—that I will get hit again or fall and be unable to work. This fear comes often, sometimes on the commute, when the escalators are slick with rain or the ice is coming down. None of this is in the annual report. But the one thing I'll no longer do, not even on the clock—in part thanks to Connie—is mask my illness.

No, I will not deny us that.

probable vulnerability

Two players in 1.5 inches of foam and candy-shell helmets run at each other at up to 20 mph for a 40 mph collision. If they were in cars, we'd stop everything to check and see if the men inside needed medical attention. But in America, we watch the clock wind down as they get into formation to do it again.

On April 7, 2021, Phillip Adams, former NFL cornerback, shot and killed six people. He drove the short distance from his house to the home of Dr. Robert Lesslie and shot the doctor; his wife, Barbara; and two of their grandchildren, ages nine and five. Adams also killed two air-conditioning technicians from nearby Gastonia who were doing repairs. The next day, police found Adams dead from a self-inflicted gunshot wound. Phillip Adams was thirty-two. He played for six NFL teams in as many years, including the 49ers, the New England Patriots, and most recently the Atlanta Falcons. He retired in 2015, one year too late to join the broad settlement between the NFL and the 4,500 retired players who had suffered repeated head trauma, and as a result he was excluded from the $1 billion class-action lawsuit that has since been distributed disproportionately to white players.

In December 2018, nine months after Phillip Adams killed six and then turned the gun on himself, a neuropathologist at Boston University reports that Adams suffered from chronic traumatic encephalopathy (CTE), the aggressive neurodegenerative disease linked to repeated hits to the head and concussion.

The night the Eagles win the Super Bowl in 2017, I am on mom's couch, along with every member of my family. Her face has been painted green since noon; now, it's smeared and makes me think of the milk in a bowl of Lucky Charms. She looks awesome. The room is covered in green streamers and balloons, the kids' tongues green. We've done this since I was a kid, chips and Carmen's hoagies, shouting "Earn your paycheck" when a play goes bad. Never have our Eagles made it as far as the Philly Special. Never have we felt the promise of underdog redemption quite like this. We hold our breath those last moments, knowing—as any re-spectable Philly fan does—that victory can be snatched away at the last second: and then we erupt as only six grown women watching football can do.

In 2018, a postmortem study of 110 out of 111 NFL brains show signs of CTE. In the scans, the brains of these young athletes bring to mind the lungs of a chronic smoker. Two years later, in 2019, there are 224 concussions, up 4.7 percent from 2018, for a total of 15.22 percent concussed active players. A high percentage of these injured athletes, many of whom are not yet twenty-five years old and who thus do not yet have fully developed brains, go on to get a second, a third, a fourth concussion. Many will continue to incur TBIs. Concussed athletes are four times more likely to sustain subsequent concussions within seven to ten days. A player who has one concussion is one to two times more likely to get a second. A player who has had two concussions is two to four times more likely to get a third. A player who has had three is three to nine times likely to get a fourth. This is not within a single season;

this reflects ongoing, exponential vulnerability. Concussions aren't just recurrent, they're intractable. After every injury, symptoms grow more severe. Athletes who have three or more concussions struggle with long-term cognitive impairment, aggression, anxiety, depression, difficulty handling emotions, as Phillip Adams did. Rates of depression in retired football players with a history of three or more concussions are threefold. It can start long into retirement, and last forever. The real danger is the subconcussive hits, which over a time can yield long-term neurodegenerative disease, such as CTE. Unlike concussion, CTE is irreversible. Dr. Ann McKee, director of the Boston University CTE Center, cautions, "The problem is the subclinical hits—the nonconcussive injuries that aren't detected, you don't pull the player off the field—and they can be in the hundreds or even the thousands in a single season." No matter what we think we see, every hit is a hit to the brain.

Halfway through his career, Phillip Adams incurred two concussions over three games, only a week or so apart. Who could say how many hits he took over a lifetime.

"I can say he's a good kid—he was a good kid, and I think the football messed him up," Phillip Adams's father, Alonzo Adams, told WCNC-TV. His sister, speaking of Phillip, said his "mental health degraded fast and terribly bad," and that she had noticed "extremely concerning" signs of mental illness, including an inability to manage anger and personal hygiene.

Gerald Dixon, the former NFL linebacker who coached him in high school, calls Phillip Adams a team leader, mild-mannered, humble.

At a writing workshop for teens, I say, A head injury can really mess you up. William, the young running back, meets my eye and says into the quiet room, Yeah, it does. He seems surprised that I know something about it; his look also says You have no idea.

ooooo

The human skull is a surprisingly hard bone, almost wood. The brain: Jell-O floating in water. It is not always the impact that creates the concussion, but rather the brain knocking around the skull. A concussion, what our own body does to our brain.

Unlike us, when the woodpecker hits its head, it's protected. The woodpecker has special eyes, a tiny brain packed tightly into its skull, stabilizer muscles in the neck, a small skull area, a long bony tongue that wraps around its spongy skull and acts like a seat belt. Whereas a person might incur a concussion at 60 to 100 gs, the woodpecker goes at a tree head-on at forces of 1,200 to 1,400 gs. It pecks a tree 20 times per second, 12,000 pecks per day, and can reach 4,000 gs before it needs to worry about brain trauma.

The ram ritually slams its head against its foe, looking to dominate. Its horns, which hold air and are connected to its respiratory system, allow it to re-breathe, drawing on carbon dioxide in the blood, filling the intracranial space—swaddling the brain in Bubble Wrap. Nature here, too, takes care of its own.

ooooo

At the Neuroscience Is . . . Cool fair, I hold a human brain. It's the size of a grapefruit but looks like a large gelatinous pink-gray walnut. There are many folds and creases, and it is squishy, though not so much as when alive, when just a little pressure can leave a permanent dent. It weighs one pound at birth, two pounds in elementary school, three pounds in adulthood. Holding the brain, I cannot help but think of my brain, of the brains of all the people I know.

But when I watch football, I am not thinking of the brains of the mostly Black men on the field. Like others, I only wonder if an injured player will be ready for playoffs, will be back for preseason. These men, who are cast in commercials as sources of entertainment, seem impenetrable when they show us how to use body spray, drive cars furiously in a seven-film franchise, swipe a pizza from a delivery driver, charge at a scrawny white guy until he switches insurance companies. I am unable to imagine them off the field in pain—I am not supposed to—so like most Americans, I neglect it. I am enamored of the fiction of extra-human strength; while in reality these men, who constantly put their bodies on the line, are the most vulnerable.

Five years into my own head injuries, I watch quarterback Patrick Mahomes get hit head-on. His eyes roll back, his feet get pulled out from under him as if by an invisible wave. I say out loud to the screen: Why is there nobody out there protecting him?

The next weekend, I am right back on the couch, Mahomes back on the field.

ooooo

The ancient Greeks loved a good hit to the head. It's in the songs and all over the literature. The *Iliad* is poetry and brain injuries. During the siege of Troy, 37 of 190 traumas are to the head and neck, while three are from wild boar bites. Eighteen are by spear, one by arrow, four by stone, five by sword. A little later on, Euryalus is concussed in a boxing match, "spitting out clotted blood, and letting his head hang to one side." Amicus gets concussed in the ring with Dioscorus Polydeuces: "He became like a drunk man from Polydeuces' blows."

At the Louvre, there is a red crusted hydria (jug) on view, showing Polydeuces treating Amicus with laurel root, having just beaten him in the face.

In 401 BCE, Plutarch writes about King Kryos, who "struck by a dart into one of his temples . . . swooning and senseless, fell off his horse." He comes up "dizzy in the head and reeling." Pyrrhos, who lightly wounds a soldier, is killed by that soldier's mother when "watching from . . . a nearby roof and fearing her son would be killed, [she] threw a heavy tile on Pyrrhos' head." His concussion makes him vulnerable, and he is overtaken by the enemy. Pyrrhos wins the battle, loses his life, gives us "Pyrrhic victory," a win that comes at great cost.

ooooo

Bayes' theorem calculates the probability that something is true. For example, what is the probability that (a) we are the only intelligent life (b) in five hundred solar systems. What is the probability that you (a) are hungry if (b) it's noon. What is the probability that you will be hurt if (a) the human body is built for destruction and (b) you are on the football field in America and (c) you are a young Black man.

This problem can best be expressed as:

$$P(A|B) = \frac{P(B|A)P(A)}{P(B)}$$

Of course, with brain injury, there are not just two variables. There are many, many determining factors:

Probability of (trauma | isolation) = Probability (structural vulnerability | re-injury)

Probability (fear of being perceived as weak | losing money | losing self as you know it)

_____

Probability (go back onto the field, take more hits)

What is the probability of suffering, what is the risk that it will take you down, your loved ones with it, how many linemen are you really facing at the end of the day?

In 2014, an anonymous survey conducted by NFL Nation asked

320 players if they would play in the Super Bowl with a concussion. Eighty-five percent responded yes.

ooooo

In 1912, Dr. Isaac Adler observed that as cigarette dependency rose, so did rates of lung cancer—a disease once so rare it was seen as an anomaly. By the 1940s and '50s, the medical industry was in agreement, facilitating several studies on etiologic factors that linked tobacco and carcinogens. They identified smoking as the leading cause of lung cancer among men. In 1964, US surgeon general Luther Terry issued a definitive report to that effect, and there was no more pretending that cigarettes wouldn't kill you. Today, even though we know the risks, 30.8 million adults in the United States are addicted to nicotine.

Coincidentally, also in 1912, the *Rodney & Otamatea Times* warned of "Coal Consumption Affecting Climate." The article noted, "The furnaces of the world are now burning about 2,000,000,000 tons of coal a year," and then went on to explain how this, coupled with oxygen in the atmosphere, yields 7,000,000,000 tons of carbon dioxide. "The effect may be considerable in a few centuries," it concluded. Except, of course, in 2019, carbon emission reached 33.2 gigatons, and climate deniers are aplenty.

It is rare that we do not know the science. It is not that we do not have data. But it is not the numbers that change the culture, it's the narrative.

In 2017, the House Committee on Energy and Commerce accused the NFL, which had gifted the National Institutes of Health an "unrestricted gift" of $30 million in 2012 for a study on CTE in living players, of pressuring the NIH to remove their expert in neurodegenerative disease and instead funnel money to researchers connected to the league. The NFL denied the accusation. It also ended its partnership with NIH.

In 2016, only a year before the congressional inquiry, a report entitled "Somatization in Post-Concussion Syndrome: A Retrospective Study" asserted that 55 percent of sixty individuals who suffered physical and emotional sequelae following concussion "were found to be somaticizing." This included a thirteen-year-old girl who, in their estimation, "most likely fell into the sick role after being out of school for so long." The study blamed an increase in somatization—psychological concerns expressed as physical symptoms—on "the overwhelming media attention that concussions have received."

At the bottom of this particular study, a disclosure stated that one of the authors was "a consultant to the New York Jets and the New York Islanders."

∞∞∞∞

For decades, when a football player got injured on-air, the camera would linger, the sportscasters would hope aloud for a speedy recovery, for the man to rise to his feet. What does it mean that, now, when we are even a little more aware of what a head injury means for a person, the camera cuts away and we go to commercial?

Luke Kuechly, linebacker for the Carolina Panthers, suffers three concussions over three seasons, retires early. He says he wants to hunt, fish, relax, be with family.

∞∞∞∞

Fifteen-year-old Berto Garcia, too injured to play the sport he loves, outfits a football helmet with custom-made force sensors and works with his physics teacher to calculate g-force equations. What is the necessary minimum protection if, every season, an average high school lineman takes the equivalent of a 25 mph car crash in hits to the head? The helmet, inspired by the woodpecker, reduces whiplash, a common cause of concussion. It is currently being pursued as possible intervention by the US Navy. But research into advanced helmets has thus far proven that concussion-free football is a fantasy. Even the Riddell 360—built of hard polycarbonate and energy foam lining—achieves only an 85 percent rating. An unsolvable math problem. No helmet in the world can protect the human brain in collision.

High school players suffer twice as many concussions as college athletes—67,000 a year—since most injuries go unreported or the young athletes are pushed back into the game. School administrators are anxious to change the culture of athletics and increase awareness, but many injured young people have already gone on to join college football, the military, the police academy. Most of these former athletes bring their strength, determination, discipline, grit, heart to the job, the workforce, the community, the home. But what about those who have been forever changed by the game? What is the probability that, having been hurt, they might hurt others?

Probability of (aggression | on the job) =
Probability (father | rookie | rage) Probability (violence)

———

Probability (generations)

What is the likelihood that a young man, multiply injured on the field in high school, will carry aggression into his future? That he will inflict it upon his girlfriend, wife, boyfriend, ex? That he will take it into school? Into the service? Onto the streets he is patrolling? That he will teach it to his children?

In the 2013 TedxOrangeCoast talk, Daniel Amen, *New York Times* best-selling author, says, "Mild traumatic brain injury . . . ruins people's lives." Amen uses SPECT (single-photon emission computed tomography) imaging, a nuclear medicine study that looks at blood flow and activity, across 83,000 brain scans, the first and largest study of active and retired NFL players. The damage looks like mold on bread. He says: "We have to look at individual brains, not clusters. ADHD, anxiety depression, addiction, these are not single disorders but are expressed multiply and variably across brains." He put the players on a brain-smart program, and 80 percent improved in blood flow, memory, mood—essentially reversing damage by engaging neuroplasticity.

We wonder, how would things have ended for Phillip Adams if Dr. Amen had gotten to him first?

Players talk about how hard Phillip Adams worked. He didn't drink. He didn't do drugs. Charcandrick West, former running back, sometimes ran drills with Adams. He said, "I never saw him get mad at anyone. He was all about his business, washing and folding his clothes, real neat."

Phillip Adams liked cars and sometimes drove too fast. He stayed close to home, taking care of his mother, a former high school teacher, after a car accident left her paralyzed. He worried about money, had plans to open a smoothie shop. His friends used to say, Easy, Phil, you don't have to do so much. He worked out three times a day, afraid that what he wanted most was impossible, afraid his injuries would leave him behind.

ooooo

We tell my sixteen-year-old nephew he cannot play football. At six-foot-three, G is built like a running back, looks as if he can take hard hits, wants to go into the military as special ops. He has fine blond hair, the chin of a Ken doll, a sweetness he prefers to hide. He is a great big brother, and on any given day you're likely to find him tending to one of his young siblings. The women in my family, even his mother, who does not believe in coddling, all say: no football! Don't even think about it! It is, of course, an American hypocrisy, a consequence of white privilege.

The men being drafted into the NFL—boys, really—they're no less vulnerable than G.

I have a harder time with the game these days. I wrestle with ethics and tradition, and even the economics of the decision to boycott the NFL, what it would mean for these mostly Black men we've groomed, for their families. What it means for the generations of young players coming up. I can't say I've sworn football off. Walking around Philadelphia, I love seeing people in Eagles jerseys, love how there is instant friendship anytime one of us brings up the victorious 2018 Super Bowl, which happens in Ubers even now. The fact that, during the 2023 Super Bowl, people reported for jury duty by calling out "Go Birds!" If the game is on at a bar, at a friend's house, I don't always turn away. But I don't yell at the players when they drop the ball. I see a particularly brutal hit, I cringe. A man lies on the ground for a long time, too long, the camera cuts away, I keep watching through the forced commercial break: I tell myself, If you're going to watch, then watch.

the lost word

Hairphones for x[1]
Bathing Suit for x
Yellow Knobs a Monkey Eats for x
Quick Joke for x
Punching Rings for x
Shirt for x
Grand Central for x
Post Office for x
Mug Hole for x
Clean Hole for x
Ejaculate for x

---

1 Hairphones for Headphones
Bathing Suit for Seat Belt
Yellow Knobs a Monkey Eats for Bananas
Quick Joke for Trick Question
Punching Rings for Brass Knuckles
Shirt for Chair
Grand Central for Great Lakes
Post Office for Airport
Mug hole for Cabinet
Clean Hole for Sink
Ejaculate for Eject

Tampon for x
Big Dead for x
i-pod for x
x for x
Tori Spelling for x

A student asks me the name of the writer we discussed two days ago in class. The one from the syllabus. I can picture the writer she's talking about perfectly—suave, bearded, gentle, blue eyes, big heart, tells us of our deepest friendships, "you couldn't do all that and not be a little bit in love." I could point her to the passage in the memoir where I am humbled by his enduring love for his best friend Denise (though I've forgotten her name, too), whom he has elegized in a book I share with students for multiple semesters. How beautifully he writes closeness, the barbs and jealousy, all his careful noticings of who Denise is. But I am blanking on the writer's name. The student—the entire class—stares at me, wondering if this is a joke, if their professor really can't answer such a simple question. You just taught him to us two days ago.

It is strange for a writer to lose language, but this is one of the things that can happen after brain injury. Sometimes the words you want slip away, as when a cloud passes across the sun and swallows it up.

Talking to my father-in-law, I say *strip joint* when what I mean is *strip mall*.

The writer my student is asking about—the one whose name eludes me while the class looks from her to me—this same writer once sent me

---

Tampon for Tight End
Big Dead for Die Hard
i-pod for Airpod
I've forgotten what x is
Tori Spelling for Toni Morrison

illustrated drafts of the work he was doing in Provincetown, sketches of little creatures. He is a vegetarian, is kinder than most people, loves animals. Not long from now, he will lead a book club on Taiwanese novelist Qiu Miaojin's *Notes of a Crocodile*, and we will trade crocodile memes, tweets about queer attunement and being full of love that nobody wants.

(This writer, not so long ago, sat across from me at a beer garden. The sky was pink, he wore a colored shirt that highlighted the flecks of gray in his short beard. We shared a plate of squeaky cheese, growled at some loud drunk girls sitting nearby. We reminisced about growing up gay in South Jersey, how we sometimes felt our throats close up when we walked by the buzz-cut lawns and the squat little grandma houses. Once, he noted of a Famous Writer posed in a photograph beside a Famous Barn, *He is the kind to believe his pain is more deserving than yours.*)

But for the life of me, I cannot think of this man's name.

ooooo

A gap is a blank we can't help but fill. Whatever is missing—a word, an idea, somebody's name—we rush to close, to stuff our own language into the holes. Gaps, pauses—these are not mere ellipses in conversation. Rather, if we're working out of a psychoanalytic framework for communication, Suzanne Keen tells us a gap indicates a fundamental asymmetry that is inevitably, if unconsciously, acted upon by others. For instance, when I blank on the writer's name that appears on my syllabus, you might have assumptions about my intelligence, my competency. When I am too sick to come to the party, the meeting, the door, you close the gap with your own explanations. You go straight to x for x. The minute we are gone—even when we are still here—people rush in to fill the space that once belonged to us.

Maybe the gap is actually an invitation.

It is between the * * where our words meet.

ooooo

My therapist's eyes are the gray-blue of an ocean cliffside. Her Irish accent has softened considerably over the years, unless she's saying "ye" or "row" or is slipping into laughter. Her hands are small, freckled, active. Her face, which has always been as clear as a creek, has more smile lines than worry lines. Long ago, she converted to Islam; peeking out from her head scarf are wisps of hair that have whitened over our many years together. I have seen her in no more than a dozen outfits, one of them a T-shirt celebrating science, one a T-shirt honoring jazz. Once, I told her about having sex in a train station parking lot and she roared with laughter. On occasion, she has picked up the phone to talk me through some snag when I'm on deadline. The night I told her about my first head injury, I heard her voice crack on the line, hurrying off the call, afraid not just of what had happened to me but of her own feelings about it.

Whatever you say, don't say anything—an Irish aphorism that captures just how deeply private Dr. G is. I know she knows I know she's queer, that she was once married to a man, but we're not supposed to talk about it. She does not know that I know her father was a celebrated footballer, that her brother is a doctor and a governmental minister, the other brother a judge. There are culture and faith differences between Dr. G and me that might have but never did get in the way. When she was in her thirties—the years following her divorce and her mother's death, two of the few biographical facts she has shared with me—Dr. G had such a bad year that she listened exclusively to Mozart on headphones she never took off. Wandering through her house, doing the dishes, walking to work— tuning out everybody but Mozart. Piling stuff next to her on the bed, books, clothes, bags, and sleeping with it, because somehow it assuaged the loneliness. Things are not so bad that they can't get worse, another one of Dr. G's Irish aphorisms. She is a strange bird, it's why I love her so much.

A great therapist raises you from the dead. Mine knew what to say when I was plagued by the same annihilating thoughts, when I came out, when I got married and my father disowned me, when my mother died, when my father died, when my writing flailed, when everything I held dear was threatened. When I showed her photos of me in drag, trying to explain how sometimes it's not about man or woman, but rather centaur, she got it. Beautiful, handsome, she said. She used the word "luminous."

But after my injuries, Dr. G no longer understands me. It is not her fault that she is baffled: I do not know what words to use to explain brain trauma to her. She is all grace and wisdom and perplexity. I keep coming back anyway. I am grateful that she was one of the first people to show me what it means to live without seeking permission. I interrupt one of our more contentious sessions, frustrated that we are not even speaking the same language anymore, to go out to my car and eat a sandwich. Then I walk back into her office with and-another-thing energy.

Every session ends with me saying, How do you not get it, x for x, x for x?

ooooo

Frequency, a good trick poets use, is a way to elongate or echo for effect. Frequency, the amount of times a thing occurs, the number of times it is told. For instance, how many times I have replayed forgetting my writer friend's name, how many times this replays in my own head. How many times I forget someone right to their face, how many times I fail to explain why.

(This writer whose name I lost, I can hear him saying, *You have to get the blood onto the page.*)

Another student notices me messing up. This one makes a tally for every time I say "uh." This goes on for weeks before I realize what they're doing. Uh, uh, uh, I say, flustered. / / / , they scratch into their notebook. For every five uhs, they make a slash across the vertical lines, as if we're playing hangman and keeping score, and I always lose. Blue ink all the way down the page in neat rows, reminding me of all the words I've lost along the way.

To be honest, not my favorite pupil.

ooooo

It's the thought that vanishes that counts, my friends and I joke.

ooooo

On a department Zoom, I misspeak my boss's name. This is a woman I respect, who I have a great affinity for and occasionally eat pancakes with. She has light hair, a tender heart, cute outfits, and a propensity for saying plainly what most people around the watercooler are thinking. When I call her the wrong name during the meeting, there is a pause—the Zoom people all smile, more surprise than malice—until somebody else jumps in to redirect the conversation. A few minutes later, I say the wrong name again. This time the pause grows longer, the eyes shuffling across the screen—Is she serious?

At a gathering for people who have head trauma, a presenter gives us some tips. Remember these five words, she says, I'll be testing you! Person Man Woman Camera TV. A few minutes later, she asks, Did you remember the words? We yell them out en masse. Good! she says. You are already changing your brain!

A joke—

If concussions can cause short-term memory loss, what can concussions cause?

One day in a hotel room, I'm flipping through channels and land on the 1987 movie about an Italian American widow. This film was one of the

first movies that the adult women in my family enthusiastically introduced me to, Mom leaning close to say, *Once a cheater always a cheater*.
"Look," I say to my wife, pointing with the remote: "It's Cheryl."

"Cheryl?" I whisper to myself. No, Cheryl is not right. Somehow,
Cheryl is the exact opposite of what I'm trying to say.

My wife erupts with laughter—still laughs every time she thinks
about it. I do, too.

You know, Cheryl. The gay icon. From *Moonstruck*.

ooooo

In my nonfiction workshop, after I tell my students about the informed
memoir I've been working on, a student writes about her own injury
during a minor car accident. Her junior year is lonely, brutal. Sometimes
she looks at a fork and doesn't know what it's called, what it's for. I recognize the confusion, the darkness, and have to keep putting the pages
down, find that all I'm writing in the margins is uh, uh, uh. It is meeting
someone in the rawness of their grief and realizing how close you still
are to your own.

What a false word, *concussion*. It means one thing to one, another
thing to another, and absolutely nothing to most. The Latin origin—
concutere—gets us a bit closer: shake violently. In Spanish, the reso-
nantly consonant *conmoción cerebral*. We add the antecedent *post* in the
1920s, when soldiers come home from the Great War, in agony and
unable to explain what's happening to them. Then the veterans all die,
and we lose the word again. *Post*-concussive, after you have been dashed,
after you've been forgotten. Untold suffering because there is no way to
plead, *Stay with me, I am shaken*.

I say *brain injury*; they hear coma. I say *concussion*; they say, Can it
really be all that bad, if you're writing this? I say: *Neuroplasticity. Good
and bad days.*

I say, *I cannot get out of bed today*, they hear the voice of their own mother, who has yet again shut herself in her bedroom rather than join the family.

This nothing word, this nonsense word—culturally indeterminate—has been stripped like a screw. We might replace it, if only we knew how.

∞∞∞∞

The first word I actually remember learning, I hope I never forget. The word: lukewarm. It appeared in a picture book about an armadillo who lives alone in a tree. His tea is lukewarm. The rain droplets that hit his precious books are lukewarm. And somewhere deep inside the well of himself, he starts to feel a sliding, all his bones coming apart because of this cloudy, tepid water.

∞∞∞∞

One day, my therapist asks me to tell her about the rabbit. We found him in the alley near our house, and he has been at our heels ever since. He is the color of wheatberry. He naps with the dog below our desk, likes to wake the dog. When I rub his nose, he chitters. When I pet him, he runs his little pink tongue across my jeans. But we cannot keep him, we already have the dog and the cat, and he has gone to a new family.

"Do you love him?" Dr. G asks.

"Well, I don't know if you would call it that," I say.

"What would you call it then?"

You cannot hold a rabbit, I want to say. It won't let you. You must imagine its soft, warm body in your arms. But such a thought makes me feel childish.

Instead, I reply, "Is there supposed to be a word for it?"

There is a pause. She asks, "Have I ever told you the story of Rumi and Shams?"

It's November, the year 1244. A man in a black suit has come to the famous inn of the Sugar Merchants in search of something he has been missing all his life. This is the wandering dervish Shams Tabrizi, a man who takes on masonry jobs simply to feel the calluses on his hands, who slips his wages into the pockets of other workers when they aren't looking, who out of humility disappears into his black cloak when adoring students flock, and then ghosts his fans. Faith has brought him to the outdoor market in Konya. He wanders the stalls in bewilderment, passing the cotton vendor, the vegetable booths, his heart pounding, saying Yes, yes, this is the way, what you seek is just around the corner. Then there is a clatter, the punch of hooves into the dust. Shams looks up, speechless. Finally, after all this time, he has found him: Rumi on a horse, a mere shadow of the mystical poet the man will become, but already a drink of cold water for a man in the desert. Shams feels his own heart beating in another man's chest. At once, Shams knows: the two belong to each other.

And what will you give in return for him? asks a voice—maybe God's—to which Shams, watching Rumi ride off, replies: My head.

The two scholars meet again some days later, by chance, when Rumi is hanging out by a bubbling fountain. Whatcha reading? Shams asks. Rumi looks up from his page and takes in the stranger—poorer than him, a yokel. People have taken to calling him the Bird.

You wouldn't get it, Rumi answers.

Shams snatches the book out of Rumi's hands, throws it into the water. Rumi plunges in after it, astonished to find the pages are all dry. But how? he asks.

You wouldn't get it, Shams replies.

The young poet falls at the feet of Shams, his mentor, his other: teach me, teach me.

Or sometimes, depending on who is telling the story, the book catches fire but never burns. So much about Shams and Rumi still shrouded, their love a mystery.

The two become one of God's great secrets. It is almost like they have a language all their own. No one knows what words to put on it—Are they friends? Is this infatuation? Is it a con, Shams after the inheritance meant for Rumi's sons? The men fawn over each other until no one can say who is the lover and who the beloved. There is harsh talk, jealousy, for we are threatened by any love that has a face we fail to recognize. Rumi's family, incensed, worries about what will become of the riches. They say, What are you doing with the Bird? Are you mad?

No, stop, don't call him that: he is mine, not yours. You could not touch one hair on his head.

Three blissful years, not caring what anyone has to say. Those who don't feel this love, Rumi says— You know what? Let them sleep.

Then, one night, there is a noise at the back door, Shams goes to check. He never comes back.

Rumi, grieving, goes looking for his lost teacher, his friend, the man whose face he touched in the quietest moments. Shams! Shams! he cries. He dresses in black. He scribbles in his pain, "Because I cannot sleep / I make music at night. / I am troubled by the one." For years, his sense of object permanence stripped, he searches for the man who once searched for him—only to find himself alone at the end of each night. Then, one day, Rumi awakens to sunlight on his cheek, or maybe the sound of a fly buzzing. He sits up. He reaches for a pen and parchment. He writes three thousand love poems, trying to keep Shams in the room with him, where, it turns out, he has been all this time.

"You and I unselfed, will be together,
indifferent to idle speculation, you and I.
The parrots of heaven will be cracking sugar

as we laugh together, you and I . . .

In one form upon this earth,

and in another form in a timeless sweet land."

Three thousand and one poems later, Rumi realizes: Shams never left. He is me, I am him.

What does it mean that, after all these months, the rabbit comes home to me?

ooooo

x for x

It's come to me!

The writer I am thinking of is:

Paul Lisicky.

ooooo

A year has passed since Dr. G and I have seen each other in person. She's slighter, frail, and I have to look into her eyes to find her. Dr. G has watched me grow up; I have watched her age. Now retired from formal practice, though not from our sessions, Dr. G says she has stopped pretending that death won't come for her. Yet, still, she will keep the door open to me for as long as she can.

Is that because I'm your rabbit? I ask.

Well, yes, she answers.

ooooo

Let's not call it Minor or Mild. Let's not call it Expectation as Etiology. Let's stop saying Silent Epidemic, let's put actual words on it, words like neurodivergent, words like not-what-you-think. Let's call it what it is: it will have its pound of flesh.

Let's never say concussion again. Let's say: More Absent-Minded,

More Agitated, More Angry, Less Calm, Less Carefree, Less Cheerful, More Complaining, More Concerned, More Confused, More Irritable, More Depressed, Way More Depressed, More Distractable, More Easily Upset, Less Energetic, Less Enthusiastic, More Less, more or less (though, also More, More, More depending on the day). More Resilient. More Resolved. More Careful, Less Guarded. Less Fucks, More Awake. More Joy, even when there is less of it.

Let's say Salisbury steak. Let's say it's the Salisbury steak you spill down the front of your shirt in seventh grade with the whole cafeteria watching. Let's call it the Salisbury Steak Incident, and there are the days before Salisbury and the days after, the *post*-Salisbury, when you look and feel like a mess, and it makes you all the more furious that there is an inexplicable silent "i" in Salisbury, and then Thursday, when you thought there could be no more Salisbury steak, you smell it, thickening the cafeteria air. Let's put this on the menu every day, for an indeterminate duration.

No one is sacred, my neuropsychologist says. Think of how we once—maybe still—talked about patients. A "dirtball," someone who signs out of treatment against medical advice. A "gomer" ("get out of my emergency room"), a chronically ill patient. LOLINAD, "a little old lady in no apparent distress."

Day to day, we stare right into each other's face, but we don't actually know what human names to call each other by.

Let's call it How to Be Lonely.

Hippocrates tried to give us the right language. "The whole bone of the head," he said, "is like a sponge; and the bone has in it many juicy substances, like carbuncles." Do we think of the word "juicy," the word "carbuncles," when it comes to concussion?

Prehistoric peoples knew the brain. They invented the drill—one of our oldest tool's, derived from rubbing a rod between two palms to start a fire—and then they used it for surgeries. We keep finding evidence of early craniotomies being practiced for religious ritual, initiation, headache relief. Of 120 prehistoric skulls found in France dating back to 6500 BCE, 40 had trepanation holes. Of 411 skulls found in territories of the Incan and Paracas cultures, dated 400 BCE, 16 percent had trepanation—far surpassing the medical knowledge of the Spanish conquistadors, who didn't even know of the Incan achievement of anesthesia through herbal extract, cactus, other juices. These early civilizations, they had the knowledge and the procedures and, even if they are lost to us now, they had the words.

More Fearful, More Forgetful, Less Friendly, More Gloomy, Less Good-Natured, Less Happy, More Impatient, Less Patient, Less Pleasant, Less Polite, More Sad, More Shaky, More Short-Tempered, More Slow, Less Strong, More Tense, More Tired, More Grateful, More Human, Totally Invisible.

Let's find new words.

My therapist suggests: Let's call it a fight for survival.

Dr. G reads TBI memoirs. She reads scientific articles about head trauma. "I'm trying to understand what it's like for you. At the same time, I don't want to know what it's like to have a brain injury."

She says tentatively: So what would you call it, when you have to decide every part of your life in advance? When you are always on edge because you could get hurt far easier and worse than most of us? You think you don't have a disability because you've always been so able. But imagine if other people didn't have a single image of disability in their head? If you gave them something else to look at?

I resist this until the thought arrives like a bang: What does it say about you that you wrote a whole book about this?

One day Dr. G tells me that she has landed a grant to work with pa-tients with brain injury. She is helping them to heal through Mindfulness-Based Stress Reduction (MBSR) and meditation. She is doing this because she thinks brains are "cool." She is also doing it so that she and I might finally, hopefully, speak the same language.

Maybe the word is not therapist: maybe it is spiritual guide, and I am merely a disciple.

Let's call it awe.

ooooo

I will tell you a true story that you might not believe—

I go to a witch. She is certified in a hands-on technique that uses light touch to move the fluids of the central nervous system and pal-pates the synarthrodial joints of the cranium. The witch says to me, What would it look like to be better? I'm not sure how to answer this, so I say, Tequila. She laughs, That's what everybody says. The witch is not the same witch each time. Sometimes she has a French accent. Some-times her teeth are crooked, other times straight and white. I trust her because she is not precious about healing like other healers, and because the look in her eyes reminds me of Dr. G. The sign on the window says she does this same technique on babies, and I think I would be a big baby to not at least give it a try. But also—she has been hurt like I have been hurt. (For her, it was the jumping out of planes and subsequent whiplash that did it. Years later, on her birthday at the beach, she will be hurt yet again when a wave knocks her over. Let's call it: one rogue wave.) The treatment is not cheap. I am lucky to have found the witch, lucky to be able to pay for this. I think about how many people need the witch but can't get to her.

The witch works on my head. It means hardly moving a muscle, hers or mine. It happens over many months, then years, as does my learning to let her into the in between (**). You are still in fight or flight, she says. Your cells are buzzing. Your parasympathetic system is the Jack that we have to put back in the Box. There is some kind of black spot behind your left eye. Those light switches you ran into, they had teeth!

Together, wordlessly, the witch and I find open spaces for us both to enter, a touch that goes where language cannot. Some days it feels like surgery. Some days she puts her hands in my mouth. People comment how light my eyes look after a session. My best friend asks, Does it feel like deep tissue? No, more like when the dentist is drilling and the Novocain starts to wear off. I leave the first session and go eat a baked potato and it is the best baked potato I have ever eaten, makes every other potato seem like pulp. I curl up on the couch, lying there as if I've recently been beaten. Despite instructions for rest, I write for hours. Without the witch, I doubt I would have been able to say any of this.

One day, the witch goes very still. I feel it—the frozen spike in my head, a thousand years old. I don't realize it just yet—another millennia will go by before I do—but the witch has felt it, too, this invisible thing between us, lodged in my skull. She hesitates. She will later tell me that, when she does this, people sometimes throw up on her. But first, an eternity passes. Then the witch swipes at the air, and without even touching me, yanks the spike right out. I cry out, a word never spoken before.

Let's call it reincarnation.

post-it/yr phone

Is in the fridge
Is in the trash
Is in the mailbox
Is in the garden
Is in the car—not your car, somebody else's
With the dog food
Is in your hand
No, your other hand
On the charger, where it's been all day
On the charger, where it's been for the last four minutes
(That book you are trying to plug your charger into is not your
*   phone)*
A random drawer, no, not that drawer, the drawer you just searched
*   two drawers ago*
With the dinner, in the oven
What phone?

q&a with my wife #3/ against regret

We begin again. And again. And again.

> ME: Horse or boat?
> YOU: What?
> ME: Horse or boat?
> YOU: Horse. ████████.
> ME: Of course you'd pick horse.
> ME: Tell me again about the snake you wrapped around your body.
> YOU: It was my freshman year in college. Back then I was a pre-vet major, I had a work study job in the lab. We kept a single boa constrictor. I don't remember her name. My job was to clean her tank. One day, I wrapped her around my waist and she stayed. Like a really big thick belt. She was gentle—she seemed kind of sad actually.
> ME (but only in my head): Horse, boat, or snake?

ME: What's one nice memory you have of us?

YOU: I remember going to get Andy. Which car did we have? We had found him on Craigslist. You were a little nervous because you hadn't really had pets and you thought you were allergic to cats. You two fell in love right away. ████████████████████████. We paid thirty dollars for him. Then we went to the pet store and I was doing supermarket sweep to get what we needed and you were showing him the fish in the tanks. We were a little family. We had just moved in together, and that was really the start of our life together, just the two of us.

ME: What about a particularly bad day? A time after the head injuries, when you came home and I was in bed, or something you were looking forward to became a disappointment because I was sick.

YOU: I can't recall. That whole time is a fog. But ████████ ██████████████████—yeah, there was a constant sense of sinking. Disappointment. Fear.

ME: Can I jog your memory?

YOU: Oh, yeah, could you? I'm excited about it, I'm closing my eyes so I can go back there.

ME: Imagine—imagine a failed witch's house.

YOU laugh.

ME: One day ████████████ and I went ice skating. I was feeling good. It was my first time back on the ice and I came home really excited about it. I couldn't do it at all before that. ████████ was supposed to stay for dinner. I came in to tell you and then ██████████████, and then I was sick again, immediately.

YOU: I don't remember any of that.

ME: We had this moment when I walked in the door, we were both so happy because it was a break in sickness— and then that dumb little thing happened, a nothing thing. I remember you being so upset. I remember you feeling loss for both of us, because that night was another night gone.

YOU: That happened more than once—the hope being ripped away.

ME: The hope for?

YOU: The hope for normalcy and happiness and being close. It was like, okay, nothing about this is going to change, this is how it is now.

ME: Part of that sense of inevitable catastrophe was that I had the first injury, and then two more in the span of a year. What was that like for you?

YOU: Terrifying. That year—it was the edge of hell. We were so unsettled; we didn't have a home. You were still in California. We were being forced to move ██████████████████ and I was trying to pack us up while you were away. That first concussion, we were across the country from each other. That was such a startling thing. We were trying to ████████████ ██████████████████. I was at work, I remember. I was in and out from my desk to the hallway freaking out. You called me on the side of the road. You said that you'd been in an accident. You said, I think I hit my head, but then you immediately said, I'm fine. And I think you were trying to protect me from panicking but I was already panicking. I let you assure me that you were okay when you weren't. I felt like ██████████████████. I felt ██████. I couldn't take in the fact that you were so far

away going through this. I immediately went into denial:
She's fine, she has to be fine, we're too far apart, I can't get
to her. You sounded mostly—normal? I didn't understand it.
Everything was ██████████████████████. I felt a little
disassociated from life for a long time. And at the center of
it all was you unwell in this way where we didn't know when
or if or how you would get better, and the distance that put
between us was really, really hard.

ME: What about when it kept happening? Not just that I
wasn't getting better but that I was being reinjured. What
was it like for you to deal with that over and over again?

YOU: There was definitely a fog over that whole period,
straight through ████████. Two and a half years ██████
████████████████████. Lay onto it that I was working
at ████████████████ and essentially being emo-
tionally abused. This is from a selfish perspective, but I felt
there was nowhere in my life that felt safe. Not my home,
not my marriage, not my job. ████████ had just died. I could
barely get through a day. I could have handled any of those
things, even ████████, but your unwellness was a huge
trigger for me. The idea that I could lose you by either you
never getting better or us splitting up—I just think I reacted
to that in a lot of different ways. It was the capstone of all the
instability and terror at that time.

ooooo

Later, crossing these lines out, you'll confess that it is hard to read the
words back to yourself. You have to take breaks, take the dog out for
walks. It is hard to sit in it for too long. You ask for an extension, an
extra few days. I say take your time. I say I know what you mean: it's

like moving through soup. I feel guilty for making you do it. But I do not tell you to stop.

◦◦◦◦◦

YOU: Now I feel very much that the lesson of those years, or the advantage, is that I've come out of it much more grounded in the moment. Whatever happens, ███████████████ ██████████████████████████████ ████████████.

ME: I really feel that now, too. But it took nearly five years to get there. I'm thinking of people who are in your position. Who are still in the early days when you don't know how long your partner is going to be sick, how hard it's going to be, if it will be okay, what's going to have to change. How does the partner of someone who is suffering also suffer?

YOU: It's one thing to have a doctor give you a ██████████ ████████████████████ and there's this kind of guide through it all and an understanding of what the sickness is. That's not what it's like with head injury. No one can tell you anything. I don't know about partners in general, but a lot of my stuff came up with this whole experience, when that hope was ripped away. We'd almost have normalcy and then ████████████████████.

ME: You're saying when we'd had a good day?

YOU: Yeah, or a moment that was changed because of reinjury or you not feeling good. It echoed a lot with my younger life, which never did get better. It made me feel panicked and trapped. And it made me question what was going on and whether you were being overly sensitive to things because you were afraid. I got all wrapped up in that and in the fear—and

a desperate, desperate need for ███████████████. I
wonder all the time if it could have played out differently, but
it was a really dark time—360 degrees of a dark time, from
██████ ████████████████████████████████
██████████—I missed you. ██████████. I worried that you
were gone in a way. That you were inaccessible to me. And
that things would never be the same. And of course things
aren't the same.

ME: Do you feel like your relationship to doubt has changed?

YOU: Yes. ███████████████.

ME: What did that for you?

YOU: Therapy. Almost breaking up. ████████████████
██████████████████████—I am programmed, I think, to
be very reactive to the person I'm closest to (███████████)
being sick or injured. The programming is a very deep fear,
um, and I think that turns into a kind of ████████████
███████████. I'm going to lose everything.

ME: So best to deny it's happening at all.

YOU: No, ████████████. It's more complicated than that.
There are a couple different things happening simultaneously.
There's the fear of you dying, ultimately—of losing you—and
therefore just a fear reaction whenever anything happens to
you. I think where the doubt comes from is the erasure of my
experience. The complete erasure of my feelings, my sensations, my traumas, my sickness.

ME: Because my sickness is so big.

YOU: Yeah. ████████████████████████, because someone else's was so big.

ME: But in real time, my sickness—it *was* so big.

YOU: Definitely. ████████████████████. But also—████
████████████████████ I'm hardwired in every arena of my
life to feel like I'm about to be erased, and so I'm grateful for
the experience that has made me have more perspective on
that. Don't give up, trust in each other and the healing power of
time and each other's resilience. ███████████████████.
You're meant to be, and that's bigger than anything. But if
you just ████████████████—wait, work on it, and
work every day to get through it. You can. I still believe that
about us.

ME: How would you characterize who we were before the injuries and who we were after?

YOU: That's a really hard question. I think we were ███████
—we were a lot younger, too.

ME: This was a big catalyst, though, right? It changed things
between us forever.

YOU: The intimacy is actually greater, trust is greater. Having been through that and continuing to go through it—it's
something we live with now—maybe it's silly, but I do believe we could ███████████████████████
██████████. We saw each other pretty raw. ███████████
███████████████ we were threadbare and we were
exhausted and just really raw.

ME: Nothing left to lose.

YOU: Raw. Like open wounds everywhere.

ME: What do you forgive me for? What can't you forgive?

YOU: What do I forgive you for? [Long pause]. ████
████████████.

ME: Think about it this way. The accident was an accident,

or whatever. But there were things on both sides that could have made coming through it easier.

YOU: But that would mean you put me through something you didn't have to put me through.

ME: I was not up-front with all my injuries. I was withholding certain information—

YOU: Why?

ME: Why was I? I—doubted you in your ability to endure it. Part of that was conscious, but part of it was ███████████ of people who capitulated or turned away. For me, it was a lifetime of ███████████████████████ so yes, I could be in this marriage and join you but only if I was always somehow also on my own. I don't think I understood that that was what I was doing. I think I thought I was protecting both of us. But it created a lot of distance between us.

YOU: I felt that. ███████████████████████████. We were magnets facing the wrong way. We were ███████ ██████████████████. Our deepest stuff was really coming up and at odds.

ME: As it does for most people who are going through something like this.

YOU: In terms of forgiveness—███████████████—I don't think of any of this as something that you did wrong. ███████████████████████. I never thought of this through the lens of forgiveness.

ME: Even the small choices, day to day, made to not include you?

YOU: But I understand that from the perspective of your own survival and not something you were doing to me. I think I did learn a lot more about who you are.

ME: Like what?

YOU: Just who you are in trauma and sickness. Your inclina-
tion to pull away was very on display at that time. A previous
me would have thought that that was about who I was, but
I understand that that is a survival mechanism for you. That
came into clearer focus and now I have a better understanding of that.

ME: What else?

YOU: Maybe a little inverse to the pulling away is being very
open about what's happened to you. That wasn't true in the
immediate moment, but now you're very forthcoming about
███████████████████████████████. I mean you're
writing a book about it.

ME: Do you see that in our private lives, too?

YOU: With our friends, maybe. Whereas I would want to
push it down. If I was going through something like that, I
would suppress it.

ME: It sounds like you think that's better.

YOU: No, I don't think it's better. You taught me about how I
can be judgmental about people who talk about their physical struggles. ██████████████████████████.

ME: What about regret?

YOU: I regret you flew home right after it happened.

ME: Why?

YOU: Because you shouldn't have gotten on a plane.

ME: Why?

YOU: Because it was trauma on trauma. ██████████████
██
██████. I should have gone out there. That's what should have
happened. What's more important than that? And I could

today. I would do exactly that without a minute of hesitation today. I felt like I was drowning in that moment. "Well, she says she's fine. It's fine, it's fine, it's fine." ██████████████ ████████████████████████████████████. Are these the right answers?

ME: These are great answers.

YOU: Do you █████████?

ME: I do. But sometimes it seems like it's the regrets that stay most silent between people in a marriage. Not talking about them gives them a lot of power.

YOU: What are your regrets?

ME: I regret ████████████████████. I regret not telling you about ██████████████ though I honestly ███ ████████████, I remember being very shocked you didn't know. I regret ██████████████ over and over again. Which is maybe why I've had to learn to talk about my sickness, my condition. I've had to force myself to do it because not doing it only jeopardized me more—at work, with family, at home, in spaces where I'd be physically compromised. It took three big hits to the head and then tons of subconcussive hits to be like, "Okay, you have to ████████ even if you don't want to and accept how people react, and that includes your wife." I regret ████████████████████████████. But I mostly regret ████████████████████████████████ ██████████████████████████. Lately I've also been thinking against regret, too. If we regret what we did, we regret those prior selves, too. Without those flaws, there's no us now.

YOU: If we had broken up, I think I'd be steeped in regret, but ██ ████████████.

ME: What don't I know about you?

YOU: ██████████████████████████████████
██████████████████████████████████
████████?

ME: ████████████████████████████████.

YOU: There's nothing you don't know about me that I want to tell you.

ME: What do I hide from myself?

YOU: Not too much anymore ████████████████████ [pause]. I think sometimes ████████████████████. Sometimes you want to be assertive about knowing something rather than being curious about it and revealing that you don't know something. [pause] Maybe you didn't mean that question like, "What's something I know about you that you don't know about you." Is that hard to hear?

ME: Only because I think you think I do it for different reasons than I do. You think I need to be ███████████.

YOU: No, ███. Sometimes I wonder if you've become more afraid of the unknown. Even on a day-to-day basis with really small things. I wonder if it sprang out of the feeling of being out of control. You must have felt that way, even though we never really talked about it. Must still feel that way sometimes.

ME: Was there something you thought you wanted and it turns out you didn't?

YOU: I have a lot of what I wanted. I wanted to be married to ██████████████████.

ME: You did? Is that true?

YOU: I wanted my partner to be ███████████
    ██████. I wanted to travel a bunch. I wanted to live in a
    city. I wanted a job I believed in where I thought I made a
    difference.

ME: But are there even little things you had wished for that
    you don't any longer?

YOU: ████████████████████████████
    █████. I let go of the disappointment of not being able to do
    them. I'm just better at knowing my limitations. I thought I
    wanted ████████? I don't know if I still do.

ME: Who will you be in five years?

YOU: I keep picturing our house in Asbury Park. I'm doing
    a lot of woodworking with the dogs in the yard, and you're
    writing in the studio.

ooooo

For the first time in a while, there is silence—the good kind. You are
smiling and petting the dog, who is always as close to you as he can get.

There are questions, still, which I don't ask, and know I never will.
Maybe that is part of it, too.

ooooo

I think back to something you said over email, in a time when we could
feel the sting of what we nearly lost—were, without realizing it, still
in the process of losing. Boat rocking, waves surging, convinced it was
somehow the other person's doing. I don't know why, but we kept reaching for each other even when it seemed doomed.

ME: Everything will be ████████████████

██████████. Some things are lost, but ██████████
██████████. I don't like anybody as much as I like you.

YOU: Oh, 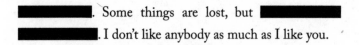 I love you so much. I
want to know you again. I'm nauseous from this instability
for over five years. But I won't lose you because of it. We have
been so tested. I've been very sad and very scared at times. I
know you have, too. I have let you down. I want to be there
for you. I want to trust you and you to trust me, intrinsically,
with our whole hearts, again. I want you to feel safe with me.
I want us to be side by side every day, through all of this, all
the ██████ to come, and all the beautiful things, too. I look
ahead, and still I wince. But there is brightness ahead.

Sometimes I think this is all a marriage is, this try-and-try-again, an
act so maddening and true, it transcends regret. The thin strip of land
appears on the horizon, and still the boat might sink, and still we make
for the coast.

ME: I pick horse, too.
[I do not add "to be with you."]
YOU: It's too late. You picked boat.

So we will just have to make it there by land and by sea, each looking
constantly for the other, even if they are a tiny speck. Don't worry, you
say, we'll recognize each other. Like that time you were walking toward
me down ██████████ and I couldn't quite make you out from that
distance: but I knew it was you.

clocked time

Draw a clock. Begin with the almighty 12. Where does the 2 go? What happens after the 6, exactly? Are you picturing a pizza pie? Are you imagining a clockface like a moon, with bright spots and blue shadows? Are you seeing a baby's face?

Draw a clock. But I did not know how. The 2, 3, 4 were so bunched up on the page they could have been minutes instead of hours, whereas my eight o'clock lasted for half the day. I looked up at the woman who was here to help me. Her eyes, mouth, and blond ponytail told me I was being ridiculous. Come on, you can do this. She was more amused than annoyed. I had stared at big silver clocks all through elementary school, followed the little hand until it hit the three p.m. bell and released us from our pens. I had checked for the time everywhere, in houses, airports, hospitals, offices. But I could no longer remember where the numbers lived. It was the brain injury, it was scrambling me up. The woman in the white coat had to show me what to do. Together, we traced out the arc of the 4, 5, 6, 7 on the sheet of paper. She made it look so easy, as if we were both on the same trip around the sun.

Illness, like fiction, is all about time. In both, there is the temporal un-folding of the narrative (i.e., will she get better or won't she). In both, there is biographical time (i.e., a lifetime). There is a lot of boredom in sick time. A lot of lying in bed pretending to be Virginia Woolf. When you are Virginia Woolf, you become an expert at repetition, at dwelling. In story time, you might begin with the phrase "Later that day," or "Five years later." But in illness time, you must live out every one of those moments over the five years.

The blue scarf. It is wrapped around your head and eyes to block out light. The blue scarf holds the same smell as your pillow. The darkness that makes even reading and escaping into fiction an impossibility, and thus makes you wonder if you are still among people. The scarf tells you what time it is, the actual time, not the treadmill of time everyone else is running on. You spend so much of your day in this scarf, you begin to wonder if the scarf is actually a source of pain. If it is what makes you sick, wrapped up in it day after day, hour after hour. The scarf takes on the sweetness of ripe fruit. This is how your wife will find you tonight, again, when she comes home from work, the smell of business on her, carrying her foreign objects, her keys and the like: wrinkles on her pants from all that productivity. Years from now, you will wear the scarf in public to convince yourself you've lost no time, but the scarf will make you feel jet-lagged and it will have to come off. But for now, over the course of an hour—Is it six o'clock? Is it three? Until she comes through the door?—you lose yourself in the scarf. You pro-ject little movies onto the theater of the blue scarf, memories, thoughts, fascinations, revenge plots, redemptions, fictions. In a single afternoon, you've walked through someone else's life.

How long does a head injury last? A few days? A couple of months? Years? One migraine goes on for an ice age.

The sun is out. The friend comes by. The first few moments go at a trickle—but actually that's just me, it's the friend who's rushing. They are thinking that I can no longer tell a coherent story distinct from my illness story, and this makes them uneasy. So I make a joke: we laugh, blood flows through the veins. Then the door closes, night breaks the windows, I am alone.

The thing I forgot I said, so I said it twice. I probably say it three, four times, until the words become, I suspect, nullified.

Wait forever for the pan to get hot, then everything speeds up, the meat burns.

A page takes three pages to read, as it must be read thrice.

The drive to the grocery store, radio off, takes months. A wheel on a grocery cart goes on for a thousand wheels.

The walk from parking lot to door, which should take three minutes, lasts forty.

According to Einstein, it is impossible to say in the absolute sense that two distinct events, separated in space, are occurring at the same time. While she is at work and I am at home like this, there is nothing simultaneous about us. When I am in the blue scarf, I am nowhere, I am on the moon, trying to remember how movement feels in all this stillness.

> *A riddle: So little of it, yet it's everywhere; so much of it, but none*
> *of it yours.*
> *Answer: Your bed, the wall, the sun sliding down the wall, the tea*
> *gone cold, the blue scarf, the sweat drying on your back, the key*
> *in the door that tells you another year has passed through the*
> *keyhole since she left this morning.*
> *Answer: Time.*

In sick time, there are the days that hold all the normal scene and summary of life, days that feel okay. Then there are the days that are measured by gaps, days full of expansion and pause. Those go on forever and still are somehow entirely lost. The story, though it is continually unfolding, feels very much stopped. You will believe you have no control, and you will be correct; even this lack of control requires pacing, the variety that is resistant to momentum. "An hour, once it lodges in the queer element of the human spirit, may be stretched to fifty or a hundred times its clock length; on the other hand an hour may be accurately represented on the timepiece of the mind by one second." Virginia Woolf, who would know.

To play with time, you can—as narratologist Suzanne Keen tells us—be "repeating details, dwelling on some events to the exclusion or reduction of others, employing story-stopping descriptions or leaping over events with gaps." This is called pacing. Compression, speeding up, lingering, skipping—these are all normal, natural rhythms.

ooooo

I lie here and think about the past because the present is inscrutable. Those early days together, many lifetimes ago, when I was surprised by how fine S's fingers were. They made me think of sparrows. I pressed my beer bottle against her thigh to say what my mouth wouldn't. Slipping into sheets, like diving into ocean waves.

And then, already awake, I wake up, and the shadows have moved across the wall, another day is gone.

ooooo

Once . . .

But what do you want me to say about once?

What is the significance of once when I have played once in my head until it multiplies. Once, I got onto a plane I shouldn't have.

Once, I was trapped on a train, I had to make them stop and let me off, the train kept moving but I was going through a tunnel of my own. Once, very hurt, I rang home and got a busy signal, all the while we were still talking on the phone. Once, I asked for help, some groceries; they replied, I'm sure you're a big girl. I slammed my head onto asphalt and *once* froze, once became years (years), and in past-present-future time I am still lying on that street in California, with the busy signal.

This thing all things devour,

Birds, beasts, trees, and flowers.

I turn forty, jumping right over thirty-five to thirty-nine.

ooooo

Draw a clock. It's common sense, Hipparchus says.

Twelve hours of daylight, twelve hours of darkness. Chop those up into smaller bits, like the Babylonians did and before them the Sumerians, and we get the Western sexagesimal counting system for mathematics and astronomy, we get minutes and seconds.

When the first clock—the sundial—is brought back from conquered Sicily and mounted onto the Forum, the Romans mistrust it. Plautus, the Roman dramatist, dismisses it in favor of the oldest and best clock: his stomach. But time marches on, the sundial is followed by water clocks, mechanical clocks, clock towers that use bells and drums, then the Maragha observatory in 1259, built almost four hundred years before the telescope by Genghis's grandson Hulagu Khan. Big Ben in 1859, whose pendulum is calibrated each year by using pennies. Coordinated Universal Time at the Royal Observatory in Greenwich. All this marking of time, yet something feels off, as if you're a second ahead, and I'm a millisecond behind. In 1982, Larry Dossey, author and physician, coins "time sickness" as a way to explain the feeling that time is always slipping away, that we scramble to keep up.

In temporal structure, calendar and clock time are gods. Every single living and nonliving thing on earth must answer to them, with the exception of the sick and fluorescent lighting.

Yet there is past-present-future time, social time, outer time, time in memory, ecstatic temporality, almost none of it mimicking clock time. There is the ringing alarm of the biological clock. There is the sun, the biggest baddest clock, making tears and empires fall. There is false time.

Those with an illness that lasts for years (chronic, from *khronikos*, because the Greeks could tell human suffering would last a long, long time) have imperceptibly unique temporal rhythms. They may have a different relationship to time altogether, and as a result a strange relationship to others. "As rhythms of bodily life alter, a person's expectations for the future might change," offers Tanisha Jowsey, time theorist and lecturer at the Faculty of Medical Health and Science at the University of Auckland. "And their relationship with other people (who have their own temporal rhythms) might also" crash. This is the real reason I can no longer see the face of the clock: it no longer belongs to me. The doctor asks: Do I see double? No, what I see is what a drunk behind the wheel sees, past peeling from present. This is hard to explain to people, until pandemic obliterates clock-time for much of the human race.

If the trash cans that line the street are full, it's Tuesday. If they're empty and rolling around, it's Tuesday again. Different rooms are for different tasks, to stop the blurring. I move furniture around as the shadows switch places on the hardwood floors. Only the church bells down the block are a sure sign that it has been hours.

My therapist and I have an ongoing argument wherein I say I lost time and she says no you didn't. Her message is basically: the house was still lived in, even if it was haunted by ghosts. Maybe she is right—in ten, twenty years, maybe I will re-conceive this period as a necessary departure that all the while was en route. But I have to take a break in the middle of our session, and I pace the narrow hallway between her office and the hair salon. When I return, the silence between us smells like hair straightener. Then she says, Okay, no, I do not agree with you that this is lost time. Maybe I can't stand the idea of that. It's a devastating thought.

I am not saying that we would definitely have had children between ages thirty-five and thirty-nine. I am simply saying that I looked up—*we* looked up—and now it suddenly feels late.

ooooo

What is the clocked time of a head injury? This should be a simple question. Is it one George Clooney? Two George Clooneys? A Lady Gaga? After his concussion, an eon of agony, George Clooney wonders how long this will go on before he really thinks about suicide.

ooooo

Normalcy is being in time with others, but in illness we are in time with no one. This is not simply because a week must now be measured by doctor visits, sessions with the neurologist, physical therapy in twenty-minute increments, five minutes a day of pills that add up to two and a half hours a month, the thankless part-time job that is recovery. Rather, our cultural understanding of what our lives should look like—which we unconsciously base on what others our age get to do or be—becomes corrupted. Those familiar temporal rhythms we have marched along to become meaningless, all habitual experience of time distorted. In 1982 (the '80s are obsessed with time—*Bill and Ted's Excellent Adventure, The*

Terminator, Back to the Future not once, not twice, but three times), so-
ciologist M. Bury described illness as "biographical disruption." We are
yanked out of our rightful place in youth or adulthood.

This loss of time means a reckoning of consciousness. Kathy Char-
maz, the expert and theorist on grounded theory and hypothesis, and a
scholar of chronicity and death and dying, says, "The struggle for control over illness and for control over time is a struggle to control the
defining images of self."

After a head injury, everybody wants their old life back, says the
comedian, swinging her mic. Everybody had such perfect lives before
all this, no problems at all, not one bad choice in men.

Every clock cries wolf.

Maybe the trouble is not time, maybe the problem is how we think of
language and telling: as only forward and back, story as straight line,
words as sequitur, words as finite and precise. But Suzanne Keen asks,
What about *contradictory narratives*, wherein incompatible or irrecon-
cilable versions of the self appear, namely You and the You you could
have been, had you not hurt your brain; *conflated narratives*, in which
two different times coexist, that is, you are here sick in bed and you are
also not here, you are anywhere else, anything to escape the awfulness
of here; *differential narratives*, in which you age at a different rate than
the people around you; *circular narratives*, which return you to the beginning, to where you were when this all started, the day of the accident,
only now, after all that has happened, you have irrefutable insight.

ooooo

My wife and I wait for who-knows-how-long until we know each other
again. In the interim, she speaks with more honesty, I handle her less
with kid gloves—ask myself why I have been handling her at all. We

celebrate the day we walk past a man with bees for a beard: one of our first nice days together in a long, long while. The wounded have strange anniversaries.

How funny, time always arriving on time. If we had had to face this injury any earlier—even a year earlier, two years, or maybe two, three years later—we might not have made it.

For the unwell, time travel is possible. I go back to an earlier time, which is somehow still now. All these echoes, which are not repetition but recursion. Listening from the other side of the door as shower water runs off my wife's body, a sound I have listened to for years, a sound to hold on to, not to remember S but to recall myself. Her long blond hair, the way she pulled it to the side of her neck, the bracelets on her wrist tinkling. Her closemouthed smiling: Why are you so far away? My beer pressing against her. Jump ahead twenty years, her hair is short, shaved in the back. Strands of gray catch the light. Lines around her eyes, softening her face. Where did our time go?

For the upright soldiers, those who are not sick: time is freedom. What they have—what I am lucky, five years after the injuries, to be getting back—is so-called ecstatic temporality. It is interconnectedness with past, present, future. It is mutuality, something made right in the rhythms of the body, an imperceptible anchor in the self that connects me to others.

At a friend's wedding, lamplight floods the marble room. A woman's shoe against the hard floor. The waiters coming out of the kitchen one after the other. I watch water shudder glasses across the table, thinking of jewels. S in a black suit jacket, her hand stroking my back even as she talks to the person beside her. Only a year or so ago, I would have had to close my eyes to all of this. In a past lifetime, really not so long ago, I wouldn't have been able to draw S to the dance floor, wrap my arm around her waist. If you just wait—sometimes if you just stay long enough, even when you are desperate to flee—you find you're ex-actly where you are supposed to be, at exactly the right moment. And she is there with you, in your arms.

Here is how to draw a clock. Do not think about the numbers: think of all that white space that only you can see, think of the hands and what they catch, release. Think of water glasses on the table at the wedding. Chatter in the room. This is how we measure time. What they mean by counting the seconds is do not count at all.

memory loss

Hit in the head with a rock: 117
Hit in the head with a bottle: 105
Hit in the head with a fire extinguisher: 80
With a shovel: 33
With a shoe: 13
With an opening door: 22
With a gun: 40
With a pot: 11
With a stick: 13
With a rock: 117
With a brick: 34
With a pipe: 14
With a crowbar: 19
With a hammer: 84
With a chair: 56
With a frying pan: 38
With scissors: 2

As of this date, there are 1,360 film titles in the IMDB database sub-categorized as "hit on the head." Among the most popular are *Rambo Last Blood*, the Joker spinoff *Birds of Prey*, and *Paddington 2*. A fan favorite—one close to my heart, and most of America's—is *Home Alone*. The 1990 film stars mischievous and lovable Macaulay Culkin as Kevin McCallister, the eight-year-old boy who brutally maims and burns two grown men who have broken into his house, discovered him to be without parental supervision, and become nearly deranged in their need to hurt him. During the hours of the assault, Kevin never incurs so much as a paper cut. The Wet Bandit burglars, however, suffer eighty-five serious injuries, according to internist Dr. Diego Ponieman. There is one particularly cringe-y scene involving a blowtorch, a pile of snow, and the pink head of Harry the Wet Bandit. There are many brain injuries, thanks to Kevin's booby traps, which result in staircase falls, tree house falls, irons to the face, BB gun pellets to the forehead, paint buckets to the face, shovels to the back of the head. "Another concussion is definitely probable, causing serious, long-term neurological damage at this point," advises Dr. Diego Ponieman—and the movie still has forty minutes to go.

In slapstick comedies, violence is on loop. The Wet Bandits get hurt, advance, get hurt again. In order to walk into the next room, the next trick, the Wet Bandits must forget what has just befallen them at the window or in the doorway. This forgetting is the only way the movie can keep them moving through Kevin's gauntlet. There is excruciating momentary injury, but no accumulation of pain; scene after scene, the film obliterates agony and vulnerability. The forgetting becomes not a mercy, but a curse. Like the damned in Dante's *Inferno*, the Wet Bandits are never made to sit in their pain, nor are they allowed to become accustomed to it. The next trap is tripped, they endure some sharp stabbing, burning, or heavy blow. Then they go after Kevin McCallister with the blindness of the damned.

The children watching *Home Alone*—including me, when I was the

same age as Macaulay Culkin when he starred in the film—do not care
that the Wet Bandit just got brained. We want him to get up, go back
into the house, get his face smashed again. Sadistic as this sounds, there
is evolutionary justification for our amnesiac delight. A hit in the head,
after all, is not a spear through the head, spike through the head, bul-
let in the head, or mace at the head. The Homo sapien part of us that
laughs is the part that knows the trauma could have been much worse:
it could have happened to us.

"It is a fantasy," Barrie Oldham of the Brain Injury Rehabilitation
Trust says about head injury and Hollywood: "Someone gets hit, recov-
ers, gets back on the horse. In real life, it doesn't happen like that."

ooooo

But have you seen Seltzer Bro? Dude on TikTok tries to chug a spar-
kling water, then cracks headfirst into a partially opened garage door,
falls to the floor. Somebody posts, "I don't think I have ever laughed
harder in my life. This isn't ok, I'm in pain." As of this writing, Seltzer
Bro has been liked more than 2.7 million times. There is a debate over
whether it was a stunt. Still, everyone agrees: the funny part is when he
slams his head. The funny part is that we don't see what happens next,
just his head smashing into the door on loop.

ooooo

One of the hardest things for me when telling people about my injuries
is not only that I have been hurt, but that I am likely to get hurt again.
This is also the toughest thing to remember, myself: mostly because I do
not want to. My conceptualized version of self has always been closer to
a ship captain or a soldier, or even Sir Ernest Shackleton, about whom
the explorer Apsley Cherry-Garrard wrote in 1922, "If I am in the devil
of a hole and want to get out of it, give me Shackleton every time."

Shackleton leads three expeditions on endless, treacherous slogs to Antarctica. One of his ships gets impaled by ramrods of ice, while his crew on land pushes through blizzards and gale-force winds in homemade clothing to deliver supply depots for the mission—but does that stop Shackleton from going back to the uninhabited, frozen continent? No.

"Anytime I am not sick, I forget that I've ever been sick," I tell my wife. I say, "I have to tell myself the story all over again." It's what I've come to think of as *healing amnesia*. I feel a little better, I immediately start to think nothing is wrong with me. The pain was entirely imagined, and now I am cured of something that wasn't real. I pack my bags again for Antarctica. Only when I'm back in it do I remember. I knock my head against a wall or a shelf, get a migraine—get hurt—and have to admit, yet again, that I am still somewhat off. The vulnerability becomes character weakness.

"That's crazy," S says. "How can you forget? I never forget."

"It's as if it happened to somebody else, like an identical twin."

"Great," she says, "now I have to worry about two of you."

This makes me feel guilty. I want to ask, But if you could make it all go away? If you could wipe your memory clean, would you? If I didn't have to plan for every eventuality, if you weren't alert to every looming danger? If you could get off the ship, would you? Aren't you sick of this? Read: aren't you tired of me?

Sometimes, the answer is yes even when it's not.

She says, in her way: We are on this ship together.

ooooo

But look at how much Sir Ernest Shackleton forgot!

His *Discovery* expedition to Antarctica in 1901, according to Royal Navy commander Robert Falcon Scott, was "a combination of success and failure" and, according to many other people, mostly a failure. It ended with twenty-two dead dogs, Shackleton so weakened that they had to carry him on a sledge (a fact hotly contested by Shackleton, to no one's surprise). Seven years later, in 1908, he forgot all that, and launched the *Nimrod* expedition. Shackleton and friends reached a new Farthest South latitude, becoming the first documented human beings not only to traverse the South Polar Plateau but to discover the location of the South Magnetic Pole. Then, conveniently, he forgot how they starved on the journey home. That he had to give away his last biscuit to Frank Wild, an explorer often photographed in sweaters and smoking a curled pipe. Shackleton returned home, hoping to get rich off his new fame and title as commander of the Royal Victorian Order. He wrote to his wife, "I am never again going South and I have thought it all out and my place is at home now," though we can be confident that Lady Shackleton read that letter and said to herself, Yeah, okay, Ernie, and then secretly pulled his snow boots out of the donate pile. She was not at all surprised when Shackleton dusted off the boots, which had not gathered very much dust at all, and began preparations for the 1914 "Imperial Trans-Antarctic Expedition." This mission—enlisting ships *Aurora* and *Endurance*— would be Shackleton's most famous, and a disaster. He would make it home only a little frostbitten after giving up his mittens to a sailor who had lost his gloves, but men would be left behind. Stranded for nearly two years on the uninhabited continent, sleeping beneath ten-pound reindeer fur that weighed thirty pounds after ice melted into freezing puddles. Three would not return. And while their deaths haunted Shackleton to his own dying day, eventually, he would forget this, too.

ooooo

Close your eyes, do you see it? The movie playing in your head? Soldiers come home from war, probably a world war, bandages wrapped around their heads. There is an intense need for quiet and trees, and they are so unlike themselves. Someone is pulled from wreckage by the jaws of life after a horrific accident, the car having gone into the ravine or into the opposing lane of traffic. For a long time, this person is unable to walk, unable to feed himself. Maybe he is never "quite right" again. Doctors walk around whispering the word "serious." This is our only image of brain injury.

We have no image of mild head injury, which means we have no real concept of it, which is why it might be so hard for me to remember my implicit fragility. Is it a clown being whacked by another clown? Is it the antics of Moe, Curly, and Larry? The 1955 "Concussion Mambo" by Chuy Reyes and His Orchestra? In 1947, Donald Duck is hit with a flowerpot, gets amnesia, forgets he loves Daisy. In 1959, Quick Draw McGraw shouts "Kabooooong" and smashes his enemies over the head with an acoustic guitar. In anime, bandages indicate a weak spot to strike, which of course is often the head. In Looney Tunes, a head injury immediately results in an angry red lump that pushes through the scalp. There are no fewer than 2,282 sound effects that mimic someone being bonked in the head. Wile E. Coyote after the anvil is dropped on his head; Wile E after he smashes into a brick wall, boulder, speeding train. Next frame, he is back to chasing the Road Runner. Next frame, the football player is back on the field, the construction worker rejoins the crew. Next day, filming *Syriana*, George Clooney hits his head against the floor during a torture scene when his chair is knocked out from under him; struggling through the very real concussion, he contemplates suicide. Next day, Briana Scurry, Olympian, gets a knee to the head and has to give up tending goal for the US Women's National soccer team, next day she pawns her medals to get treatment, next day she contemplates suicide, has to pull herself back from the edge.

Or how about the skull breaker challenge that was started in Spain. It's easy to do, it guarantees likes. Get two friends, put one in the middle, say to them, "All you have to do is jump." When they jump, kick their legs out from under them and watch them eat it. One Arkansas teen gets concussed. One New Jersey thirteen-year-old is hospitalized. When he lands on the blacktop, his body still, his friends are still laughing, not realizing he is no longer awake.

Head trauma is not extraneous to a society in which it appears; rather, the culture tells us through film, through stories passed down—what it spurs or manifests, the way it sees and treats its athletes, workers, women—exactly how humane it is. The evidence surrounding TBI, incomplete as it is, has always been there. But it slips our minds, our policies, our medical practice, our sympathies. *It looks different in the movies.* This cognitive dissonance—what we're shown vs. how we suffer—is our inherited amnesia.

We are a country that knows with certainty what it is at the end of the night but which, come morning, forgets all over again. We remember, we forget, we remember, we make our coffee, we go to our jobs, we set off to conquer continents, both knowing and not knowing our own weakness.

ooooo

Annie Dillard says that whatever memory you put on the page, it becomes fossilized—thus, no longer a memory at all, but an object to hold in our hands and examine. A gift, I think, to take something that has been harboring inside you all this time, cast it out.

ooooo

Tig Notaro delivers jokes about death in deadpan. She speaks so slowly, it would be maddening if it were not the entire draw of the act. Her dark brown hair is cut in a messy shag, her body thin, her arms lanky. She has cheekbones to rival my wife's, the kind of wide smile that grows only in the Midwest. She is best known for *One Mississippi*, the semi-autobiographical television series about returning home to take care of her dying mother. In the past, Tig Notaro's stand-up has been dark, sardonic, but she stayed away from anything personal. These days, she is talking about her mother. In *Boyish Girl Interrupted*, Tig tells a joke about how, after her mother's passing, her stepfather bought six burial plots—because they were having a special. One of the plots was for him, the other two were for Tig and Tig's brother. And the last two? "I guess that's where you'll be gay buried," quips Tig to her girlfriend, pointing at the invisible patch of grass on the stage.

Soon enough, Tig will be diagnosed with breast cancer. The girl-friend will leave her. Tig speaks openly about this with her audience. After the double mastectomy, Tig elects not to get reconstructive sur-gery. She tells a joke about a TSA representative too nervous to pat her down because she wasn't certain that Tig was a woman ("I just did not . . . want to help her out," says Tig). And maybe because the audience doesn't think she'll do it, and maybe because they do, Tig begins to un-button her shirt to show them the scars. She toys with us, saying mostly in gesture, "I'll do it/What, no, of course I won't take off my shirt!" The air thickens. There is nothing slapstick about this, even though we are laughing hard, cheering harder. The awareness in the room, electric—the sense that we are about to altogether see that which is usually kept hid-den. Every viewer holding their breath, even when that viewer is one of fifteen students in my creative nonfiction class watching the screen. The act becomes something else, something new. Not merely performance, but deeply personal public demonstration, a strange and unexpected gift.

Tig stands before us, topless, her chest flat and concave. You can see her ribs, her breath pressing against them. The skin is puckered in places. It is as if we are simultaneously witnessing Tig's injury and recovery—as if we are joining Tig in a fearless act of remembering. What this shared knowledge does to us, how it astounds us. We are stunned to realize that memory is collective, not singular or private, as we are led to believe in our daily lives. Tig does not allow you to forget that she is only human. She has been deeply hurt: here is the proof. We expect such an act of vulnerability to take away her power. Instead, it delivers it back to her tenfold. It binds us to her.

Without missing a beat, Tig launches into a bit about small planes, and we erupt at so mundane a fear in the face of her ferocity. She delivers the rest of the show half-dressed.

Watching Tig Notaro, I am aware that the comedian has done this before. We are not the first people to hear about her double mastectomy, her mother's death, her girlfriend at the gravesite. She toys with us, as she has toyed with past audiences. We are not the first to see her remove her shirt, will not be the last. It is an act, she is a professional, she has worked this material for months. Yet somewhere along the way, we must concede . . . there was a first time. There was an initial impulse on stage to reach for the top button and undo it, to move on to the second button, despite the feelings—exhilaration? shame? fear?—that rose up. Does that fade for Tig over time? Does Tig ever forget that she is exposed? And is it any less raw if it's done twice, three times, a hundred times before an unsuspecting audience? Does it make her any less vulnerable to bare herself to new strangers, this queer woman who reveals what most keep concealed? Or does she need to do it time and time again so she can hold on to the truth of her own body in the face of erasure?

I do not want to be Shackleton, I realize. I want to be Tig.

ooooo

Annie asks: But, seriously, did this have to be a work of nonfiction?
Annie replies: Yes. All we have of concussion are false stories.

ooooo

Maybe this will give you a new image of head injury—

Think of the cell phone you keep dropping. Maybe it's fine the first time it lands on concrete, maybe it's not, maybe you will get a call and the voice coming through the speaker will be warped. Maybe after three drops, it starts to glitch: the screen is cracked, the receiver doesn't work. It can't really load apps. For some unknown reason, it keeps dialing your boss. You fumble to explain yourself, and only some of what you say comes through. What you hold in your hands is recognizable as a phone, and yet you are perhaps the only person who understands it is not a phone the way that other people's phones are phones. But there's no way you can get another one, you're stuck in this contract. So you hang on to it. You use it to call out.

ooooo

After everything—the dead dogs, the dead men, the sunken ship, the failed mission—Shackleton goes back to Antarctica for one last hurrah. Who knows what he says to his wife this time, maybe he says nothing, maybe he takes out his traveling cloak and they both know what that means. Maybe he puts on the old boots she keeps for him in a chest. The enlisted men of the 1921 Shackleton-Rowett crew—most of them from the *Endurance*, who never received their wages—are waiting for him.

Shackleton, one last time, off to sea—erasing the knowledge he carries in his bones, the memory of every other brutal voyage, every failure. His heavy wool coat is not heavy. The ice is not cold, the wind is not a blade, I have never suffered, nor starved, I have never accidentally poisoned dogs, never nearly lost a finger to frostbite, never led and left men to their deaths in the most brutal landscape on earth.

What's wrong with your heart? the crew asks Shackleton in Rio de Janeiro after a suspected myocardial infarction.

Nothing: I have never had a heart.

They land on the island of South Georgia on January 4, 1922. The expedition's physician Alexander Macklin says maybe Shackleton should go home, live a normal life. Shackleton responds, "You are always wanting me to give up things, what is it I ought to give up?"

"Chiefly alcohol, Boss."

They await the orders to push off, but the forgetting is adding up—ice, cold, hunger, dead dogs, dead men. At 2:50 a.m. on January 5, Shackleton's heart gives out. Forgetting has brought him here. His death means the end of the Heroic Age of Antarctic Exploration and mounds of debt for Lady Shackleton.

Macklin, physician in mourning, writes, "I think this is as 'the Boss' would have had it himself, standing lonely in an island far from civilization, surrounded by stormy tempestuous seas, & in the vicinity of one of his greatest exploits."

Trying like the devil to remember.

bent lace

for Ursula

"We don't know the contour of feeling;
we only know what molds it
from without."
—Rainer Maria Rilke (1875–1926),
"Fourth Duino Elegy"

There is nothing tame about Ursula von Rydingsvard: Ursula wants to be the wind that cuts through forest. When she touches wood, this is precisely what she becomes. Communion with the world, with nature, is her art. Most of her pieces are built from cedar, because Ursula long ago fell in love with the wood, but some are bronze, copper. The sculptures, in their craggy abstractness and rough cuts, say, Do not turn from what makes you human. The sculptures rise up like geological monuments. The life expectancy of each piece, anywhere from fifty to two thousand years. We'll go, they'll still be here. Ursula's work offers the same semi-permanence as the stars. When I look up at the massive sculptures, I feel blissfully insignificant.

To shape them, Ursula uses circular saws, buffers, drills. She uses her hands. She does not use the word "beauty." A refugee of Nazi labor camps, she doubts that anything like beauty—an idealized state—can exist. Anyway, it is art that has saved her, not beauty. Making work is how you stay alive, she says.

During my recovery, I go looking for Ursula. Thus far, I have only encountered her in books, or online. It is like seeing the Grand Canyon on paper your whole life, but feeling its shadows and depths call to you. This has been a hard year, my thirty-seventh, the most frayed of the five plus bad years. I have spent most of my days either sick or scared. I am on the wrong frequency, and I am trying to listen for the right one so I can rejoin those I love. Thus far, that has been nearly impossible. I have had to say aloud to my wife, to my doctor, What if I can't work anymore? I have heard my wife say, What if we don't work out?

Okay, yes, a lot has been taken, but not everything. What I have learned about bravery is that it is not a skin that you are born with. Rather, you must put it on little by little, like sunscreen. Even on the worst days, I still have color, shape, form. An orange lily opening in the darkest corner of my room. A ripe red tomato. And art, of course, which, in its truest expression, turns no one away.

The night before we are supposed to go see the sculptures, in a moment of cognitive overload, I mix up olive oil and dish soap and ruin fifty dollars' worth of meat. We try to wash it off, cook it off in the fire, but I have thoroughly soaped the steaks. We take small bites, throw out the rest. I stare at the slim branches of trees, which spread across the darkening sky like alternate lives. The next morning, we explore Storm King, an open-air museum in New Windsor, New York. It is a gray, blustery day, moody after hours of rain—a canvas Ursula might herself have dreamed up—and there are less people roaming the grounds than expected. I bury my face in the collar of my coat and tune everyone out, looking for her. I only have so much time before I have to go back and rest. I give up on the map, just try to feel my way toward her. I need to sit in her shadow, feel her towering presence, and remember aloneness is not an eternal state.

I remind myself that Ursula calls most of her works "she," not just the twelve-thousand-pound *Ona* (*Her* in Polish) with the bumpy textured surface cast in tinted bronze, nor the seventeen-foot *Mocna* (*Mocna* is "'strong,' for a woman"). Even *Bent Lace*—the bronze statue gifted by one obscenely rich person to another rich person on his hundredth birthday that, though elegant and haunting in the tradition of Louise Bourgeois, brings to mind a slackened scrotum—is a she. Each of Ursula's sculptures coming into her own.

And then, halfway across the field, there she is: *For Paul*. She breaks from the green mound like a surprise volcanic cliff, dark and solid, nearly fifteen feet of glued cedar planks in graphite. What is permanent? What is lasting? How can you feel yourself part of something eternal even when you walk around trapped in a body of immaterial materials? I press my back against Paul, feel her there, feel the cold ground beneath my feet, an ache in my chest. I experience a quaking that, for the first time in years, is not about my own brokenness. This is watching the world slide and change and be reborn, and feeling yourself a part of that. I cry tears, the good kind. This is how you stay alive, I think.

ooooo

After Storm King, I go looking for Ursula elsewhere. At the Philadelphia Art Museum, I find *Now, She*, cedar cast in bronze and urethane resin, an iceberg coming awake. I seek out the *Contour of Feeling* at the Fabric Workshop and Museum, where Ursula is artist-in-residence. I am too sick to attend the opening and listen to the artist in her own words, but I can feel her talking through the wood a week later when I walk through the nearly empty gallery. *Zakopane*, twelve feet high, looms like a church organ. *Seven Mountains* invoke seven buddhas. *Nine Cones*, hollowed cedar from which nine spirits have escaped. *Ocean Floor*, a cedar basin, ripples and pulses as if filled with water. *Ocean Voices*, humped and large as a whale, is sorrowful and nearly breathing.

And—for fun—there is *PODERWAĆ* ("Tearing Apart"), an eleven-foot leather jacket sewn together from 150 vintage jackets found at thrift stores and flea markets. Of course she would go for a biker jacket. What, you think I died already? Ursula seems to be asking. You think I put myself in a wooden box for good?

Her father was abusive. He brutally beat the nine children in the tub, where they huddled and covered their heads. Ursula saw the worst of it trying to shield her little brother Stas, who still speaks of his big sister with the wonder of a child once protected by another child. In the displaced persons camp in Germany, where Ursula grew up, everything was made of rough wood—floors, walls, ceilings, staircases. ("Everyone around me looked ravaged by the war, including the Germans.") (Including her father.) There was no insulation, little food. Ursula slept atop a metal spring bed, grateful for the wood that kept her from the violence just feet outside the door.

In 1950, the family emigrates to America, to a blue-collar town in Connecticut. On the porch, dozens of boxes of donated clothes: my god, the riches in this country. Her father gets two factory jobs, at one point loses a finger, receiving $500 for it. Over the years, his rage and paranoia deepen. It is possible he loves no one, only his favorite axe, which will be buried with him. During one holiday gathering, he turns to Ursula, proclaims: May you suffer. Her first husband is a similar trap. Ursula flees to New York City, to Columbia University, to save herself and her young daughter, and to make art.

The moment the saw hit the wood, she said "Oh my god" and covered the metal shop in a snowstorm of dust. It was an Irish monk who, in 1975, delivered Ursula the gift of beams of cedar. The monk was a friend, an artist in his own right (the abstract painter Michael Mulhern, who would later witness 9/11 from his apartment and create the series "Ash Road" from the paint and dust that blew in when the towers came down). The cedar was soft. It was the color of skin. It was sexy, sensual, toxic to breathe in, and Ursula knew it would always answer her.

"If art hasn't saved your life in some essential way," says sculptor Sarah Sze, "then you probably won't continue making it."

This is how you stay alive, by giving yourself to it even when it takes your life from you.

ooooo

Look at all that grace, all that power. In photos, Ursula looks as if she herself might have been sculpted from raw materials—thick hands of a carpenter, fingernails black with graphite. A beautiful carved face that I wish I could touch. You could almost miss what's beneath it all: the anger. The anger is there, the fuel for her art. It is as present as the wood that feeds the fire when you peer through the flames. "Yes, it is there," Ursula says. "And there is nothing like putting a circular saw in your hand when you're angry. It is such a healer—it so does the trick." This is taking the pain and breathing life into it. It is not meanness in Ursula, in Ursula's art, but largesse.

I think of Thornton Wilder: "Without your wound, where would your power be?"

A concussion cannot live and thus never really dies. It sticks around for years, like ruins overtaken by new growth, the ground never quite forgetting the weight of what once was there. I would never wish my injuries on anyone, but it is a mistake to think they are only destructive. I am not merely my suffering or rage, just as Ursula is not her anger, her pain, her loss. Putting one word after another is, for me, an audacious act of hope. This is not about happiness, which is flat and white, which is too often simple and dull. This is about joy, which is far more precious for its impermanence, and which bubbles up to contain everything—yearning, desperation, elation, celebration, excitement, nostalgia, desire, possibility, transfiguration. Joy is bent lace.

Fleeting as it is, the feeling lasts months, even years after I've said goodbye to Ursula and Storm King: I see a tree in its proximity to another tree, how they crisscross in conversation over a patch of blue sky. I see a thousand winterberries on the edges of slim branches, how they huddle together to make red redder just because I move closer to them. This is a gift from Ursula, this new capacity to see the edges of the living world—but it is not only a gift from her. I come to realize that this new sight is another invisible, lasting touch of the head injuries.

At times, I may be reduced to a childlike state, but this means that now I experience an openness and wonder I have not known since I was just a little thing coming to America. I am awakening to a part of me that has been quieted for so long and that has finally emerged with new sight. Gratitude, this is the gift Ursula has given herself, and that I have come to claim for myself, too.

David Brooks once wrote, in a stunning response to an impossible question posed by a stranger in pain, "We all know cases where suffering didn't break people but broke them open." How wonderful, to be broken in this way.

ooooo

One day, I email Ursula to tell her that I, too, am a foreigner and an artist, and that I will seek out her art as long as I live. I send her the piece I am writing about her. The next day, I receive a response back—

"I have rarely had a person who wrote about my artwork with such a deep understanding," Ursula writes. "Your honesty fits mine."

This is how you stay alive, I think.

She invites me to her studio in Brooklyn, a warehouse surrounded by warehouses, with a long, hazy view of Manhattan. The number 78 is spraypainted on the door. A hanging medallion reads "UVR Studios." I ascend a flight of metal stairs, at the top of which stands Ursula, arms open. We hug. We will hug many more times during my visit. "I am so happy," she says, before I can get those exact words out. At the end of the four-hour visit, I will be so stupefied and overcome that I will stumble into a sex toy shop on the Lower West Side, come face-to-face with a towering wall of fake penises and think, These, too, could have been made by Ursula.

Walking into Ursula's workspace is like stepping into the world on the sixth day of creation. Steel beams, clamps, pallets, adhesives, ladders, sawdust. The scent of cedar forest. Two dozen hulking wooden shapes rise up out of the floor and walls. The studio is full of her "monstrous" pieces, as she calls them. Some are old, most are new, a number of them created in the last few years since her husband's death, and then her daughter's. Grief demands much of Ursula: I wonder if she sleeps. She tells me about her new pillow, large enough to wrap her arms around. Forty years, they were together. Losing Paul is like losing a part of myself, she says.

We begin with a demonstration—this is how you seek the shape the wood wants to be. Ursula draws on a block of cedar and her assistant Mike (she calls her cutters "princes") brings it into being with a circular saw. The blade is specially designed for the studio, able to make angled cuts that would otherwise be impossible. Jo gives us a tour, talking about each sculpture with intimacy and precision, and Ursula nods. She adores her assistants; they are like family to her, especially now.

Pavel, a hanging piece, is puckered with holes that run across eight boards in rivers and tributaries; it commemorates Paul's discovery of the neuron that led to SSRIs and the research that earned him a Nobel. Another (*OBUDOWAĆ*) is a storm blowing in, "all force," with the wood giving way. A third is a mountain hacked at by the elements until it becomes vulnerable. (Difficult cuts, narrow bridges—Ursula describes the process as "shedding.") This one near the back, shaped like an elephant trunk, is a "he." Ursula tells me to grab hold of it, can't I feel the testosterone and the energy it's getting from the wall, spilling out at the top. A favorite, *Dottir*, is "she," muscular, strong; we joke how that must be true of all daughters. When we reach the glue room, kept at sixty degrees even in winter, Ursula shows me her newest work, as yet unnamed. It has two selves, "the one piece will be enamored of the other." According to Ruben, who has been with Ursula for twenty-six years, it is one of the most difficult they've ever built. I touch them all, run my fingers along the sharp edges and grooves, graphite coming off onto my fingers.

But the one that calls to me and which makes my chest swell—the unknown rising from dark recesses—sits close to the ground like a tomb. Because it was made by Ursula's hands, it cannot be still: there is movement here, as there might be in a movie theater or church. The piece makes me think of prayer, Pompeii, an elephant separated from its herd, how photographs are attempts to keep time and motion already lost to us. The staff affectionately calls this one *For Paul*, too, but its true name is *Where Are You*. Ursula made it after her husband's death. It is the length of his body. Inside, tucked away but not impossible to see, two pairs of Paul's hiking boots.

"It helped me work through something," Ursula says.

I am invited to stay for lunch. Hayley makes mushroom ravioli and salad and arranges some pink flowers. It is just Ursula and me, the cat Malutka, and Paul, in a framed photograph. Ursula pulls from her bag some "special" brown bread for us to eat. We talk about *The Year of Magical Thinking*, the shoes that Joan Didion could not throw away after her husband's death, and Ursula nods with recognition. ("I could not give away the rest of his shoes," Didion writes. "I stood there for a moment, then realized why: he would need shoes if he was to return.") We talk about soul mates. The old wounds that never go away. What art demands. We lose words together. (Ursula has aphasia, too—x for "apartment," x for "sorority," miming the word "grenade" when she talks of her first husband, calling him "dangerous" in such a way that makes me think this is a word she will never forget.) When Ursula speaks about her daughter, the stage four cancer, she squeezes the air as if clutching a heart in her hand.

The end is never the end, Ursula says. Finishing one piece tells you where to go next, it knows you are "begging" to go on. "There is a feeling that tells you that you can let go of this now. Or you never get that, and then the work is in trouble. I'm in trouble." Sometimes, that piece follows you for thirty years.

She keeps telling me I am fearless. She reads my own words back to me—*the same semi-permanence as the stars, making work is how you stay alive.* I do not have the heart to tell her I live with the fear every day, but that I have learned from her how to mold it into a different shape. She says, You allow yourself a kind of freedom in your writing that I don't usually see—the kind of freedom to have your say. You make your own life. That is what I do, too, she says.

Would you call this true love? I wonder. What else would you call it? In the rocky shores of Ursula's art, I find I am home.

"I keep saying, Ursula, this is your last one. It never is," she says. "I don't know, I'm probably going to die with the cedar."

Me, I'm probably going to die with the words. But first, I will live through them.

the healing algorithm

The first time I went ice skating after my injuries, I had trouble going in circles. My brain only understood backward and forward, even after months of vestibular therapy, and was throwing dizzy spells at me. My skates were fat gray bricks on my feet. I could do four clumsy laps around the rink before I had to get off. My heart was a lump. But it wasn't just my body's relationship to proprioception that I was re-learning, it was its proximity to danger. A light fall could mean another concussion, even if I didn't hit my head. The next time I went skating I made sure the rink was nearly empty, and managed a few additional laps, passing an older man who was wearing a helmet. My third time back on the ice, I watched someone go down and come up with a bloody nose. Then another girl fell, bad. When they cleared the rink, I hid in the rubber-tiled bathroom. I didn't know if she hit her head. Was it a sign? Should I go back home? Crawl into bed? Forget altogether the feeling of gliding? When they let everyone back onto the ice, I sat on the bench, watching others do the thing that I was desperate and terrified to do.

I love skating. I didn't take to it early the way some kids did, lining up at the rink's edge like little ducklings. One of the first times I went ice skating—ninth grade—I was on my ass so much I may as well have sat on the ice for the full hour. It mystified me, why anyone would strap thin blades to their feet and then intentionally walk out onto a slippery surface. I was in my thirties before I tried again, at Bryant Park with my nephew, who was enthralled. He took me by the hand and that's when I felt it—the chill coming off the ice, the effervescence of moving with and between strangers, the athletic little girls who cut the surface with no mercy. What an amazing gift, to discover something so electric after three decades of living. Lap after lap, I felt an invisible string pulling me, a rightness in the body I had not thought possible. This was what it must feel like to surf a wave. I looked over and saw the smile on my nephew's face. Here was something we could share, he and I, despite being very different people—me with my books, him with fascination with the military; me barely reaching five feet, him with his long spider legs. Here was something I could do with him that almost no one else in my family can. It's how we spend Christmas Eve.

Sitting on the bench, staring at the people going around and around, I thought about those times my nephew and I raced each other at the cost of splatting across the ice. I thought of the nickname I gave him the day my sister gave birth to him—*Pepponi*, Greek for melon, for his big head, which makes balancing on skates improbable, though he looks graceful doing it. I thought of my other nephew Fish Stick, who we joke I gave birth to, and who I also taught to skate. I thought of my nieces Queenie, and Sweet Charli, and cousins Puffin and Chicken, the latter of whom I took shopping for her first bra. All those years I could have been playing with them, getting to know them better, but was too fragile, too vulnerable.

I said to myself: What are you going to do, cry baby? You can't sit on the sidelines forever.

I go back out on the ice. I go week after week. I hold on to the words of Jon Kabat-Zinn, founder of the Center for Mindfulness in Medicine:

"We never know what might be possible in the mindscape and the bodyscape."

One day, the ice beneath me becomes a window, I the pelting rain.

ooooo

You can skip this ad in 5, 4, 3, 2—

Congratulations, you're having a good life! but then you went and hit your head. Now your brain is about as good at filtering as the hot tubs at the Jersey shore. Touch, smell, movement, questions, the taste of your beloved's mouth, the taste of your own mouth—it's all too much. Your concussed brain works a little slower, darts around like a child through traffic. No need to start crying! Even if Western medicine is failing you, the human body is built for destruction. Now, with just a few thousand efforts—and more time than you thought possible—you'll be able to aim for happiness again.

ooooo

They say heal. What they mean is retrain. And everything trains your brain after an accident. Walking down a street. Counting change. Dealing with your mother. Recalling the name of your cousins. Talking on the phone. Listening to directions. Going in circles. Being back out in the world is free therapy for vision, cognition, emotional regulation, stamina. The brain is plastic, in a way—is moldable. Every time you think, feel, attempt something new, neural pathways light up and make new connections. The axons—that is, neuro fibers that connect various parts of the brain—give the high fives so you keep going, champ! This is neuroplasticity, this learning of new skills and approaches, this doing things differently. Think of Mom after she and your father divorced, when she quit smoking, joined kickboxing (you didn't even think she knew how to kick, let alone punch), took up Italian, and started going out, posting photos of her dinner plate, never the date. The brain, especially after injury, is as surprising and facile—as plastic—as this.

We discovered the potential for neuroplasticity in 1793, when Italian anatomist Vincenzo Malacarne determined that the cerebellums of trained animals were substantially larger than those of animals not forced into tricks. Then we promptly forgot about it for a good two hundred years. Neuroplasticity, as recently as a decade ago believed to be possible only in the very young, is actually for everybody.

But like us, because it is part of us, the brain can be lazy, easily slipping back into familiar pathways: Netflix on repeat. If what you're doing is boring and mindless, like many jobs in America, the brain's plasticity mechanisms simply won't kick in. The brain has to be coached to try something new. Reading fiction, for instance, creates heightened connectivity in the brain. Taking up a new instrument, learning to juggle, picking up a new language, using your nondominant hand, traveling—these are all ways to remodel the brain.

My wife says, Say one nice thing about yourself, I blurt out: I like cheese.

Once a week, Dr. E has me follow moving orbs on the Sanet Vision Integrator until I can hit all the Cs floating on the touchscreen. The program has the same chunky, four-tone interface of the 1999 Minesweeper. The display is intentionally jittery. It feels like the 1980s, when teachers tried to trick you into learning with video games that were not really video games, and were locked inside beige boxes. But Dr. E insists this is how we build neuroplasticity in vision and address oculomotor issues. The shape of our skull is proof of how plastic we are, eyes at the front of our faces so we can communicate with one another, peripheral vision to detect predators. Of course, since visual pathways account for more than 50 percent of the brain's pathways, the eyes are almost always implicated in head trauma. I struggle to locate a small, moving object in a stretched-out, pixelated seaside, a place I instantly hate because it makes me nauseous. Then, in the Saccades—a peripheral awareness game that encourages sustained visual attention—I have to hit numbers in sequence as fast as I can. In Round Two, the computer speaks to me so I can find letters on the screen as she calls them out. The point of the exercise is to fatigue the mind, push myself so I start to mess up, go brain-numb, but not so much that I get blown. When I get an answer wrong, a buzzer goes off. This, they tell me, is how you get better.

"Keep that side vision, that magic vision open," one of the doctors calls out.

Think of it this way: You'll crash into fewer people on the ice.

At the end of each session, I feel as if I've been cramming for a test all night.

ooooo

You can skip this ad in 4, 3, 2—

It's six months after the first concussion. You're at the mall to buy your beloved a present. Things are going well until the fifty-five-minute marker, when you begin to get nauseous from all the people walking toward you/away from you, swinging shopping bags, making the marble floors shake. The retail lights are hot enough to cook a chicken. Everything is a reflective surface, every conversation overheard but only 2 percent audible. All you want to do is run out the door.

Or maybe it's two years after the concussion: you are at the grocery store picking up ingredients for your beloved's favorite dish. You are holding up two cans. The lines and edges are vibrating because you are at the breaking point and can't see what is right in front of you. An entire wall is corn, and yet none of it is corn. The creamed corn, especially, cannot be corn. By some miracle, you make it to the checkout, only to realize you're pushing someone else's cart.

After the accident, don't believe anyone who says you owe them money from before. The people who liked you in the good old days might not like you now. Those who didn't like you back then will probably like you less.

Side effects may include: recoiling at a bag of chips, flinching at the sound of a zipper, the prickling sensation of having bitten into a lemon, head spinning, head floating, total blank out, can't connect two thoughts, can't follow conversations, can't make it two blocks, disturbed, heat wave, having a fit. But now, maybe, you can recognize the danger before it overtakes you. You can drop the can of corn, rush home, where your beloved is waiting for you.

Good job. You're doing a good job.

ooooo

Anything can be an algorithm. Tying your shoes. Doing the laundry. Sorting papers. Baking a cake. Anything can be the foundation on which you rebuild.

A few years into recovery, I enrolled in Introduction to Japanese. In the Zoom room was the sensei, a good ten years younger than me, and a dozen undergraduates, most in their first semester of college. I was told on day one that Japanese has three different alphabets, all of which are used interchangeably in newspapers and other media, and that we'd be learning two in their entirety plus a little of the third, which contains thousands of words. The undergrads outperformed me at an astonishing pace. One said, with an air of wonder, *You really see why they say to study a foreign language before age twenty-five*. Most nights found me finishing worksheets and practicing my hiragana at ten p.m. I bombed

30 percent of our eighty quizzes, embarrassed myself at least once a session, and went nearly a month before I figured out that *watashi* meant "I." It took all semester to place the verb at the end of a sentence. But with each class, four days a week, I felt my brain changing, stretching. Learning a new language reshapes neural networks, with most of the action happening in the frontal lobe, improving global cognition and increasing functional connectivity. It makes your thinking faster, more flexible. I was now working in an Eastern language highly reliant on context and employing a syntactical construction entirely unknown to me. It felt like the furniture in my brain was being rearranged to let in new light. Over time, I started to make sense when I spoke, figured out how numbers work in Japanese, and delivered a three-minute speech about my favorite restaurant. I got a B+ and ordered sushi to celebrate.

Shortly after, as a gift, I received a Daruma, a Japanese traditional doll modeled on Bodhidharma, the founder of Zen Buddhism. The Daruma was red, the traditional color, the one often associated with sickness and encouragements for cleanliness around the ill. It was accompanied by the phrase *nanakorobi yaoki*: seven times down, eight times up.

One day, deep into recovery, when I'm doing much better and have big plans, I slam the back of my head against a wall. This is not a concussion but it is definitely a blow, injury #3.5. My wife consoles me while I cry like a Teddy Ruxpin doll on stuck. I wander the house wearing a blanket like a robe. Here comes the pain, the Fixations, the anger, blah blah blah. I go see the witch. I am lucky she can see me, the witch says. I can feel your head trying to suck me in but uh-uh, I'm not going there. She tugs on a string above my brow, and I feel how deep my eyeballs go. She does a thing to my temples, to my eyelids, and a rocket flies up my nose and singes all the little hairs. Afterward, all I smell is chocolate, a big mug of hot chocolate after a long day on the ice.

When I get home, my wife wraps the plush red blanket tighter around me and pulls on my hair because she knows how much relief it brings. Nobody, not even the witch, knows how to touch my head like she does.

I hold on to the poetry of Zach Savich: "Can delicacy be enough / If insistent enough to endure / Is it delicacy then?"

We are getting better all the time, little by little—both of us. This is what #3.5 teaches me: that even when I go backward, I am still moving ahead.

Years out, I begin to realize that leaving my marriage would not have brought freedom. Rather, it would have made me far more brittle, capable only of a shrinking love, closed to any means of forgiveness. Of reinvention.

ooooo

You can skip this ad in 3, 2, 1—

Make a list of triggers. Choose one of the lesser ones, such as being in a room with people who are like family. Be with these people a few times a week, a few minutes at a time. Go on to the next mildest trigger and give that a try. Go get the corn together at a time when the grocery store is calm and most people are home asleep. Avoid the mall entirely. Walk trails. Paint. Look up flow state, then try to achieve flow state. Visit the past. Reread "The Allegory of the Cave." Be glad you are not the woman in Veria, Greece, 1,800 years ago, who was conscious during brain surgery when doctors tried to treat her for a blow to the head.

Cut everything by half: meetings, children, hours in the day. Too many people talking at once, too many words, too much cross-talk—get rid of them, even your mother, lie if you have to—too many T-shirts, too many faces! Too many trees, too much highway, too much wind, too hot,

too cold, too many steps, sunshine, streetlights all in a row, the water running down the windshield, the movie too big on the screen, the voiceover,
the music at the restaurant, people chewing at the restaurant, anything
that pops out when you look to the left. Switch out your cotton sheets for
CBD-infused ones, weighted sheets, sheets that reduce electromagnetic
fields and help increase melatonin. Try this Grocery Store Walk-Through
Optokinetic Training on YouTube, which takes you through aisle after
aisle of goods, before you go looking for cans of corn in actual stores by
yourself. Pass multiple challenging tests with corn, do many rounds of bio-
feedback. Try Sudoku, solve crosswords, get a decoder ring, take one of the
Great Courses in nonfungible tokens or game theory. Turn off the office
fluorescents. If they turn them back on, cite cases #xyz in NJ, PA, MA.

ooooo

But also: take more, take back what you love. Look up at the clouds
and think about how we shape them as much as any other natural force
does, when we see ourselves in them.

Keep, for as long as you can, the job that brings you joy. For me,
that's teaching. For me, that's young people.

Keep writing.

Collect success stories. What about the man who got a TBI and
when he woke up, he was a brilliant piano player even though he had
never played a day in his life and couldn't even read music. Maybe you
could be that guy now? Or what about Jerry Jemmott, who was only
an "okay" musician before his multiple head injuries (pole, stairs, car
accident), but afterward—he heard the notes between the notes. One
day apathetic about everything, and the next—music sounds different.
Couldn't hear out of the left ear because of a crushed cochlea, heard
only the horn players and the singers, and the notes the bass should be
playing between them. Played with Aretha Franklin and Ray Charles.

Maybe, like Jemmott, you could invent a whole new style, plucked right out of your damaged brain.

Another unexpected success story—Roald Dahl. Beloved by all children, the writer did not exist as we know him until he crashed a Gloster Gladiator on a WWII mission to Libya, having had zero training in aerial combat. Couldn't find the airstrip, tried for the desert, smashed into a boulder. Dahl was an unhappy man, so much so that his own wife, the actress Patricia Neal—who he cheated on with a friend of hers in a years' long affair—named him Roald the Rotten, then divorced him. His oldest daughter died from measles, his son survived a car crash but suffers from brain damage. Dahl was difficult, temperamental, misogynistic. Dahl was anti-Semitic, justifying as late as 1983 the genocide of Jews by Hitler (his family is deeply sorry about this as well). He didn't even like children very much, yet children love him, will love him for a hundred years. Dahl sells three hundred million books worldwide. Tells friends that the little bang on the head when he crashed his plane is what unleashed his creative spirit, though privately he suspected the crash was also part of what fueled the rancor, grief. Sudden artistic output syndrome, he called it, and his doctor agrees: this was the tipping point, the damage to the frontal lobe ignited a disinhibition that made Dahl fearless and dark on the page.

You fantasize about going back in time, erasing the injuries, being the person you once were. But when you meet you again—your sureness, your impenetrability—you realize there is no room for you here. The old you is as ungiving as a wall, as flat as a sleeping bag, and cannot speak your new language.

ooooo

A writing conference comes to town. It feels like a traveling circus, to those of us who have been stuck at home for so long. At first, everyone is shy—and then there are hugs, everybody thawing at the hotel bar. I am feeling pretty good, myself. I walk my city, I am in step with myself every moment, run into a friend eating pasta at a sidewalk café. I keep going, discover a delicious new restaurant in my own city, keep going, meet a doodle pup, keep going, end up sitting on the floor of an underground arts space where there is an excellent reading about sex by women and TGQN folks. None of the people who said they'd be here show up, but I don't care, I stay for the after party. I peel off layers and dance by myself, who cares if the famous writers are trying to categorize what sort of animal I am. I get slick and sweaty. I know how I look but I don't care, I have been waiting years for this moment. One thing I would whisper to the me lying in bed, You might not get back all the days but you will get some really good ones. Outside, a few grad students say, Whoa, it's you from the dance floor! And they invite me to karaoke but I keep going, to another party, on the other side of the city where there are samosas and more dancing. I meet a gay man I fall in love with, and I dance some more. When I finally get on the trolley for home, I run into the grad students again, however unlikely in a city of a million people. I hear them say: That was wild! Young ones, you have no idea.

○○○○○

A 2021 study analyzing functional MRI screenings shows that elite ice skaters have higher gray matter than nonathletes like you and me. Neuroscientists have found that such complex motor skill training—speed, coordination, balance, the fine-tuning of neural connections in the cerebellum with each subtle adjustment of the body moving across the ice—yields structural and functional plasticity.

Don't forget joy, I want to say. That's part of getting better, too.

"Beloved, I believe all theories / reduce to the horizontal. Consider / a gardener hosing hanging plants / clearing the horizon / Or wildflowers / immoderately set. Ice with no one skating there."—Zach Savich, from his sickbed.

I meet a friend in Chinatown for chicken wings but there are six screens around the bar, and the K-Pop dancers are eight feet tall. It's too much for me. We leave: no wings, no beer. The next week I meet a friend at another bar: more screens, all sports. We leave. I push her down the street, we wander the city. No apps, no drinks. Just clean, cool air.

Love and plastic, love and plastic, little by little by little.

I am not naïve. I know love and physical therapy can't cure all. I know what likely awaits me twenty, thirty years down the line. In 2021, the Perelman School of Medicine at the University of Philadelphia warns that a single head injury can lead to dementia, let alone my multiple ones, which mark me more than twice as susceptible.

Before my injuries, I had already been alerted by 23andMe that I inherited the e4 allele in the APOE gene attributed to late-onset Alzheimer's. There is standing evidence of this: my *yia yia*, locking the door against my aunt because she thought she had come from the village to steal her husband. I joke to my friends that they better not come for my wife when I'm *yia yia*'s age, but privately I have always been terrified of such a future. This only gets worse when I learn that those with moderate traumatic brain injury have a 2.32 times greater risk of developing Alzheimer's than seniors with no history of head injury. Even now I can picture my *yia yia*, how greasy her thin hair, how gray her face, a rag wrung of all moisture, how unable she was to care for herself.

My best friend says, So I'll pull you around in a red wagon.

ooooo

You cannot skip this ad.

Side effects include nightmares, such as the one where doctors insert a black spider the size of a cat into your shoulder, the one where the doctors on *The Love Boat* hook you up intravenously to a boot full of blood, or the one where your opening an abandoned fridge signals the end of the world has begun. Stop, walk away, leave the corn. Do something for you today: nap and cry, knit and cry, sit in a bath and cry, sit alone in a room and stifle your cries so your family can't hear you, cry so the neighbors hear. Choose one person to talk to and ghost everybody else. Sit with your beloved, even if they can't bear to hear you speak a single word. The sentence is long, and no one can say when you will be free again. But dreams about water—gliding over the ocean in a grapefruit pink sky with friends coasting nearby on their own large sails—are a good sign. They suggest healing.

No. The vulnerability will probably never go away. Yes, there will probably be more hits, #3.75, #4, and—bite your tongue—#5. Still, *poco a poco a poco*, my wife says, and she's right: a bike ride, a day in the sun, a crowded bar, and what has only thus far appeared as a fleeting mirage: a jalapeno margarita. Old gifts wrapped in fresh paper. Things lost given back, new things discovered. Everyone wants you to get better. Annoying as that is, sometimes it is the only thing that cures. As is loving—taking care—of something outside of yourself. That, too, is a part of the recovery.

Your wife might want a dog—she might have wanted one for sixteen years. You're not sure if you should get the dog: get the dog. Train the dog not to go near your head. The dog, laying its head on your chest, will remind you that you are not all sharp edges. It may know—be weary of—the darkness that sometimes overtakes you. Still, you will be instantly loyal to it, and it will love you—will know instinctively to be gentle. Being with it will change you in ways you cannot really explain, not even to yourself, except that you will realize that you have too often sought out love like a mouse who has to sneak down to the kitchen at night. You have other ways now.

You're not sure about the cat. You are correct in this. The cat will aim for your head and swerve only at the last minute. It will also, when you most need it, curl up around you on the pillow like a winter hat.

Sex, too. Go right up to the edge, remember that you cannot get where you need to go without letting yourself fall.

Fall.

We falsely think of memory as a flat activity—retrieval. We have this idea that pulling up a fact, remembering a moment, that feeling of flying across the ice, is as simple as hitting Next Episode. In fact, we do not gather memories: we re-create them.

Daniela Schiller of Mt. Sinai's Icahn School of Medicine argues that a memory is a story that we edit each time we return to it. With every retelling, there are new or omitted details, determined by our evolving emotional relationship to the memory. Anytime we tell the story, our feelings about it change, if subtly, and those feelings ultimately reshape the memory. The revision creates a new little pathway in our brain, like streetlights blinking on.

Memory, the ultimate neuroplasticity. Proof that we can, and do, constantly reinvent ourselves. There are all kinds of ways to rewrite the brain, there are many pathways to take.

I am learning to skate backward.

The day after concussion #3.5, my wife and I go to the fertility clinic. We walk slowly, hold hands. We pass the old brown church with the very bright yellow tree, its leaves falling around us and making us glow a little, like jack-o'-lanterns. HGTV is on in the lobby, as if to say, You, too, can build a family. We are excited when she sits pantsless waiting for the doctor. We are excited when they start up the screen. We are excited when the bubbles shoot through her fallopian tubes. I am grateful that she is opening herself up to this. We watch her reproductive organs pulse on the grainy screen, healthy and strong. I make jokes about her being beautiful inside and out and she rolls her eyes. I hold her hand for the fifteen painful minutes the doctor rustles inside her. Then the procedure is done, my wife lets go of my hand: and I almost pass out. One minute I'm standing beside her, the next I'm in the chair, and she is standing over me in her long shirt and bare legs, worry on her face. My fingers are tingling, my chest drenched. The medical professionals are fanning my face and draping me in ice packs. I'm sorry, I'm sorry, I keep saying through the gauzy view to the woman I love, who is putting her body on the line for our little dream. Please believe I would be stronger for you if I could.

Later, we joke about it. When her water breaks, we say, she'll be in one bed, giving birth to Baby, and I'll be in the bed next to her having my own hysterical pregnancy, pushing out Heavy Baby.

Love, too, is a pathway.

works cited

The Life Cycle of a Concussion

Duncan, Kelli A., and Sarah Garijo-Garde. "Sex, Genes, and Traumatic Brain Injury (TBI): A Call for a Gender Inclusive Approach to the Study of TBI in the Lab." *Frontiers in Neuroscience*, 15 (May 2021).

Ferry, Benjamin, and Alexei DeCastro, *Concussion*. Treasure Island, Fla.: StatPearls Publishing, 2023.

Jauk, Daniela. "Gender Violence Revisited: Lessons from Violent Victimization of Transgender Identified Individuals. *Sexualities* 16, no. 7 (December 2013): 807–25.

Mollayeva, Tatyana, Shirin Mollayeva, and Angela Colantonio. "Traumatic Brain Injury: Sex, Gender and Intersecting Vulnerabilities." *Nature Reviews Neurology* 14, no. 12 (December 2018): 711–22.

"Roseanne Talks About Being Impaled by a Hood Ornament," *Joe Rogan Experience*, October 11, 2018. https://www.youtube.com /watch?v=q6EsPjN2xw0.

Safer, Joshua D., Eli Coleman, Jamie Feldman, Robert Garofalo, Wylie Hembree, Asa Radix, and Jae Sevelius. "Barriers to Healthcare for Transgender Individuals." *Current Opinion in Endocrinology, Diabetes, and Obesity* 23, no. 2 (April 2016): 168–71.

Woolf, Virginia. *On Being Ill: With Notes from Sick Rooms by Julia Stephen*. Middletown, Conn.: Wesleyan University Press, 2012.

Sex with a Brain Injury

Sander, Angelle M., Kacey Little Maestas, Todd G. Nick, Monique R. Pappadis, Flora M. Hammond, Robin A. Hanks, David L. Ripley. "Predictors of Sexual Functioning and Satisfaction 1 Year Following Traumatic Brain Injury: A TBI Model Systems Multicenter Study." *Journal of Head Trauma Rehabilitation* 28, no. 3 (May–June 2013): 186–94.

Doubt, My Love

Descartes, René. *Meditations on First Philosophy*. Translated by John Cottingham. Cambridge: Cambridge University Press, 1996.

Descartes, René. *Meditations on First Philosophy*. Translated by Michael Moriarty. Oxford: Oxford University Press, 2008.

Forster, John. *The Life of Charles Dickens*. London: Chapman and Hall, 1892.

Holdorff, Bernd, and Tom Dening. "The Fight for 'Traumatic Neurosis,' 1889–1916: Hermann Oppenheim and His Opponents in Berlin." *History of Psychiatry* 22, no. 4 (December 2011): 465–76. https://doi.org/10.1177/0957154X10390495.

Lee, Hermione. *Virginia Woolf*. New York: Alfred A. Knopf, 1997.

Lowes, Richard. "Grace—Somatic Symptom Disorder," BLB Solicitors. https://www.blbchronicpain.co.uk/case-studies/somatic-symptom-disorder-claim/.

Luckhurst, Roger. *The Trauma Question*. Abingdon, U.K.: Routledge, 2008.

Macnab, Aidan. "When the Mind Fails to Heal," *Canadian Lawyer*, February 11, 2019. https://www.canadianlawyermag.com/practice-areas/personal-injury/when-the-mind-fails-to-heal/275824.

Reed, Robert C. *Train Wrecks: A Pictorial History of Accidents on the Main Line*. Seattle, Wash.: Superior Publishing, 1968.

Scarry, Elaine. *The Body in Pain: The Making and Unmaking of the World*. New York: Oxford University Press, 1985.

Shoot, Brittany. "The Brain Injury That Helped End Slavery," *Folks*. https://folks.pillpack.com/brain-injury-helped-end-slavery/.

"The Staplehurst Railway Accident," Charles Dickens Info, originally published July 5, 2012; updated June 13, 2023. https://www.charlesdickensinfo.com/life/staplehurst-railway-accident/.

Whitman, James Q. *The Origins of Reasonable Doubt: Theological Roots of the Criminal Trial*. New Haven, Conn.: Yale University Press, 2008.

Woolf, Virginia. *On Being Ill: With Notes from Sick Rooms by Julia Stephen*. Middletown, Conn.: Wesleyan University Press, 2012, pages 53, 111.

"The Wrong Side of the Tracks," Notes from the Frontier, April 8, 2020. https://www.notesfromthefrontier.com/post/the-wrong-side-of-the-tracks.

Duplicity

Kashy, Deborah A., and Bella M. DePaulo. "Who Lies?," *Journal of Personality and Social Psychology* 70, no. 5 (1996): 1037–51. https://doi.org/10.1037/0022-3514.70.5.1037.

Meyer, Pamela. "How to Spot a Liar," TEDGlobal, 2011. https://www.ted.com/talks/pamela_meyer_how_to_spot_a_liar.

Schaarschmidt, Theodor. "The Art of Lying." *Scientific American*, July 11, 2018. https://www.scientificamerican.com/article/the-art-of-lying/.

Dancing in the Dark

Corrigan, John, and Rachel Sayko Adams. "The Intersection of Lifetime History of Traumatic Brain Injury and the Opioid Epidemic." *Addictive Behaviors* 90 (March 2019): 143–45. https://doi.org/10.1016/j.addbeh.2018.10.030.

Dunkley, Benjamin T., Leodante Da Costa, Allison Bethune, Rakesh Jetly, Elizabeth W. Pang, Margot J. Taylor, and Sam M. Doesburg. "Low-frequency Connectivity Is Associated with Mild Traumatic Brain Injury. *NeuroImage: Clinical* 7 (March 2015): 611–21. https://doi.org/10.1016/j.nicl.2015.02.020.

Drowning

Broshek, Donna K., Anthony P. De Marco, and Jason R. Freeman. "A Review of Post-Concussion Syndrome and Psychological Factors Associated with Concussion." *Brain Injury* 29, no. 2 (November 2014): 228–37. https://doi.org/10.3109/02699052.2014.974674.

Elliott, Clark. *The Ghost in My Brain: How a Concussion Stole My Life and How the New Science of Brain Plasticity Helped Me Get It Back.* New York: Viking Penguin, 2015.

Foxhall, Katherine. *Migraine: A History.* Baltimore: Johns Hopkins University Press, 2019. https://www.press.jhu.edu/newsroom/migraine-history.

"How a Concussion Can Lead to Depression Years Later," Newswise, December 9, 2013. https://www.newswise.com/articles/how-a-concussion-can-lead-to-depression-years-later.

O'Connor, Flannery. *Mystery and Manners: Occasional Prose.* Selected and Edited by Sally and Robert Fitzgerald. New York: Farrar, Straus & Giroux, 1969.

Pearce, J.M.S. "Historical Aspects of Migraine." *Journal of Neurology, Neurosurgery, and Psychiatry* 49, no. 10 (October 1986): 1097–1103. https://doi.org/0.1136/jnnp.49.10.1097.

Sacks, Oliver. *Migraine: Understanding a Common Disorder.* New York: Vintage, 1999.

Shenk, Joshua Wolf. "Lincoln's Great Depression," *Atlantic*, October

2005. https://www.theatlantic.com/magazine/archive/2005/10/lincolns-great-depression/304247/.

On Anger

Abramson, Ashley. "The Science Behind Your Child's Tantrums." *New York Times*, October 15, 2020. https://www.nytimes.com/2020/10/15/parenting/kids-tantrums-advice.html.

Corrigan, John D., and Rachel Sayko Adams. "The Intersection of Lifetime History of Traumatic Brain Injury and the Opioid Epidemic." *Addictive Behaviors* 90 (October 2018): 143–45. https://doi.org/10.1016/j.addbeh.2018.10.030.

Dalton, Hannah. *The Tudors: England 1485–1603*. Cambridge: Cambridge University Press, 2015.

Damasio, Hanna, Thomas Grabowski, Randall Frank, Albert M. Galaburda, and Antonio R. Damasio. "The Return of Phineas Gage: Clues about the Brain from the Skull of a Famous Patient." *Science* 264, no. 5162 (May 20, 1994): 1102–1105. https://doi.org/10.1126/science.8178168.

Dyer, Kevin F., Rob Bell, John McCann, and Robert Rauch. "Aggression After Traumatic Brain Injury: Analysing Socially Desirable Responses and the Nature of Aggressive Traits." *Brain Injury* 20, no. 11 (November 2006): 1163–73. https://doi.org/10.1080/02699050601049312.

Hathaway, Bill. "Did Henry VIII Suffer Same Brain Injury as Some NFL Players." *YaleNews*, February 2, 2016. https://news.yale.edu/2016/02/02/did-henry-viii-suffer-same-brain-injury-some-nfl-players.

"How Jousting Made a Man of Henry VIII." History Extra, August 3, 2015. https://www.historyextra.com/period/tudor/how-jousting-made-a-man-of-henry-viii/.

Sachar, Louis. *Sideways Stories from Wayside School.* Avon Camelot Books, 1978.

Schwarzbold, Marcelo, Alexandre Diaz, Evandro Tostes Martins, Armanda Rufino, Lúcia Nazareth Amante, Maria Emília Thais, João Quevedo, Alexandre Hohl, Marcelo Neves Linhares, and Roger Walz. "Psychiatric Disorders and Traumatic Brain Injury." *Neuropsychiatric Disease and Treatment* 4, no. 4 (August 2008): 797–816. https://doi.org/10.2147/ndt.s2653.

Living in the Basement

Babb, Kent. "Driven to the End." *Washington Post*, July 29, 2019. https://www.washingtonpost.com/sports/2019/07/29/kelly-catlin -death-cyclist/.

Boren, Cindy. "Cyclist Kelly Catlin's Family Donates Her Brain for Concussion Research." *Washington Post*, March 13, 2019. https:// www.washingtonpost.com/sports/2019/03/12/cyclist-kelly-catlins -family-donates-her-brain-concussion-research/.

Doty, Mark. *The Art of Description: World into Word.* Minneapolis: Graywolf, 2010.

Hussain, Danyal. "Tragic Snowboarder Ellie Soutter's Father Says Concussions and Head Injuries May Have Contributed to Her Taking Her Own Life." *New Zealand Herald*, September 23, 2018. https://www .nzherald.co.nz/sport/tragic-snowboarder-ellie-soutters-father -says-concussions-and-head-injuries-may-have-contributed-to -her-taking-her-own-life/CWBQE5BBWWK3MYPU2O5K PDZBNI/.

Ingber, Sasha. "Olympic Cycling Medalist Kelly Catlin Dead at 23." NPR, March 11, 2019. https://www.npr.org/2019/03/11/702206 945/olympic-cycling-medalist-kelly-catlin-dead-at-23.

Korfmacher, Carsten. "Personal Identity." Internet Encyclopedia of Philosophy. https://iep.utm.edu/person-i/.

McLaughlin, Ann Marie. "'I Am Not Me': The Impact of Concussion on Emotional Adjustment." Mind Your Brain Conference, Penn Medicine, April 3, 2018.

Myles, Stephen M. "Understanding and Treating Loss of Sense of Self Following Brain Injury: A Behavior Analytic Approach." *International Journal of Psychology and Psychological Therapy* 4, no. 3 (November 2004): 487–504.

Parfit, Derek. *Reasons and Persons*. Oxford: Oxford University Press, 1984.

Sacks, Oliver. *An Anthropologist on Mars: Seven Paradoxical Tales*. New York: Vintage, 1996.

Woodyatt, Amy. "These Young Female Athletes Died by Suicide. They All Had Head Injuries in Common." CNN, February 6, 2023. https://www.cnn.com/2023/02/05/sport/head-injury-suicide-female-athletes-intl-spt-cmd/index.html.

The Big Sleep

Benjamin, Marina. *Insomnia*. New York: Catapult, 2018.

Brooks, Gwendolyn. *The Near-Johannesburg Boy and Other Poems*. Chicago: David Co., 1986.

Me vs. The Bear

Gonzales, Laurence. *Surviving Survival: The Art and Science of Resilience*. New York: W. W. Norton, 2012.

Van der Kolk, Bessel. *The Body Keeps the Score: Brain, Mind and Body in the Healing of Trauma*. New York: Penguin, 2014.

Woolf, Virginia. *On Being Ill: With Notes from Sick Rooms by Julia Stephen*. Middletown, Conn.: Wesleyan University Press, 2012.

Q&A with My Wife/Horse or Boat

Cowley, Christopher. "Regret, Remorse and the Twilight Perspective." *International Journal of Philosophical Studies* 25, no. 5 (2017): 624–34. https://doi.org/10.1080/09672559.2017.1381410.

Danaher, John. "The Wisdom of Regret and the Fallacy of Regret Minimalism." *Philosophical Disquisitions*, January 1, 2019. https://philosophicaldisquisitions.blogspot.com/2019/01/the-wisdom-of-regret-and-fallacy-of.html.

Tolstoy, Leo. *The Death of Ivan Ilych*. Translated by Louise and Aylmer Maude. Oxford: Oxford University Press, 1935.

Professor X and the Trauma Justice League

Bickford, Melissa. "The Criminal Justice Issue Nobody Talks About: Brain Injuries." Marshall Project, January 6, 2022. https://www.themarshallproject.org/2022/01/06/the-criminal-justice-issue-nobody-talks-about-brain-injuries.

Gorgens, Kim. "The Surprising Connection Between Brain Injuries and Crime." TedxMile High 2019. https://www.ted.com/talks/kim_gorgens_the_surprising_connection_between_brain_injuries_and_crime.

Gorgens, Kim A., Laura Meyer, Judy Dettmer, Molly Standeven, Cory Marchi, Emily Goodwin, Hollis Lyman. "Traumatic Brain Injury in Community Corrections: Prevalence and Differences in Compliance and Long-Term Outcomes Among Men and Women on Probation." *Criminal Justice and Behavior* 48, no. 12 (December 2021): 1679–93. https://doi.org/10.1177/00938548211010316.

Hayasaki, Erika. "Teaching Prison Inmates About Their Own Brain Trauma Could Help Them Rehabilitate." *Newsweek*, June 29, 2016. https://www.newsweek.com/2016/07/08/prison-inmate-traumatic-brain-injury-research-475615.html.

Hillstrom, Christa. "The Hidden Epidemic of Brain Injuries from Domestic Violence." *New York Times*, March 1, 2022. https://www.nytimes.com/2022/03/01/magazine/brain-trauma-domestic-violence.html.

"Inmate Race." Federal Bureau of Prisons, May 20, 2023. https://www.bop.gov/about/statistics/statistics_inmate_race.jsp.

Lash, Marilyn. "TBI and PTSD: Navigating the Perfect Storm." *Brain Injury Journey*, 2018. https://www.brainline.org/article/tbi-and-ptsd-navigating-perfect-storm.

Lyon, Edward. "People with Traumatic Brain Injuries More Likely to Commit Crimes." *Prison Legal News*, June 2019. https://www.prisonlegalnews.org/news/2019/jun/3/people-traumatic-brain-injuries-more-likely-commit-crimes/.

Maass, Brian. "Colorado Prison Inmates Now Ordering from Amazon, Walmart—'Sounds Like a Five-Star Hotel,' Says Prosecutor," CBS News, March 17, 2023. https://www.cbsnews.com/colorado/news/colorado-prisons-amazon-walmart-prisoners-ordering-honor-house-la-vista-correctional-facility/.

Misciagna, Vanessa. "Two Former Inmates Say Better Traumatic Brain Injury Treatment Behind Bars Could Prevent Recidivism." Denver 7 ABC, July 23, 2021. https://www.denver7.com/news/national-politics/the-race/two-former-inmates-say-better-traumatic-brain-injury-treatment-behind-bars-could-prevent-recidivism.

Mollayeva, Tatyana, Shirin Mollayeva, and Angela Colantonio. "Traumatic Brain Injury: Sex, Gender and Intersecting Vulnerabilities." *Nature Reviews Neurology* 14, no. 12 (December 2018): 711–22. https://doi.org/10.1038/s41582-018-0091-y.

Sarai, Tamar. "Brain Injuries and 'the Revolving Door' of Incarceration." *Prism*, May 26, 2022. https://prismreports.org/2022/05/26/brain-injuries-incarceration/.

"SB 21-138 Improve Brain Injury Support in Criminal Justice System." Office of Planning and Analysis, Colorado Department of Corrections, January 2023.

"See AYBOS Advocacy Services in Action Here." Rebuild Your Mind. https://rebuildyourmind.org/aybos-advocacy-services/.

Hit Like a Girl

Hesketh, Ian, and Cary L. Cooper. "Leaveism at Work." *Occupational Medicine* 64, no. 3 (April 2014): 146–47. https://doi.org/10.1093/occmed/kqu025.

Hillstrom, Christa. "The Hidden Epidemic of Brain Injuries from Domestic Violence." *New York Times*, March 1, 2022. https://www.nytimes.com/2022/03/01/magazine/brain-trauma-domestic-violence.html.

Mollayeva, Tatyana, and Angela Colantonio. "Sex, Gender, and Traumatic Brain Injury: Implications for Better Science and Practice." Brain Injury Association of America. https://www.biausa.org/public-affairs/media/sex-gender-and-traumatic-brain-injury-implications-for-better-science-and-practice.

Mollayeva, Tatyana, Shirin Mollayeva, and Angela Colantonio. "Traumatic Brain Injury: Sex, Gender and Intersecting Vulnerabilities." *Nature Reviews Neurology* 14, no. 12 (December 2018): 711–22. https://doi.org/10.1038/s41582-018-0091-y.

Mollayeva, Tatyana, David Stock, and Angela Colantonio. "Physiological and Pathological Covariates of Persistent Concussion-Related Fatigue: Results from Two Regression Methodologies." *Brain Injury* 33, no. 4 (2019): 463–79. https://doi.org/10.1080/02699052.2019.1566833.

Taylor, Margaret. "The Perfect Number of Hours to Work Every Day? Five." *Wired*, June 15, 2021. https://www.wired.co.uk/article

/working-day-time-five-hours#:~:text=%E2%80%9CResearch%
20indicates%20that%20five%20hours,shorter%20working%20
hours%20and%20productivity.

Vingård, Eva, Kristina Alexanderson, and Anders Norlund. "Sickness Presence." *Scandinavian Journal of Public Health* 63 (2004): 216–21. http://www.jstor.org/stable/45205748.

Woodyatt, Amy. "These Young Female Athletes Died by Suicide. They All Had Head Injuries in Common." CNN, February 6, 2023. https://www.cnn.com/2023/02/05/sport/head-injury-suicide -female-athletes-intl-spt-cmd/index.html.

Probable Vulnerability

Blanc, Shirley. "Athletes with Previous Concussion Have 4 Times the Risk of Another." Concussion Vision Clinic, September 28, 2021. https://www.concussionvisionclinic.com/2021/09/28/athletes -with-previous-concussion-have-4-times-the-risk-of-another/.

"Coal Consumption Affecting Climate." *Rodney and Otamatea Times*, August 14, 1912.

"Current Cigarette Smoking Among Adults in the United States." Centers for Disease Control and Prevention, May 4, 2023. https://www .cdc.gov/tobacco/data_statistics/fact_sheets/adult_data/cig_smoking /index.htm#:~:text=This%20means%20an%20estimated%20 30.8,with%20a%20smoking%2Drelated%20disease.&text= Current%20smoking%20has%20declined%20from,every%20 100%20adults)%20in%202020.

Fainaru, Steve, and Mark Fainaru-Wada. "Congressional Report Says NFL Waged Improper Campaign to Influence Government Study." ESPN, May 22, 2016. https://www.espn.com/espn/otl/story/_/id /15667689/congressional-report-finds-nfl-improperly-intervened -brain-research-cost-taxpayers-16-million.

"Global Energy Review 2019." International Energy Agency, April 2020. https://www.iea.org/reports/global-energy-review-2019.

Konsolaki, Eleni, Elisabeth Astyrakaki, George Stefanakis, Panos Agouridakis, and Helen Askitopoulou. "Cranial Trauma in Ancient Greece: from Homer to Classical Authors." *Journal of Cranio-Maxillofacial Surgery* 38, no. 8 (December 2010): 549–53. https://doi.org/10.1016/j.jcms.2010.02.009.

McFadden, Josh. "At the Head of the Issue." *Journal of Emergency Dispatch*, October 16, 2016. https://www.iaedjournal.org/at-the-head-of-the-issue.

Mez, Jesse, Daniel H. Daneshvar, Patrick Kiernan, et al. "Clinicopathological Evaluation of Chronic Traumatic Encephalopathy in Players of American Football." *JAMA* 318, no. 4 (July 25, 2017): 360–70. https://doi.org/10.1001/jama.2017.8334.

Perrine, Kenneth, and James C. Gibaldi. "Somatization in Post-Concussion Syndrome: A Retrospective Study." *Cureus* 8, no. 8 (August 2016). https://doi.org/10.7759/cureus.743.

Rae, Haniya. "A Helmet Inspired by Woodpeckers Could Save Football Players from Concussions," *Popular Science*, September 12, 2016. https://www.popsci.com/inspired-by-woodpeckers-this-helmet-could-save-football-players-from-concussions/.

Ruegg, Tracy A. "Historical Perspectives of the Causation of Lung Cancer: Nursing as a Bystander." *Global Qualitative Nursing Research* 2 (2015). https://doi.org/10.1177/2333393615585972.

Wamsley, Laurel. "NFL, NIH End Partnership for Concussion Research With $16M Unspent," NPR, July 29, 2017. https://www.npr.org/sections/thetwo-way/2017/07/29/540238260/nfl-ends-partnership-with-nih-for-concussion-research-with-16m-unspent.

Woodyatt, Amy. "These Young Female Athletes Died by Suicide. They All Had Head Injuries in Common." CNN, February 6, 2023.

https://www.cnn.com/2023/02/05/sport/head-injury-suicide
-female-athletes-intl-spt-cmd/index.html.

The Lost Word

Dans, Peter E. "The Use of Pejorative Terms to Describe Patients:
   'Dirtball' Revisited." *Proceedings (Baylor University. Medical Center)*
   15, no. 1 (January 2002): 26–30. https://doi.org/10.1080/0899828
   0.2002.11927811.

Keen, Suzanne. *Narrative Form.* London: Palgrave Macmillan, 2015.

Rumi. *The Essential Rumi.* Translated by Coleman Barks. New York:
   HarperCollins, 1995.

Rumi. "Rumi Quotes and Poems," 2020. https://www.rumi.org.uk/.

"Rumi and Shams." The Art Blot, October 22, 2013. https://artblot
   .wordpress.com/2013/10/22/rumi-and-shams/.

Clocked Time

Gleick, James. "Toll of the Clock." *New York Review*, September 23, 2021.
   https://www.nybooks.com/articles/2021/09/23/toll-of-the-clock/.

Keen, Suzanne. *Narrative Form.* London: Palgrave Macmillan, 2015.

Memory Loss

Fisher, Margery, and James Fisher. *Shackleton.* London: Barrie, 1957.

Fulton, Wil. "All 85 Potential Injuries in 'Home Alone,' Assessed by
   a Real Doctor." Thrillist, December 24, 2014. https://www.thrillist
   .com/home/all-injuries-sustained-in-home-alone-assessed-by-a
   -real-doctor.

"Hit On Head: Sound Effects." Pond5, https://www.pond5.com/search
   ?kw=hit-on-head&media=sfx.

Moldovan, Alfred. Interview, *Civil Rights History Project*, Library
   of Congress, July 19, 2011. https://tile.loc.gov/storage-services

/service/afc/afc2010039/afc2010039_crhp0036_moldovan
_transcript/afc2010039_crhp0036_moldovan_transcript.pdf.

Morreall, John. *Comic Relief: A Comprehensive Philosophy of Humor.* Oxford: John Wiley & Sons, 2009.

Notaro, Tig. *Boyish Girl Interrupted.* HBO, 2015. https://www.hbo
.com/movies/tig-notaro-boyish-girl-interrupted.

Tyler, Kelly. "Shackleton's Lost Men," *NOVA*, PBS, March 2022. https://
www.pbs.org/wgbh/nova/shackleton/1914/lostmen.html.

Bent Lace

Ursula von Rydingsvard: Into Her Own. Icarus Films, 2020.

The Healing Algorithm

Dobrin, Arthur. "Your Memory Isn't What You Think It Is." *Psychology Today*, July 16, 2023.

"Head Injury 25 Years Later—Penn Study Finds Increased Risk of Dementia," *Penn Medicine News*, March 9, 2021. https://www
.pennmedicine.org/news/news-releases/2021/march/head-injury
-25-years-later-penn-study-finds-increased-risk-of-dementia.

Kabat-Zinn, Jon. "Neuroplasticity and the Unknown Limits of the Possible." *Mindfulness* 10, no. 2 (January 2019): 1–5. https://doi
.org/10.1007/s12671-018-1080-3.

Pierce, Gabrielle. "Grocery Store Walk Through Optokinetic Training." July 29, 2016. https://www.youtube.com/watch?v=C-OAFv5uGOw.

Savich, Zach. "Poetry by Zach Savich." *The Spectacle*, 2015. https://
thespectacle.wustl.edu/?p=53.

"Traumatic Brain Injury (TBI)." Alzheimer's Association. https://
www.alz.org/alzheimers-dementia/what-is-dementia/related
_conditions/traumatic-brain-injury#:~:text=One%20of%20
the%20key%20studies,a%204.5%20times%20greater%20risk.

"Welcome to the Northern Brain Injury Association." Northern Brain Injury Association. https://www.nbia.ca.

Zhang, Keying, Yu Liu, Jianxiu Liu, Ruidong Liu, Chunmei Cao. "Detecting Structural and Functional Neuroplasticity in Elite Ice-Skating Athletes." *Human Movement Science* 78 (August 2021). https://doi.org/10.1016/j.humov.2021.102795.

acknowledgments

Thank you to my reader—whether you're one of the Walking Wounded, or you've watched someone close to you suffer, or you're thinking of a stranger as you sit with these pages. Writing this book has been no small part of my recovery. It is my greatest hope that it will make others feel seen.

My deepest gratitude to the people who helped bring this work into the world:

Thank you especially to my editor, Kara Watson, for her brilliant insights, care, empathy, humor, and for seeing the true heart and potential of this project (and for pulling off publishing miracles)! Every page we make together is, and will always be, precious to me.

Thank you to my agents, David McCormick and Bridget McCarthy, for their encouragement and faith and support. Thank you to Kate Loyd and Georgia Brainard, who steward this book with heart and enthusiasm. Thank you to fact checker extraordinaire Hilary McClellen. Thanks, too, to the entire team at Scribner, especially: Joie Asuquo, Liz Byer, Sarajane Herman, Carolyn Levin, Laura Wise, Lauren Dooley, and Jaya Miceli for her art direction.

I am indebted to the researchers, scientists, and medical professionals whose sweat, work, and dedication inform these pages. As much as possible, I have noted their contributions in works cited.

Lifelong gratitude to "Professor X," Marchell Taylor, a force of undeniable good. Our hours sharing, laughing, and creating together were truly healing.

Thanks to "Wonder Woman" Dr. Kim Gorgens, Terri Hurst, Jaime Horsfall, Dr. Chris Estep, and the entire Trauma Justice League for their life-changing work. Thanks to Candace Gantt and the Mind Your Brain Foundation.

This work could not have been possible without the generous contributions of people who offered their knowledge, expertise, personal experiences, trust, research, stories, wisdom, and empathy. Thank you to Ella Bartlett, Camille Urueta, R. Dean Johnson, Dr. Raynata Ramkhelawan, Deb Olin Unferth, Paul Lisicky, Bruce Smith, Zach Savich, Danny Atherton, Dr. Salam Hawa, Jeff Parker and Alina Parker, Nava EtShalom, Aunt Judy Baker, and Daddio Al Nordstrom.

Thank you to Ursula von Rydingsvard, who has my heart. Thank you, too, to her team—Jo Yu, Mike Leach, Hailey Blomquist, and Malutka the cat.

I could have never launched this book without the generous support of Millay Arts, where I served as Mid-Atlantic Arts Fellow. Shout-out to Gay Millay—Sabrina Imbler, Andrea Pérez Bessin, Dāshaun Washington, Lucas Baisch, and Peg Harrigan. Special thanks to Calliope, Monika Burczyk, and Chef Donna.

I could have never finished this book without the generous support of Lighthouse Works. My gratitude to Claude DeSimone, Dylan Gautier, Nate Malinowski, and my Studio 54 compatriots Carlina Duan, Enrique Garcia, Katy McCarthy, and Talena Sanders.

Thank you to everyone at Disquiet, especially Jeff Parker, Scott Laughlin, Laura Breitenbeck, Jane Dykema, and Maaza Mengiste.

Thank you to the early readers who saw the potential in the mess. Thanks, especially, to Cate McLaughlin, my best friend—the Irishman who reads all my roughest drafts, brings me meat when I'm sick, and sends links about Henry VIII. Thanks to Gwyn Knauer for joining me in the journey. Thank you to Claw for encouragement and advice, especially Camille Acker, Piyali Bhattacharya, Jessamine Chan, Emma Eisenberg, Liz Greenspan, Carmen Machado, Liz Moore, and Asali Solomon. For their friendship and community, Tracey Levine, Jessica Schiccitano, Grady Chambers, Stevie Koteff, Nana Kwame Adjei-Brenyah. Thank you to my GPP workshop, Rachel Heng, Jeanne Thornton, Sarah Marshall. Thank you to my lit friend Lito Velazquez, my compatriot in this work. Thank you to Melissa Febos for reminding us that our stories must be told.

Thank you to my wonderful, supportive colleagues at George Washington University. Our students are so blessed to have you, as am I.

Thank you, Syracuse, especially *mentoh* Arthur Flowers, George Saunders, Dana Spiotta—and Sarah Harwell and Terri Zollo, who make it all possible.

Thank you to my healers, Siobhan Gibbons, Catherine Sliman, Emmanuelle Celicout, Jonah Mink, and Emily Lerner.

Thank you to my family of origin (especially Michele Liontas, Alexis Liontas, and Damara Burke) and my chosen family.

Most of all—thank you to Sara, my soul mate. I could have never done this—made it back, come forward—without you.